'Fascinating and funny'
Sunday Times

'[Hall] has a fine ear for the myriad speech patterns of the East End's
varied inhabitants . . . pertinent and unusually insightful views on
the whole "illegal immigrant" issue . . . gripping'
Daily Mail

'He fleshes out figures that are usually little more than symbols for
political viewpoints, and the result is a Dickensian tale of the
modern underclass that serves as an answer to negative immigration
issues'
Guardian

'Tender and harrowing'
The Times

'What started out as a series of entertaining character sketches turns
into an instructive investigation of "Englishness"'
Daily Telegraph

'Entertaining . . . Hall cannily plays the bewildered public schoolboy
to a range of different characters . . . allows us to hear the wonderful
patter of the East Enders'
Times Literary Supplement

'A thought-provoking read . . . fascinating insights into fractured
lives. And Hall's affectionate portrayals of eccentric acquaintances
enhance this touching portrait no end'
Metro

'*Salaam Brick Lane* is a compelling journey of discovery by an
outsider in his own city and offers an explicit glimpse of this quarter
of London'
Traveller

'I was absolutely riveted. It's funny, enlightening and very moving – but moving in a quiet, understated, English way, without any mawkish sentimentality. It has given me lots of new insights into the complexities and nuances of "acculturation", and I'm recommending it to all my friends just because it's such a good read'
Kate Fox, author of *Watching the English*

'A gem of a book that reveals a hidden world lying right on our doorstep. As the stories unfold, so does our appreciation for Tarquin Hall's acute eye and for the gentle power of his narrative'
Saira Shah, writer and broadcaster

'Such a light, playful book and yet with a compelling tow which takes you into the myriad realities of life in the East End of London'
Yasmin Alibhai-Brown, author of *Some of My Best Friends Are . . .*

Tarquin Hall

Tarquin Hall became an under-age journalist at nineteen and spent the next ten years working in Africa, America, Asia and the Middle East. He is the author of *Mercenaries, Missionaries and Misfits*, an account of his early adventures; and *To the Elephant Graveyard: A True Story of the Hunt for a Man-killing Indian Elephant*, a BBC Radio 4 Book of the Week. He is married to the BBC World Service presenter Anu Anand. They live in East London.

Salaam Brick Lane

A Year in the New East End

TARQUIN HALL

JOHN MURRAY

© Tarquin Hall 2005

First published in 2005 by John Murray (Publishers)
A division of Hodder Headline

Paperback edition 2006

The right of Tarquin Hall to be identified as the Author of the Work has been asserted by him in accordance with the Copyright, Designs and Patents Act 1988.

10

Names of individuals have been changed in order to protect their identities.

A CIP catalogue record for this title is available from the British Library

ISBN 978-0-7195-6556-4

Typeset in Monotype Bembo by Servis Filmsetting Ltd, Manchester

Printed and bound by
Clays Ltd, St Ives plc

Hodder Headline policy is to use papers that are natural, renewable and recyclable products and made from wood grown in sustainable forests. The logging and manufacturing processes are expected to conform to the environmental regulations of the country of origin.

John Murray (Publishers)
338 Euston Road
London NW1 3BH

For my Chowti Mali
with love
and gratitude

Contents

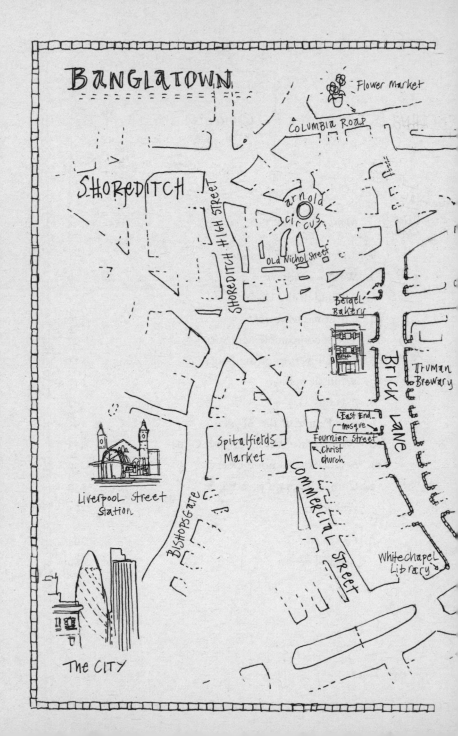

BANGLATOWN

Flower Market

COLUMBIA ROAD

SHOREDITCH

SHOREDITCH HIGH STREET

arnold circus

Old Nichol Street

Beigel Bakery

Truman Brewery

Brick Lane

East End Mosque

Fournier Street

Christ church

Spitalfields Market

Liverpool Street Station

Bishopsgate

COMMERCIAL STREET

Whitechapel Library

THE CITY

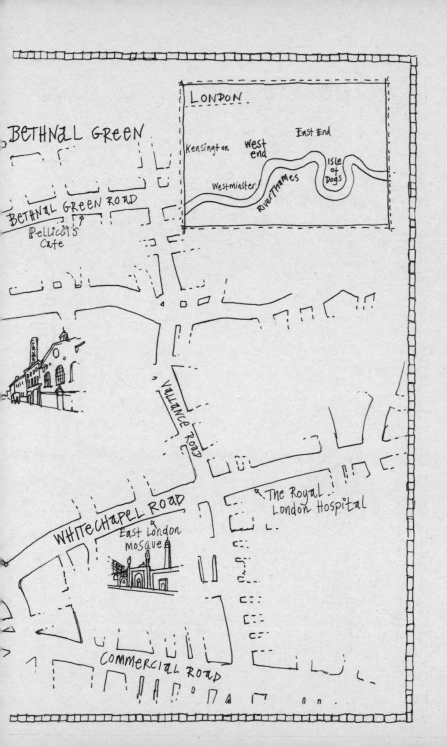

There rolls the deep where grew the tree.
O earth, what changes hast thou seen!
There where the long street roars, hath been
The stillness of the central sea.
              Tennyson, *In Memoriam A.H.H.*, CXXII

I

Toilet Seat Not Included

'"Brick Lane!" said Trupp suddenly.
They stood at the entrance of that street so much talked about.
Whitechapel! The East End in the East End! The hell of hells!'
John Henry Mackay, *The Anarchists* (1891)

'Londoners do not know their own city . . . you will meet there
frequently men who babble of foreign fields . . . but who would
never dream of leaving the square mile or the West End or their
own special bus or Tube route, to explore further in the greatest
city of the world.'

Paul Elek, *This Other London* (1951)

THE ADVERTISEMENT DESCRIBED it as 'a spacious live-work
studio'. But it was really just an attic in which I could stand up
straight providing I stayed in the middle of the room. As for the 'pan-
oramic views of the City': if you opened the single window in the
roof, which was like pushing up the hatch of a submarine in high seas,
you could catch a glimpse of the top of the NatWest tower shrouded
by the impenetrable October gloom.

And what of the 'modern furnishings'? Well, perhaps it was a
matter of taste, but tables and chairs made out of wooden pallets did
not appeal to mine, despite the originality of their design.

Only the 'separate bathroom' lived up to its description. It was
accessible from the second-floor landing (one flight of stairs down
from the attic) and had been suspended from the back of the building
in contravention of all planning regulations by a man known locally
as 'Rafik the Builder'. Measuring four feet by five, it was barely large

enough to house a toilet and a shower. This meant that in order to wash, you had first to step over the toilet, avoiding two plastic buckets strategically positioned on the floor to capture raindrops dripping from cracks in the ceiling. There was no basin and I noticed that the previous tenants had made do with the one in the kitchen, which was also located on the second floor. There, on the stainless steel draining board, amongst a stack of dirty plates and glasses filled with flat beer and bloated cigarette butts, lay a couple of bald toothbrushes and a shaving mirror flecked with dried spittle.

The Bangladeshi landlord, Mr Ali, who owned the leather jacket shop downstairs, hadn't bothered to clean the place, even though the former tenants had thrown a party on their last night, leaving the floors littered with empty cans, bottles and the odd needle. Nor had he bothered to paint over the gratuitous graffiti they had sprayed on the walls before absconding in the middle of the night.

'They were students,' said Mr Ali with disdain. 'Students are dirty bustards, innit.'

Mr Ali's accent was an unlikely combination of South Asian and Estuary, the result of having spent his first fourteen years in Bangladesh and the last twenty-nine in the East End. He dropped his Hs, pronounced nothing as 'nafing', and, when addressing white people such as myself, dispensed with their proper names in favour of 'geezer', 'guvna' or 'mate'. Anyone he didn't like was invariably referred to as a 'bustard'.

Mr Ali's choice of clothing was as much a reflection of his mixed cultural identity as his accent. He wore a long, collarless *kameez*, but in place of the usual matching baggy pants and sandals or slip-on shoes, he'd opted for a pair of Levis and alligator cowboy boots. His white prayer cap, although in need of a wash, suggested a man of faith, but was at odds with the whiff of booze on his breath, and helped complete the impression of a person of contradictions.

However, there was one thing about Mr Ali that was abundantly clear: he was the epitome of the slum landlord. His was a Heath Robinson approach to fixing everything – evident from the tape on the cracked windowpane in the kitchen – and he was disparaging of his tenants, past and present.

'I've 'ad, like, nafing but bustards, innit,' he said, complaining about how the students had stolen the toilet seat from the bathroom. 'The ones before the students was –' he grimaced as if he'd suddenly smelt something unpleasant – ''omosexuals.'

He emphasised this last word as if it was sacrilege to say it out loud.

'I 'eard 'em – you know . . .' His eyes widened and he made an aggressive action with his right fist, punching it against the palm of his left hand. 'Buggering, all day and all night! Breakfast, lunch and dinner! Always buggering, innit!'

Mr Ali's promiscuous gay tenants had disturbed the old Jewish lady who lived in the bed-sit on the first floor. She had complained to Mr Ali and he in turn had called the police.

'I says to the coppers, "It's not right, innit. The Koran forbids it, yeah." But the coppers, they just laugh. They says to me, "Mr Ali, it's the law. 'er Majesty, she allows the buggering."'

He shook his head in disgust and then regaled me with more stories of his 'Tenants from Hell'. Other occupants of the attic had included a heroin dealer and a Satan worshipper. They had been followed by a couple of Albanians, who had, in turn, invited six of their friends to live with them. The Albanians' main occupation had been selling smuggled tobacco, which in itself had not bothered Mr Ali as it had assured him a free supply of cigarettes. But when the police had raided the building and subsequently deported the Albanians, it had cast Mr Ali in a bad light. He was now on the lookout for a better class of tenant. He liked the idea of yuppies.

'They pay good rent and they don't spray the walls with "cock-sucker", innit.'

Mr Ali wanted to know if I was a yuppie and I had to admit that I was not. I was a journalist, I explained. But, no, I didn't work for the *Sun* and, no, sadly not the *Star*, either.

This came as a disappointment to him, although it did not rule me out as a potential tenant. The rate was one hundred pounds a week – 'It's monkey nuts, innit' – with a six-month lease, extendable providing the place was kept in good order. This meant no spraying the walls with graffiti and no staging of huge parties or raves. Loud music, drug dealing and the entertaining of local prostitutes were strictly prohibited. Mr Ali also stipulated that I should not sacrifice any animals on his property – the Satan worshipper had skinned a couple of the neighbours' cats – nor plan any violent campaigns against pharmaceutical companies as another of his previous tenants had done.

Above all else, at no time or under any circumstances, was there to be any buggering.

I assured Mr Ali of my heterosexual credentials, told him that I would think the matter over, and promised to call with a decision later that afternoon. Then I made my way downstairs and out into the street. I had taken only a couple of steps when I heard him calling to me from a second-floor window.

'Oi! Mate! One other fing!' he shouted. 'If you rent the place, yeah, you'll af to get your own toilet seat, innit!'

I stood outside Mr Ali's shop on the north end of Brick Lane close to the intersection with Bethnal Green Road and Redchurch Street, grimacing at the surrounding urban sprawl. Nature had been banished from the place, concreted over. There was not a tree nor a blade of grass in sight. Only a few stubborn weeds were rooted in the cracks in the brickwork.

A muddle of architecture lined the wet, clinker pavements. Crumbling Victorian terraces stood shoulder to shoulder with dilapidated warehouses and empty 1950s office blocks, which bled rust down their façades. A few houses stood empty or gutted, their tiled roofs sagging, their red chimney pots leaning perilously. Pigeons flew in and out of broken windows. Walls served as canvases for local graffiti artists. In doorways, soggy pizza flyers lay among nests of rags and cardboard boxes made by the homeless.

A black refuse bag had spilled its contents across the pavement at my feet. Chicken bones, baked potato skins and sweetcorn kernels lay amidst a slick of condensed mushroom soup. The pavement had also been fouled with dog shit, smears and smudges spread across the paving stones, causing passers-by to skip round them like children playing hopscotch.

The opposite side of the street was busy with people coming and going from Brick Lane's two bagel bakeries. Through steamed-up windows, I could make out shop assistants carving hunks of salt beef that lay on hot plates; and bakers peppered in flour pounding great hunks of dough. The bakery to the right appeared to be the more popular of the two. A queue snaked through its door out on to the pavement where customers stood devouring bagels oozing with cream cheese. They shared the space with five tramps who were drinking cans of Fosters and bumming cigarettes and change off passers-by. The loudest of them was a man with a mane of filthy black hair and a face as rough as a cat-scratched chair leg. He stood on the pavement raising his can of lager to passing drivers and making incomprehensible toasts punctuated by the word 'fuckers!' At the same time, a woman tramp sat on the kerb, picking at the dead skin on the soles of her feet and occasionally laughing to herself.

I pulled my coat tight around me against the cold winter weather and trudged off south down Brick Lane. The narrow, one-way street led past shopfronts guarded by steel shutters, and hoardings erected across gaps in the terraces. Slogans sprayed on the walls competed for attention – 'RELEASE REG KRAY'; 'LIBERATE KASHMIR'; 'FREE ABDUL-LAH OCALAN'; 'BLAIR MUST GO!' – while fairytale Indian princesses with doe eyes smiled out at me from Bollywood film posters.

The street led under a disused railway bridge where discarded mattresses lay rotting. I passed a burnt-out car surrounded by shards of shattered windscreen, and a gang of kids of ten or perhaps eleven years old who were sharing a spliff and cursing in a barrage of foul language. Further on, a SERIOUS INCIDENT police sign positioned on the pavement appealed for witnesses to an assault.

I turned left on to Pedley Street and came to Shoreditch tube-station. On the platform, I waited impatiently for a train to take me the one stop to Whitechapel. Standing there, all I wanted was to put as much distance as possible between myself and Brick Lane.

For the past ten years, I had been living away from England – the last three in India, where I had been working for the American news agency, the Associated Press, covering the major events of the region from the capture of Kabul by Taliban forces to the death of Mother

Teresa. I had returned to London just shy of thirty, somewhat weary of always being an outsider abroad and feeling the tug of home where I sought the familiarity of the past. Travel had taken me to many extraordinary places, but I had become detribalised and felt suddenly uneasy about where I belonged in the world. I hoped that returning to live in my own culture would provide the answers.

It had been my intention to put down roots in the leafy suburb of Barnes where I had grown up. But a lot had changed in my absence. My parents now lived three hours' journey outside London, my brother had emigrated to Los Angeles, my relatives were scattered across England and mostly didn't speak to one another, and many of my childhood friendships had not survived the test of time and distance.

I was also broke. The freelance journalism I had been guaranteed in London had yet to materialise. And during my last months in India, I had spent my savings travelling through the jungles and tea plantations of Assam in the company of a superstitious elephant hunter who had been on the trail of a man-killing rogue. I had even written a book about the journey, convinced that I had a best-seller on my hands. But no publisher had shown any interest in the manuscript and for now it sat at the bottom of my suitcase in the South Kensington flat where a friend was putting me up while I searched for a place of my own.

My financial difficulties aside, London property prices had shot up and Barnes was now one of the most sought-after areas. The semidetached on Madrid Road which my father had bought for ten thousand pounds in 1975 (and subsequently sold) was on the market for a cool half a million. One-bedroom flats were renting for silly money.

'You won't get a shoebox in Dagenham on your budget, sir,' one estate agent told me on Barnes High Street when I'd gone in search of a place to live.

It was a similar story in Chiswick, Kew, Putney, Richmond – all the areas I had known intimately as a child and thought of as home. Even Sheen, where my parents had lived when I was an infant (then still a working-class neighbourhood where the neighbours kept carrier pigeons), was leagues out of my price range.

Reluctantly, over the past fortnight, I had started looking elsewhere. Searching through the *Evening Standard* classifieds, I had travelled the length and breadth of the capital. And in the process, I had had a revelation. Most of London, the city of my birth, was as foreign to me as Prague.

The East End in particular was one huge blank spot. Until a week ago, I had never so much as set foot east of the City – but then again, I'd never had any desire to do so. The borough of Tower Hamlets, which today encompasses the East End proper, might as well have been marked on the map with a large skull and crossbones. My impression of the place was still coloured by childhood images of fog-bound streets stalked by Jack the Ripper, Bill Sykes, and the notorious Kray Twins, who drove black Sedans and buried their victims in the foundations of motorways. At home and at school, I had been taught that the people of the East End were different. My parents and teachers had made the Cockneys sound like a distinct race – cheery, perhaps, like Eliza Doolittle's father, but tougher, wilier and never wholly to be trusted. They even had their own language, Cockney rhyming slang, which – it was said – they had developed to fool policemen.

My father and his father before him had never set foot in the East End either. Their world had been Chelsea and Knightsbridge (where my grandmother did all her shopping at Harrods) and later, the villagey suburbs of south-west London. During my childhood, my parents had rarely travelled beyond these borders, except to go to the theatre in the West End or to visit Hampstead where, compared to Barnes, their friends were distinctly bohemian. The closest we had ever come to the East End was during a day trip to Greenwich. Standing on the Meridian, we had looked out over the Thames to the badlands beyond, a grim cityscape of gasworks and disused cranes, abandoned warehouses and crumbling wharves, and we had counted ourselves lucky that we didn't live there.

———◆———

By the time I reached Whitechapel it was nearly four o'clock and already dusk was falling. The neon signs above the shopfronts seared the gathering darkness like branding irons, while the main road, still slick with rain, began to glisten beneath the headlights of passing vehicles. I crossed over Whitechapel Road and entered the warren of narrow streets behind the East End mosque where Bangladeshi children in white skullcaps played football between rows of parked cars. Not for the first time during the past few days, I found that I was the only white face on the street. Everyone else was from Afghanistan, Bangladesh, India, Pakistan, Somalia. As I passed by, I caught snippets of conversation in some of the estimated 102 languages spoken in the East End. Only occasionally did I hear a word or two of English – and only then amid a babble of Somali or Urdu.

The area was mostly residential, the streets filled with the sounds of Talvin Singh blaring from open windows, and the enticing aromas of South Asian cooking. Among the tightly packed terraces, there were businesses too, all of them immigrant-owned. A halal butcher here, an old warehouse packed with rows of people working behind sewing machines there. And on one corner, an Islamic paraphernalia shop selling everything from leather-bound Korans to prayer mats with sewn-in compasses, designed to ensure that the twenty-first-century Muslim never fails to locate Mecca.

Looking up at the street signs, I noticed they were written in Bengali, as were the posters plastered on the lamp-posts and walls. The illusion of being back in South Asia was almost complete. But as I reached the next main road, the sight of a red double-decker bus hurtling past reminded me that this was London – just not the London I knew.

The café where I was due to meet Abdul-Haq, the Shia letting agent who had set up the appointment with Mr Ali, was owned by a Pakistani family from Lahore. Photographs of the city's famous landmarks, including the fort and Kim's gun, hung on the wall. In the window sat a pair of dusty brass samovars.

The café's *chai* was milky and sweet and flavoured with cardamoms, and as I waited for Abdul-Haq, I drank several cups and read the last few pages of Jack London's *The People of the Abyss*. I had come across the book the day before while browsing through a bookshop on Whitechapel High Street. It was an account of the American writer and adventurer's harrowing experiences living as a down-and-out in the East End in 1902. The Abyss of the title – the Victorian East End – was, to Jack London's socialist eyes, a bottomless pit that sucked the poor down into its depths and enslaved them in debilitating poverty. Much like Third World slums of today, it was a city of the damned in which young girls were sold into prostitution, destitute workers were left to rot in vermin-infested bed-sits, and broken men on the verge of starvation slept in Dickensian doss-houses.

'The streets were filled with a new and different race of people, short of stature, and of wretched or beer-sodden appearance,' wrote Jack London of his first impressions.

> We rolled along through miles of bricks and squalor, and from each cross street and alley flashed long vistas of bricks and misery. Here and there lurched a drunken man or woman . . . At a market, tottery old men and women were searching in the garbage . . . for potatoes, beans and vegetables, while little children clustered like flies around a festering mass of fruit . . .

Given that the slums had been only a stone's throw from the heart of the British Empire, *The People of the Abyss* still, nearly a century after its publication, made for shocking reading. Indeed, what intrigued me most about the book was Jack London's impression of the capital as a segregated city, with the rich, affluent and powerful living in the west, and the poor confined to the east.

This was a trend established as far back as Roman times when the area east of Londinium's walls was used as a rubbish tip and burial ground. During the period prior to the Reformation when the land was owned by the Church, it remained a transient place with leases restricted to just a few years. Later, when ownership was wrested from the Church, it was allowed to grow unchecked into the slums so vilified during Jack the Ripper's reign of terror. Its geographical position downwind from the Court, together with its proximity to the docks, ensured that the East End became London's principal industrial quarter, attracting migrant workers, immigrants, dissidents and artisans, as well as entrepreneurs excluded from the City by the monopolistic guilds.

In sharp contrast, the West End's development was homogeneous, its grand squares, avenues and parks designed and built by the rich, to the exclusion of the poor. By the time Jack London arrived on the scene, the segregation of the City had become what the historian Jerry White has called 'a mystic divide between good and evil, civilisation and savagery'. Indeed, while staying in Highgate before making what he called his 'descent' into the East End, the American was hard pressed to find a single person who had ever set foot beyond the eastern border of the Square Mile of the City.

'It is over there somewhere,' people told him vaguely, waving their hands in an easterly direction and warning him against travelling there. 'Why, it is said there are places where a man's life isn't worth tu'pence.'

In his frustration, Jack London turned to the travel agents Thomas Cook & Son – 'pathfinders and trail-clearers, living sign-posts to all the world' – for help. The company had plenty of experience in organising expeditions into darkest Africa and innermost Tibet, but of the East End they admitted they knew 'nothing whatsoever'.

Eventually, Jack London disguised himself as a sailor and, with a gold sovereign sewn into the lining of his jacket for emergencies, set off for the East End on his own. He spent the next seven weeks sleeping rough and living off a diet of tea, bread, margarine and 'skilly', or watery oatmeal. Later in life he would write, 'No other book of mine took so much of my young heart and tears.'

When Abdul-Haq arrived, he sat down next to me, ordered a cup of tea and started to complain about his life. He was late, he said, because a tenant of a property he managed had been found dead from an overdose in his bathroom.

'Suicide,' he said dryly. 'I had to go to the morgue to identify him. He'd been dead for days. He did not look his best.'

Abdul-Haq's tea was brought to the table and he took several short, sharp sips, eyeing my copy of *The People of the Abyss*, which was lying on the table.

'What is this?' he asked gruffly with a nod.

I told him about the book's premise and he picked it up, turning to a passage I had marked.

'From the slimy, spittle-drenched sidewalk, they were picking up bits of orange peel, apple skin and grape stems, and they were eating them,' he read aloud. 'The pits of greengage plums they cracked between their teeth for the kernels inside. They picked up stray crumbs of bread the size of peas, apple cores so black and dirty one would not take them to be apple cores, and these things these two men took into their mouths, chewed them, and swallowed them.'

Abdul-Haq, a diehard pessimist who never smiled, nodded his solemn nod, closed the book and placed it back on the table.

'Yes, that is most definitely Whitechapel,' he said.

'But that book was written in 1902.'

'Perhaps. But it has not changed much round here.'

Abdul-Haq had come to England in 1973 from Kenya, looking for a bright new future, but things had not gone his way, and he had grown bitter about Britain. He continually likened conditions in the East End to those of the Third World. When he did, I found myself trying to placate him.

'I admit it's grim around here,' I said. 'But surely you can't be saying that it's as bad as it was in Jack London's day. People don't starve to death in the streets any more. The Welfare State has –'

'Welfare State, huh!' he interrupted. 'There are people living in such poverty here that it would make you sick just to see it for five minutes! I have seen old women so poor that they must eat cat food to survive. Many children suffer from cholera and rickets. It is common for families of ten to live in one room with no toilet, no bath, no running water. Only recently a part of the Whitechapel Hospital was closed because it was overrun by rats. And they call this *Great* Britain!'

Abdul-Haq's voice was raised now and other customers in the café were staring. The Kenyan didn't care; an audience is what he wanted.

'This is still one of the poorest parts of Britain. You will not find rich people living here. They are all in *Piccadilly*! And because the people are so poor and ignorant, the vultures' – he meant politicians – 'are able to line their pockets with our taxes and get away with it. You will not find justice here. You will only find lies!'

Abdul-Haq was the only estate agent I had ever met who talked down the area he dealt with. The first time I'd stepped into his agency near Brick Lane, he had tried his hardest to persuade me not to move to the East End.

'Why do you want to live *here*?' he'd said. 'You are obviously educated. This is not a place for a person like you. Everyone here is a criminal!'

To illustrate his point, Abdul-Haq had shown me the latest edition of the local newspaper, the *East London Advertiser*, which was packed with news of contract killings, gruesome murders, rapes, muggings and armed robberies. One story described how a man had been found floating bound and gagged in the Regent's Canal; another spoke of a pitched battle that had taken place in a local park between rival Bangladeshi teenage gangs, the Brick Lane Massif and Stepney Posse. In one edition, a two-page spread was dedicated to a recent spate of drive-by shootings by Yardies, whose weapon of choice was the Uzi machine-gun.

During that first meeting, Abdul-Haq also showed me the latest statistics on poverty, education and unemployment for the area. They were some of the worst for any inner city borough in Britain. Eighty per cent of the population lived in state housing; the average 'official' income per household was less than five thousand pounds a year.

'People here are being exploited as they always have been. The vultures care nothing for the poor people. We are pawns in a greater game!'

It had taken a good deal of effort on my part to persuade Abdul-Haq to show me the properties on his books. Although eventually he had relented, he still seemed to be holding out hope that I would abandon the idea of living in the East End.

'So you still want to move here, to this *place*?' he said, finishing his tea and fixing me with his cold, dark eyes.

'Believe me, it's not by choice,' I said, almost apologetically.

Abdul-Haq, who cringed when anyone shortened his name to Abdul – 'My name is "Abdul-Haq", which means "servant of the truth". To call me "Abdul" is to call me "servant" ' – had another one-bedroom flat to show me. But when I looked over the property details and read the blurb, which described it as 'cosy', I told him that I wasn't interested. I had seen enough places in the past month to know that 'cosy' was code for 'very nasty indeed'. The odds that it backed on to a railway line or provided vistas of a dual carriageway were high, as were those on the kitchen turning out to be a bottle-gas stove and a clapped-out fridge housing rare forms of fungi. The bathroom was also likely to be sub-standard – if indeed there was a bathroom at all. Only that morning, I had seen a place in Bethnal Green that had been without one. When I'd pointed out this flaw to the Ukrainian landlord, he'd told me with a shrug that there was a perfectly good Victorian bathhouse around the corner.

'It's got hot water and everything,' he'd said.

The sad reality was that Mr Ali's attic was the best place I'd seen to date. It was reasonably self-contained, the rent was – just – within my means, and although I could see my own breath in the bathroom, at least I would be able to wash in privacy.

I asked Abdul-Haq to call Mr Ali and tell him that I was willing to rent the 'studio' and that I would come to his shop to sign the lease at eight o'clock the following morning. He agreed to do so, albeit reluctantly.

'Be it upon your own head.'

That evening, I returned to my friend's flat in South Kensington and called my fiancée, Anu, who was in Delhi waiting for her British work visa to be issued. Before leaving India, I had talked her into moving with me to England. I had brushed aside her concerns about the infamous British climate and the price of property, and waxed lyrical about how London was an overgrown village with quaint Victorian terraces with back gardens and parks filled with rose arbours and swans. My idealistic description had made no mention of garbage-strewn streets where tramps pissed on the walls and people dumped their unwanted mattresses.

Now I had to decide whether to come clean or to continue being economical with the truth in the hope that by January, when she was due to arrive, I could find work and provide us with a home in a better area.

I opted for plan B.

'Hi. I found a flat,' I said when she answered the phone in her spacious, two-bedroom apartment in Delhi.

'How big?'

'Not huge. But it's . . . cosy.'

'Cosy. That sounds nice.'

There was a pause as she waited for the echo on the line to clear.

'Has it got a garden?' she asked.

Anu was a keen gardener; the possibility of having her own had proven a big draw.

'It's got a big roof terrace,' I said.

This was almost true: there was a flat roof out the back with a load of junk on it.

'And what about a shower? Has it got a shower?'

Being American, Anu was big on showers.

'Yes, there's a shower.' Just no showerhead: another thing the students had stolen.

'So how big is the living room?'

'Well, it's sort of a studio.'

There was another pause; we had a crossed line.

'Sounds great,' she shouted, over the intervening jabber of Punjabi.

'Well, I wouldn't call it *great*,' I said. 'But it will do for the time being.'

Mr Ali's shop was protected as if it housed the Crown Jewels. The front door and window were covered by a set of reinforced steel shutters that looked strong enough to deflect a rocket-propelled grenade. An alarm box fixed to the wall flashed with lights just a few feet from a CCTV camera that was trained on the pavement. The upper windows were shielded by rows of iron bars.

It took Mr Ali a full five minutes to sort through his great bunch of keys and open the six padlocks that secured the shutters to a thick frame bolted into the concrete.

'It can be a bit dodgy round 'ere,' he said as I stood behind him on the pavement the next morning ready to settle the let. 'You can't be too careful, yeah. You never know what's going to 'appen on Brick Lane.'

Mr Ali was in a chattier mood. As he opened his shop, he told me about the 'dark days' of the 1970s when gangs of skinheads rampaged through the streets, smashing shop windows and attacking anyone with coloured skin. He had been in his early twenties at the time, a sweatshop worker living with his uncle in a tenement building in Spitalfields.

'One evening when I was on my way 'ome, I see this bunch of skin'eads coming down the street towards me, yeah. They was shouting, "Kill the Black Paki Bustard!" I remember finkin', thas the biscuit, innit. 'cause if someone calls me "black" it don't bovver me much 'cause, at the end of the day, I'm black, innit. But I'm not Pakistani; I'm Bangladeshi, yeah. Iss a big difference. So I says to these bustard skin'eads, "Get your facts right, yeah." But they says to me, "Fuck off 'ome, Paki."'

Mr Ali ran but not fast enough. The thugs caught up with him and knocked him down, laying into him with their steel-capped Doc Marten boots. He suffered a broken nose, five broken ribs and a lacerated ear.

'It could 'ave been a lot worse, yeah. That is if my auntie 'adn't seen 'em off.'

'What did she do?' I asked, trying to picture a veiled Bangladeshi woman taking on a gang of skinheads.

'She was upstairs cooking fish curry when she 'eard the fighting. So she carried the pot – 'uge it was – to the window and poured it out. Next fing I know, yeah, there's curry fallin' on the skin'eads, burning them. It got in their eyes and everything, yeah, so they run off.'

Mr Ali smiled to himself, still savouring the memory. But the smile quickly vanished and was replaced by a deep frown.

'In actual fact, yeah, I got off easy, innit,' he continued. 'There was another geezer my age, yeah. Altab Ali was 'is name. 'e got knifed on Adler Street when 'e was, like, walking 'ome. 'e was twenty-four. It was a tragedy, innit.'

Mr Ali told me how the murder of Altab Ali in May 1978 helped galvanise the Bangladeshi community into action against the racists.

On the day of his funeral, thousands marched on Downing Street, demanding justice and protection from the police. In the coming months, further demonstrations prevented the National Front from distributing their hate literature on Brick Lane.

'Once they knew we was ready to stand up to them, yeah, them racialist bustards backed off, innit,' said Mr Ali as he unlocked the last padlock securing the shutters. 'After that, fings got better round 'ere. But the bad feelings towards us people never went away. Not completely, yeah. 'cause a few years ago there was more trouble and fings got serious again.'

During the 1993 Tower Hamlets council elections, which saw the British National Party win a council seat in the Isle of Dogs, Brick Lane was the scene of pitched battles between white supremacists and local Bangladeshis backed by anti-fascist groups. Once again, Mr Ali found himself on the front line. Swastikas were sprayed on his shop shutters and, one evening as he drove down Bethnal Green Road, a brick was thrown through his windscreen.

Perhaps surprisingly, he didn't hold a grudge.

'Basically, I don't fink the British people are racialist, yeah,' he said, pulling up the shutters on his shop. 'There's bad people everywhere, innit. When everyone's got a few quid in their pockets, then fings are all right. People can live together, no problem, yeah. It's when everyone's, like, 'anging around, thas when there's trouble. Iss all about economics, innit.'

Mr Ali opened the front door of the shop, stepped inside and turned on the lights. A row of Indian mannequins stood in the window with red *bindis* on their foreheads and hands pressed together in the Hindu *namaste*. Their curvy figures had been moulded with saris in mind. But Mr Ali had them dressed in red and yellow leather miniskirts, matching strapless tops and studded belts, a style better suited to Hollywood kerb-side hookers.

The shop beyond was dark and cavernous, one side lined with black leather jackets which hung from the racks like sleeping bats. The opposite wall displayed rows of fake leopardskin trousers, and jackets with a glossy, snakeskin finish. I ran my fingers over the material, making a mental note where to come next time I needed a fancy dress outfit, and wondering who would pay good money for such clothing. Elvis impersonators or game show hosts perhaps?

'You don't get better quality,' said Mr Ali, who mistook my curiosity for interest. 'People come from all over the world to buy from me. I get a lot of Japanese, innit. They come down the East End for jellied eels and they come in 'ere. My leathers are big in Tokyo.'

It was this newfound, walk-in trade that had kept Mr Ali's business afloat. The days when every good Essex Girl had owned a black leather jacket and a tight little miniskirt were over.

'Now they're all shopping at Next, innit.'

Mr Ali led me into his office at the back of the shop. It was a small room that smelt of junk food and cigarettes and looked as if it had been ransacked by thieves during the night. Papers lay strewn across the carpet, and the desk was awash with files, offcuts of fabric and leather samples and dried bits of lettuce and onion fallen from hamburgers. A dustbin behind the desk was stuffed full of Burger King cartons. Up on the wall hung a black and white photograph of the Fonz astride a shiny motorbike, wearing his trademark black leather jacket.

'Right guv, this won't take long, yeah,' he said, indicating the chair in front of his desk.

I sat down and Mr Ali started to fill in a lease, occasionally asking me for pertinent details. As he did so, I noticed a repetitive thumping noise coming from the basement, which made the floorboards vibrate beneath my feet. When I asked Mr Ali what was going on downstairs, he told me that he had hired some builders to knock down a wall and that they were using a pneumatic drill. This seemed like a plausible explanation and I gave the matter no further thought. That is until about five minutes later when, quite suddenly, a secret door concealed in the wall to my left opened and the sounds of thumping machinery and raised voices spilled into the room. They were followed by a young Bangladeshi man in oil-stained clothes, his face hot and sweaty. In one hand he carried a red, lacy bra. This he handed to Mr Ali and, after a brief exchange between the two men, the worker withdrew through the door, closing it behind him.

The red, lacy bra remained on the desk while Mr Ali went on filling in the lease. Once it was finished, he pushed the document over to my side of the desk and then picked up the bra, which he stretched between his fingers, testing its elasticity.

'You must be, like, wondering waas going on, innit,' he said. 'I mean, what's this sweaty geezer doing down the basement with women's underwear, yeah?'

I nodded.

'OK guv, seeing as we're mates and everything, I'll level with you.' He leant forward in his chair and over the front of his desk. 'The fing is, yeah, I've got a bit-a-work goin' on down the basement, innit. My boys, yeah, they're making garments. Underwears, T-shirts, that sort of fing.'

He stuffed the bra into one of the drawers of his desk.

'See, what you've gotta understand yeah, is I'm creating jobs, contributing to the economy, innit. But there's people 'oo don't see it that way. Like the coppers, yeah. They'd 'ave a go at me, innit. "Oi! Mr Ali! 'er Majesty, she don't allow no factory down your basement!"'

He put an index finger to his lips.

'So keep it 'ushed, yeah. Between mates, innit. Mum's the word. Agreed?'

I nodded again and picked up the lease to check all the details. It seemed to be in order, but the thought of living above a sweatshop caused me to hesitate.

'How safe is your "factory"?' I asked him. 'May I see it?'

'Sorry, mate, no can do, yeah. But there's nafing to worry about, geezer. It couldn't be safer. One 'under per cent. I'm Mr Responsible, innit. I'll give you a ladder and everyfing, so if there's a fire, you can climb on the roof.'

I asked him about the workers. What sort of conditions were they labouring in?

'Couldn't be better,' answered Mr Ali, who made himself out to be a regular Mother Teresa. 'In actual fact, yeah, there's people 'oo'd give their arms and legs to work for me. Iss all about opportunity, innit. One of my boys, yeah, 'e came 'ere in 1988 with nafing. Now 'e's workin' for London Underground.'

Mr Ali took a set of keys out of a drawer in his desk and handed them to me.

'Remember, yeah. If anybody come round asking waas goin' on down the basement, you don't know nafing. Keep it to yourself, yeah, and I'll do you a bargain on a jacket. Them snakeskin ones are a steal at two 'under quid, innit.'

I went to South Kensington to collect my belongings and returned to Brick Lane in a taxi. My driver was a native of Bethnal Green who, like many white East Enders, had moved out of the area. He now lived in Essex where, he boasted, the French windows of his living room looked out on to open fields.

'When I was growing up, we never locked our doors at night,' he said, speaking over his shoulder through the gap in the glass partition of his hackney carriage.

A thickset man in his early sixties, he had a close-shaven head and a nose that looked as if it had been chiselled out of solid rock.

'It's not like that now. I'll tell you that for nothing. 'ardly a day goes by without a knifing or a shooting. I wouldn't want my grandchildren growing up round 'ere. Not now. Terrible it is.'

I didn't know it yet, but these were the opening lines of the-East End's-gone-to-rack-and-ruin rant made by resident and non-resident white East Enders whenever they found an opportunity. Over the course of the year I spent living on Brick Lane, I heard it so many times that I got to know it by heart.

'When I was growing up, the East End was a friendly place,' continued the driver, who had my full attention, but only because this was the first time I'd heard someone lamenting the end of Cockney culture. 'Everyone knew everyone. We was like one big 'appy family. People looked out for one another in them days.'

Encouraged by my interest, he reminisced for a while about music halls and knees-ups, about playing Knock Down Ginger in the streets and eating jellied eels in pie and mash shops. It was nostalgic, idyllic stuff that made the old East End sound more like the set of a musical than your average city neighbourhood.

'What we lacked in wealth we made up for in spirit,' he said, gunning his cab through the narrow streets of the financial district and crossing over the eastern boundary of the City into Spitalfields. 'It was a special place back then. But now . . .' He cast his left hand along the length of his windscreen and peered out at the dreary streets beyond. 'Frankly speaking, you can 'ave it.'

We sped down Fashion Street where the façades of the warehouses were dark with dirt. Steel plates were screwed over windows to stop squatters gaining access.

'Wasn't it always pretty bad round here – the poverty I mean?' I was remembering Jack London's descriptions.

The driver stared contemptuously at my reflection in his rear view mirror. 'People are always banging on about how terrible it was, 'ow the East End was this and that. People 'ave always tried to malign us East Enders, make us out to be dirty and lazy. But we've got our pride, too, you know!'

I apologised.

'No apology necessary,' he said, as he turned left on to the southern end of Brick Lane. 'Don't get me wrong. There was poverty all right; I'm not denying it. We didn't 'ave none of your creature comforts. No central heating, no indoor plumbing, none of your wall-to-wall carpeting. We were underprivileged, no doubt about it. But that's what made us resilient, helped build the Cockney character. Take the Blitz. Nowhere in London got the pounding the East End did. But we got through it, just like we got through everything – by pulling together.'

'So why did you move out, then?'

The driver pointed to a crowd of Bangladeshi men in white prayer caps standing outside the Brick Lane mosque on the corner of Fournier Street.

'*Them*,' he said.

By now, we were stuck in traffic at the south end of Brick Lane. This was the heart of what was known officially as 'Banglatown', home to some fifty thousand or more Bangladeshis, and this portion of the street was lined with Indian restaurants, sari emporiums, Asian video rental stores, travel agents advertising *Hajj* package deals, confectionery shops selling fried, syrupy *jellabies* and lamp-posts painted red and green, the national colours of Bangladesh. Touts stood outside the curry houses trying to entice passers-by with special meal offers. Inside a Pakistani-owned barbers, where a photograph of the Ka'bah lit up at night hung on the wall, a man was having his ears cleaned out with cotton buds. A couple of doors down stood a wedding goods store where prospective brides and grooms could pick up garlands of plastic flowers and red velvet-upholstered thrones for their reception.

'Just look at it!' said the driver mockingly. 'I don't know what you'd call it. But it's not England.'

The traffic began to move again and we crawled past a refrigerated truck parked up on the pavement. Bangladeshi men in bloodstained white jackets were unloading lamb carcases and carrying them over their shoulders into a supermarket called Taj Stores. Through the doors I spotted exotic Bengali vegetables and fruit for sale, and virtually everything else a South Asian family would ever need – from stainless steel *tiffins* to cooking pots the size of cauldrons.

'Don't get me wrong,' said the driver. 'Personally, I've got nothing against the Indians. I'm a bit of a curry holic myself. There's just too many of them. Britain's getting swamped. It won't be long before there's no such thing as an Englishman. We'll be a bunch of mongrels. Naa! It's no good, is it? You've got to draw the line somewhere.'

We passed more curry houses with names like 'Le Taj' and women in *niqabs*, with only their eyes and the tips of their shoes visible as they shuffled along the narrow pavements. A trio of teenage Bangladeshi girls came up the street towards us, chewing gum and smiling and chatting amongst themselves. They were dressed modestly in long black coats, loose trousers and *hijabs*, but they also wore make-up and lipstick and their nails were manicured and polished. Further on, half a dozen teenage Bangladeshi boys loitered on a street corner. All of them had the same identical hairstyle: sides shaved and tops parted down the middle and caked in gel. In their Eminem caps, Tommy Hilfiger jeans and Nikes, they looked like wannabe members of an LA gang – only they were short and thin, and, unlike the Americans they tried to emulate, not especially threatening.

Beyond the corner of Woodseer Street, we passed through the complex of buildings that once housed the old Truman Buxton Brewery, which dated back to the sixteenth century and had been converted into studios and workspaces for a young crowd of artists, video producers, fashion designers and dot com entrepreneurs. Here, in the shadow of the brewery's now defunct brick chimney, the bustling ethnic stores gave way to minimalist furniture shops and boutiques with names like 'Eat My Handbag Bitch!' There were a couple of art galleries, too, one showing an exhibition entitled 'SNOG!' – a series of photographs of couples young and old, straight and gay, pushing their tongues into each other's mouths. At the centre of the complex stood the Vibe Bar, recently dubbed one of the trendiest hangouts in London.

The traffic began to move a little faster and we entered the northern end of Brick Lane where the street changed character yet again. This was the run-down, seedier part where the old East End rag trade still survived in the form of leather jacket shops and cheap clothing wholesalers. Cardboard boxes stencilled 'Karachi' and 'Istanbul' were being offloaded from a van overseen by one of Mr Ali's competitors, a Pakistani with a pot-belly and three-day stubble.

The cab pulled up outside Mr Ali's shop and I got out and unloaded my belongings.

'You want to watch your back round here, mate,' said the driver, as I paid him through the window. 'You can't trust *them*, you know. They don't share our values. Remember that.'

I felt like telling him that it wasn't being around immigrants that worried me so much as having to blend in amongst the white Cockney population. It had been years since I had had to deal with Britain's class system, but as a former public school boy, I knew only too well how deep the hostility and prejudice ran. As a teenager I was often chased or picked on by local kids from the comprehensive near to my posh school. Once, when I was fifteen, I was beaten up and stripped naked for being a 'toff'.

The book I had been reading over the past couple of days had hardly put my mind at ease. Entitled *I Took Off My Tie*, it was an account by Hugh Massingham, a young, idealistic writer from west London, who went to live in the heart of the East End in the 1930s and was given a less than friendly reception by his neighbours. Far from the caricature of chirpy Cockneys, they jeered at him, accused him of being a spy, and one of them even broke into his flat and smashed up his possessions.

'I felt that I had stumbled on a secret society whose members were communicating with one another by signs whose significance was entirely lost on me,' wrote Massingham. 'I was in a strange land inhabited by a strange people.'

———◆———

I spent my first day on Brick Lane bagging up all the rubbish and junk that littered the floors; vacuuming, scrubbing, washing and disinfecting every inch of every surface; installing a new toilet seat, which I had duly paid for myself; and taping foam to the beams in the attic to protect my head.

As I worked, I discovered a few unpleasant surprises.

The attic was home to a family of mice who scurried about in broad daylight, merrily depositing droppings wherever they went. The electricity in each room was routed through several old meters (one above the door of each room), which, when not adequately fed with one-pound coins, cut off the electricity supply. This caused unsaved computer documents to vanish and food to spoil in the fridge, and it often meant that going to the loo in the middle of the night presented something of a challenge.

The bathroom also had its fair share of problems. When the outdoor temperature dropped to zero, my shampoo congealed. A crack in the ceiling ran above the toilet, which meant that when it rained, water dripped on to my bare thighs. And the shower alternated from freezing cold to scorching hot, but never produced anything in between.

When I complained to Mr Ali about all this and more besides, he was long on advice but short on solutions. To rid the attic of the mice he suggested I buy some traps – 'And some cheese. Mice like cheese, innit.' To ensure a constant supply of electricity, he pointed me in the direction of the nearest bank where, he said, the tellers cashed notes for coins. And vis-à-vis the faulty shower, he agreed that the water supply was erratic but urged me to wash with a bucket: 'You've lived in India. You should be used to it.'

'And what about the leaking roof in the bathroom?' I demanded.
'No problem,' said Mr Ali nonchalantly.
Reaching back behind his office chair, he produced an umbrella.
'Keep this by the toilet,' he said. 'It'll keep you dry, innit.'

The most irritating characteristic of the building was the front door-bell, which was hooked up to a fire station bell that Mr Ali had bought in a junk sale and attached to the wall of the second-floor landing. Its ring caused the windows and all the crockery and cutlery to vibrate in my kitchen, and it never failed to wake me with a start. Evidently, it also disturbed the neighbours who put rude notes through the door.

Unfortunately, the front doorbell was rung with great frequency, and because the woman on the first floor was elderly, it was left for me to answer it. I soon tired of charging downstairs to find yet another pamphleteer standing on the doorstep canvassing for the Socialist Workers Party or a drug addict hoping to score from a man called Gavin, apparently a previous tenant who had been the neighbour-hood's chief supplier of ecstasy. So I attached a notice to the door, explaining that, a) I was not interested in changing my religious or political persuasions; that b) Gavin had moved and I had no idea where he had gone; and c) I was not a supplier of narcotics.

After that the bell rang less frequently. But there were still those to whom my notice failed to speak directly, and who, not taking a hint, pressed the buzzer anyway.

One of these offenders was a Nigerian immigrant who was search-ing for someone – anyone – to sponsor him for UK residency. Another man, who represented a cult whose Prophet had been sighted on Brick Lane, was searching for eyewitnesses to the miracles which 'The Enlightened One' was alleged to have performed. And I was pes-tered on more than one occasion by a middle-aged Muslim convert from Stoke-on-Trent who wanted me to sign a petition against the use of 'half-naked' women in British advertising.

Before long, my patience ran thin and I started slamming the door in people's faces. But occasionally I made exceptions. And when one morning I opened the door to find an attractive Scandinavian woman with an infectious smile standing on the doorstep, I played nice.

'Hello,' she said. 'May I come in out of the rain?'

'Sure,' I said, opening the door.

She stepped inside and the two of us stood on the stairs where she explained she was a film location scout.

'I'm looking for a suitable place to shoot a few scenes. Could I look around. We pay £750 a day.'

'Come on up!'

I gave her the grand tour, making excuses for the graffiti, the buckets and the furniture. 'I just moved in,' I explained. But she seemed delighted and even took some pictures with her camera.

'It's perfect,' she beamed, like someone who had stumbled upon Shangri-La.

'Perfect?'

'Yes. It's exactly what we're after.'

It was then she explained that the film was about a group of junkies who caught HIV by sharing the same needles. The script, she assured me, was thick with irony and carried an important message – presumably something along the lines of 'if you're a junkie, don't share needles'.

'The kitchen would be great for the suicide scene,' she said with a squeal.

'The suicide scene?'

'When Danny, the main character, hangs himself.'

And with that she thanked me for my time, took a note of my telephone number, and made her way downstairs. That was the last I ever saw of her. This was probably for the best, because over the course of the next week or so I painted over the graffiti with white emulsion, bought some potted houseplants, and did away with the wooden pallet table in the kitchen in favour of a model from Ikea.

During my first few weeks on Brick Lane, I spent as much time away from the East End as possible. When I wasn't job-hunting, I took sanctuary in the reading room of the London Library in St James's Square, went for walks through Green Park and browsed at Hatchards.

I felt at home in the West End; this was the London I knew and where I wanted to be. But in the early evening, when the library closed and I would have to make my way back east on the number eight bus, the loneliness invariably crept up on me.

I was an immigrant in a strange and unfamiliar landscape, despite the fact that this was my city. There was no community to offer me any measure of comfort – the white East Enders of Bethnal Green struck me as wary of outsiders; the Bangladeshis and other immigrant groups seemed to keep themselves to themselves – and after dark, the streets were full of foreboding.

Watching from my kitchen window, which looked out over Brick Lane, hardly put my mind at ease. On my first night, I saw a gang of Bangladeshi teenagers beat up a black rival, leaving him bleeding and unconscious in the gutter. The following evening, a couple of bleach blondes in miniskirts and high heels got into a scrap in the car park at the junction with Bethnal Green Road, egged on by a group of onlookers who shouted encouragement as they punched and clawed one another.

I lost count of the number of times I saw pushers selling drugs, people having their mobile phones snatched, or bikes being stolen by teenagers who carried cutters down their trouser legs. Eventually I gave up calling the police, who never bothered to show up.

But still I found sitting in the window strangely addictive. It was like having my own private box with a bird's-eye view of Brick Lane's street theatre. For hours at a time, I would watch the diverse collection of people coming and going in the street below, their fleeting faces caught in the flashing yellow emergency light fixed to the wooden shack of the cab firm that was housed in a corner of the car park.

Since the two bakeries never closed, the street was never quiet. Even in the dead of night, clubbers ravenous after hours on the dance floors of Shoreditch and Hoxton would congregate on the pavement, satisfying their munchies. The bakeries were also a popular spot with taxi drivers who took breaks sitting in the backs of their black cabs, drinking coffee and chatting with fellow cabbies working the grave-yard shift. Occasionally, one of London's new armed police patrols would pull up and officers wearing body armour and carrying pistols and machine-guns would load up on snacks before speeding away to a stake-out or the scene of the latest shooting.

Dawn brought the first of the white van men, who would make quick pit stops, leaving their engines running while they bought breakfast. At about the same time, a steady stream of black office cleaners would appear en route to the City, taking away their bagels in brown paper bags which, once they'd gorged themselves on the contents, they would screw up into balls and toss into the street.

I soon came to recognise some of the regulars. Mr Ali's sweatshop workers emerged occasionally from the basement below to take a break and pick up a snack. Two Eastern European prostitutes who worked on the corner of Redchurch Street often appeared between jobs, looking cold and underfed in miniskirts and armless sheepskin jackets. Their pimp was never far behind them, his face half-hidden under the brim of his baseball cap.

At around midnight two thick-necked heavies straight out of Central Casting who worked as bouncers at a Hoxton strip joint would always appear. They both wore identical black leather jackets and chunky gold rings and, while eating their bagels, stood outside the bakeries shoulder to shoulder, backs straight and feet spread apart.

Two tramps always hung around until late into the night. The older of them, a man with red hair, would pass out on the pavement with only his threadbare tweed jacket to keep him warm. His friend, who wore a permanent silly grin, spent his nights standing in the middle of the street, trying to direct traffic and causing irate drivers to sound their horns in fury.

Eventually the novelty of sitting in the window wore off. And as my apprehension diminished, I became a regular at the bakeries myself. I also stopped hiding out in Piccadilly and started to explore the East End, reading up on the history of the area as had been my habit while living in cities abroad.

Instead of my travels coming to an end, they had in fact taken a new and unexpected turn. But still, the loneliness and sense of dislocation was hard to shake, and for months I had trouble sleeping. Often it was the noise from the street that woke me — shouting or raucous laughter, or the sounds of police sirens and car and house alarm bells wailing in the night – and I would make my way downstairs to the kitchen where I would be drawn back to the window.

Standing there, watching the endless activity in the street below, I would often contemplate my shattered nostalgia for London and read the words of Isaac Rosenberg, the Jewish poet who lived in the East End a century before me, whose 'Ballad of Whitechapel' I had photo-copied and sellotaped to the wall:

> I stood where glowed
> The merry glare of golden whirring lights
> Above the monstrous mass that seethed and flowed
> Through one of London's nights.

> I watched the gleams
> Of jagged warm lights on shrunk faces pale.
> I heard mad laughter as one hears in dreams,
> Or Hell's harsh lurid tale.

2

We Are Shadows

'The East End cannot really be called pretty. But it is, without doubt, attractive, sometimes in the broadest sense even beautiful and always, in some peculiar way, it has charm. Because the East End is not simply a place it is a people.'

Roy Curtis, *East End Passport* (1969)

'IT'S NOT NICE to wake up old ladies in the middle of the night. Not nice at all!' scolded my first-floor neighbour, squinting through the narrow gap between her front door and its frame. 'If my Mendel was alive, he'd show you. Batter you black and blue, 'e would. My Mendel was a boxer. A champion of Bethal Green!'

I stood on the first-floor landing, wondering what I had done to offend her. Had my TV been up too loud? Had I been sleepwalking again? Was she crazy?

'To think that I grew up in a respectable family,' she gasped, her voice abrasive. 'We might 'ave been poor, but respect was never in short supply. Respect. There was always respect!'

I tried to explain that I had only moved in a couple of weeks ago, that I was not one of the previous tenants and had had nothing to do with the rave that had been held before I moved in. Nor was I responsible for the disappearance of the light bulbs in the hallway. But she was deaf to all reason. Her eyes shone with anger and her pockmarked nose turned an alarming purple as she spat more insults at me.

'You're a disgrace, that's what you are. A bleedin' disgrace! Leave an old lady alone, why don't you?'

With that, she slammed the door shut in my face. Four locks clicked into place. And as she retreated into her room, I heard her cursing me as a 'bleedin' 'ooligan'.

That was my introduction to Mrs Sadie Cohen.

The next time we saw one another, a couple of days later, was on the stairs and she tried to cosh me with her umbrella.

The following week, we crossed paths in the local newsagent where she denounced me as a 'villain' in front of Mr Singh, the owner, whose warrior-caste instincts had not been tempered by his twenty-seven years as a newsagent wallah.

'Get out of my shop this instant, you dog!' he shouted at me, lobbing a Creme Egg in my direction.

Later that day, Mrs Cohen took her complaint to Mr Ali, telling him that I had been drilling holes through the floorboards for the purpose of spying on her. Mr Ali soon paid me a visit in the attic to hear my side of the story (I had been banging down a few sharp nails sticking out of the floorboards). He didn't seem the least bit surprised to hear that Mrs Cohen had got it all spectacularly wrong.

'The old bat's a bit cuckoo clock, innit,' he said, tapping his temple with one finger after he listened to my version of events. 'She's always imaginin' fings. One time, yeah, she calls the coppers telling them I've, like, stolen 'er TV aerial off the roof. When they come round, they find the lead is out the back of 'er TV set. It's just paranoia, innit.'

Mr Ali promised to smooth things over with 'the old Jew', as he referred to her, and said he would set the record straight with Mr Singh as well. Half an hour later, I heard the old lady calling to me up the stairs.

'Young man! Young man! I know you're up there!'

Despite her age, she was able to project her voice with considerable force. Its piercing quality made it all the more arresting.

'Why didn't you say something?' she said accusingly as I came down the stairs. 'You expect an old lady to be able to tell you boys apart? My eyes aren't what they used to be, you know. They're well past their sell-by date.'

Mrs Cohen, or Sadie, as she asked to be called – 'Mrs Cohen, he calls me! What are you, a lawyer or something?' – stood a little over five feet tall, although she insisted that before old age had set in, she had been much taller.

'I've shrunk,' she would say. 'Someone's put a curse on me!'

Now in her eighties, her arms and legs were a roadmap of raised blue veins and the skin above her upper lip was ribbed like the surface of a clamshell. Even in a flower print dress and tartan slippers, she didn't seem the least bit frail or vulnerable. Her arresting gaze more than made up for her diminutive stature. In fact, she could be surprisingly intimidating at times, her dark, unblinking eyes animated into cartoon proportions by her thick glasses and punctuated by two pointy eyebrows drawn in brown pencil liner like French circumflexes.

For someone so elderly, Sadie had an extraordinary amount of energy, and at times I found it hard to keep up with her. She could talk for hours on end, switching from one topic to another without so much as a pause. Her opinions were anything but sensitive or tempered. Old age had brought with it the perk of being able to say what she liked and she made the most of it.

'You're not another of them poofters, are you?' she asked me as we stood on the landing. 'If there's one thing I can't stand, it's poofters.'

'No,' I said. 'I'm —'

'Not married though, are you?'

'No, I'm engage —'

'You wouldn't be living *here* if you was married. Divorced probably. Everyone's divorced these days. Marriage isn't the sacred institution it was in my day, you know. When *we* got married, it was for life. "Till death us do part . . ." '

Sadie kept me standing on the stairs for another ten minutes before I finally summoned the courage to interrupt her and invited her to join me in my kitchen for a cup of tea.

'Tea! Are you crazy?' She glared at me as if I'd just insulted her. 'Think! I can't have tea with you in your kitchen. What would the neighbours say?'

'Which neighbours?'

'Which neighbours, he asks! Them! Across the way. They see everything. They'll be saying I'm not 'ospitable. I'll get a reputation. And a reputation's like a stain that won't come out in the wash.'

She pushed open the door to her bed-sit. A smell that I associated with old people's homes came wafting out: stale, uncirculated air laced with the odours of boiled vegetables and Nivea cream. The door led on to a large room with a carpet the colour of mud and a pair of faded red velvet curtains drawn across the window.

'You'd better come in to mine,' she said reluctantly, stepping inside. 'You can say 'ello to Mr Begleiter.'

I followed her into the room and she locked the door behind me, hanging a set of wind chimes on the handle.

'That's my early warning system. And this' – she picked up a cricket bat – 'this is for intruders.'

She prodded it in the direction of my groin, causing me to flinch.

'I can look after myself, you know! I don't need nobody mollycoddling me!' She put the cricket bat back in its place beside the door. 'Now, come over 'ere and sit down, and don't move a muscle!'

As instructed, I sat down in a burgundy armchair, which was sprouting sprigs of horsehair stuffing. I felt them pricking my backside. The more I shifted the more uncomfortable I became.

'You're in for a treat,' said Sadie standing over me, her tone suddenly sweetness again. 'I've made chicken noodle soup. It'll be ready before you can say "mazel tov".'

Sadie turned and disappeared into her kitchen, which was housed in a room off the main bed-sit and was little larger than a broom cupboard. Uneasy in the chair, I got up and looked around the room. It was like a time vault, with only a few of her possessions, like the colour TV and a copy of *Cosmopolitan*, to ruin the illusion that I had stepped back to the 1950s. The wardrobe, dressing table and drawers were all teak, the varnish chipped and cracked. The rose-printed wallpaper had long since faded and, in places, was peeling away from the walls. Moths had done serious damage to the curtains, which let in tiny beams of sunshine. The brass bed frame was tarnished green.

But despite the room's jaded appearance, it was extremely neat and tidy and no dust lay on any surface within Sadie's reach. The bed was made up as perfectly as a wrapped Christmas present. The frames on the mantelpiece were arranged as if part of an exhibition. The few dozen books on the shelf next to the door were ordered according to size. Even the old newspapers had been carefully folded and placed in a box next to the fireplace.

'Mr Begleiter's getting on a bit now,' she shouted from the kitchen. 'He 'ardly moves nowadays, poor dear. Arth–right–is. 'orrible arth–right–is.'

A tortured, drawn-out miaow from the far corner by the window alerted me to the presence of a long-haired Siamese lying on a cushion matted with hair. He had a sticky eye and a face that looked as if someone had sat on it, the mouth, nose and eyes all squashed together.

'The vet says he 'asn't long. But what do vets know? Or doctors? Idiots, the 'ole bleedin' lot of 'em. Said I'd be dead decades ago! But 'ere I am, alive and kicking. Told my Mum the same thing. "You'll be dead within the year!" Know what age she lived to? Ninety-two! She was a fighter my Mum. A tough'un through and through.'

Mrs Cohen emerged from the kitchen, carrying a couple of bowls and spoons and a packet of kosher crackers, which she placed on her small dining table. I fetched the pot of soup from the stove and she ladled it out, instructing me to try some. I ate my first spoonful and, although it tasted like salty dishwater flavoured with chicken stock, made appropriately appreciative sounds.

'See! What did I tell you! You'll never taste better. It's the oregano, my secret ingredient. I've won prizes for my soup. My Mendel loved it. "Sadie," he used to say, "I don't know what I love more: you or your chicken noodle soup."'

She took down a photograph from the mantelpiece and gazed upon it affectionately. It was of a young man with distinctly Semitic features wearing boxing gloves held up to the camera as if he was about to give the photographer a right hook.

'That's my Mendel,' she said, running a finger over the small Star of David that hung around her neck. 'We was married forty years. Imagine that. Lovely man 'e was. Sixteen years 'e's been gawn. We buried 'im out in Chadwell 'eath. A very fancy funeral we 'ad. 'orses, a carriage, flowers and a beautiful marble 'eadstone. He got a right royal send off 'e did.'

Before I could ask her anything more about Mendel, she changed the subject yet again.

'So what sort of name is "Tarquin", anyway?' Her tone was inquisitive but somehow dismissive at the same time.

'It's Etruscan,' I said.

'Etruscan!' She made a face. 'Sounds Irish. You're not Irish, are you? They're the scum of the earth is the Irish. We don't like the Irish, do we, Mr Begleiter?'

The cat let out another tortured miaow, blinking his sticky eye, and I explained that the Etruscans had been an ancient people who lived in central Italy.

'Italy! So you're Italian. Well, why didn't you say so? I always liked the Italian people. Good-looking the Italians are. Lovely olive skin they 'ave. Like that Ricky Martin.'

She pushed up the back of her hair and rolled her eyes, saying dreamily: 'What I wouldn't do for a man like Ricky Martin.'

'Ricky Martin's not Italian – and neither am I,' I protested.

'I know, you're Etruscan!' she snapped.

'No I'm not. I'm English.'

'All right, I hear you. God gave me ears, too, you know!'

She nibbled on a cracker and stirred her soup, frowning and muttering to herself. Then she looked up at me and said defiantly, 'You're not Jewish, that's for sure.'

'No, I'm not Jewish,' I admitted, sounding apologetic although I couldn't think why.

Sadie smiled mischievously, leaned forward on the table towards me and touched my arm playfully.

'Never mind, dear,' she said. '*Schwer und bitter is dos Leben.*'

'I beg your pardon?'

'That's a bit of Yiddish for you,' she said. 'My granddad taught me. It means "Life is 'arsh and bitter." '

———— • ————

Sadie had developed a phobia for the outside world and often spent up to six days at a time closeted inside her bed-sit. Her groceries were delivered to her door, a homecare worker oversaw her day-to-day affairs, and occasionally a rabbi would stop by to say prayers, although he was generally given a frosty reception – 'Bleedin' rabbis. Bloodsuckers!'

Sadie only ventured out on Thursdays when she had lunch at a local Jewish day care centre. Preparations for this weekly ritual began mid-morning with a visit to her favourite Bethnal Green hairdressers and beauty salon where her hair (which she dyed a honey colour) was arranged into a Margaret Thatcher-style bouffant. Afterwards, her nails would be manicured, and make-up applied to her face by someone with steadier hands than her own. Then it was back home to slip into a skirt and blouse, and as a finishing touch, she would douse herself in Chanel No. 5.

At twelve thirty sharp, her 'chauffeur' would arrive in the form of Ron, the one cab driver whom she trusted to take her the short ride to the day care centre. Ron also happened to be a rugged, handsome man in his early forties who played up to her flirtatiousness, joking that she was the only woman in the world for him.

'Mrs Co'en, I could eat you alive,' he'd say, causing her to 'ooh' and blush on the back seat of his BMW.

On a number of occasions during my first months on Brick Lane, Sadie persuaded me to keep her company during her Thursday morning ritual, and afterwards, as a reward, she bought me lunch at the day care centre, or her 'club' as she liked to refer to it.

The place was frequented by the last of the East End Jews, the youngest of whom were in their early eighties. Like many such centres, it had a big communal room in which old friends came to chat, watched TV, played backgammon and cards, or just sat staring blankly into space. A team of young nurses remained on hand to help with everything from adjusting pillows to emptying colostomy bags. On special days, entertainers visited and put on a show. There were karaoke and bingo nights. And on the Jewish holy days, a visiting rabbi would conduct religious services.

Being a creature of habit, Sadie always arrived for lunch at least fifteen minutes early, which ensured that she got the same seat at her favourite table. Over the course of the next ten to fifteen minutes before the meal was served, she would guard the three remaining seats for her friends. Anyone trying to take a place at the table who wasn't wanted was given short shrift, no matter how incapacitated or elderly they might be.

'Oi! Wheel off some place else!' she shouted at an old man in a wheelchair the first time we had lunch at the centre. 'This table's reserved. Get your own!'

The tone she took with her long-term friends Ethel, Gilda and Solly was less abrupt but still cuttingly sarcastic.

'Still alive then,' she said to Ethel, her close friend for seventy-five years, as she sat down at the table.

'Just about – which is more than can be said for you!'

The two of them cackled loudly, nudging one another with their elbows. Then they turned their attention on Solly, who was a few years younger than them, a fact that over the decades he had never been allowed to forget.

'Oi, Casanova! Fancy a dance?' Sadie shouted across the table at him.

Solly, who wore hearing aids, a bow tie and a trilby hat, playfully batted away her question with one hand, retorting in his gruff voice: 'Not on your life, Sadie Cohen. The last time I danced with you was in 1952 and my toes still haven't recovered!'

Gilda, who sat to my right, was less inclined to banter, but was no less of a gossip than Sadie. A former hairdresser, she liked to brag that in her youth she had known everyone in the East End. 'There wasn't an 'ead of 'air I didn't cut, curl, dye or shave. Old and young, they all came to me. I used to be known as "Silver Gilda".'

'Why's that?' I asked.

'"cause I grew up in Silvertown,' she replied. 'I'm East End born and bred.'

Gilda opened her handbag and took out a selection of old black and white photographs. Among them, she had one of herself as a young woman standing in an old-fashioned barber's shop with leather swivel chairs and art deco lights around the mirrors. She had been a striking woman with a Hollywood smile and high cheekbones, and a slim figure which must have turned many a head on Thursday evenings along the Whitechapel Road where young Jewish men and women used to go to be seen.

'All the boys were after me,' she boasted. 'I lost count of the number of proposals I 'ad.' Her voice dropped to a whisper and she leant towards me, beaming an infectious smile. 'Even Solly asked me to marry 'im. Imagine that!'

Unlike some of the other elderly East End Jews I met who preferred not to talk about the past, Gilda enjoyed reminiscing about her childhood. She remembered her grandfather vividly. He had come from Poland, one of tens of thousands of Jews who fled the pogroms at the end of the nineteenth century and settled in the East End.

'He didn't want to come to Britain. None of them did,' said Gilda as the first course of lentil soup was placed before us and Sadie turned her nose up at it, calling it 'muck'. 'They all dreamed of going to America, the "Land of the Free". But my granddad and all the others on board their ship were cheated by the captain. He told them 'e was taking them to New York, so when they reached the Thames, they thought it was the 'udson River. All of them got up on deck, peering through the fog, on the lookout for the Statue of Liberty. But what did they see instead? Tower bleedin' Bridge!'

Gilda described how her grandfather was forced to disembark in the docks where he was registered as an immigrant and his name was shortened from Wolfsheimer to Wolf. From there, carrying everything he owned in a small leather suitcase, he made his way on foot to Spitalfields.

'God only knows how he survived,' she said. 'The East End was a terrible place in them days. There wasn't no propa 'ousing or jobs, and my granddad didn't speak no English. Anti-Semitism was rife and all. But like my Dad always said, the Jews 'ad been through far worse. At least in London they didn't af to go round wearing Stars of David and they weren't thrown into camps and exterminated like they was in Germany. All in all, Britain was good to them, gave them a chance to make new lives for themselves. They was grateful to be allowed to get on with it.'

At first, Gilda's grandfather stayed in Spitalfields in a house that was chronically overcrowded and lacked even the most basic amenities. But he was not alone. Some 120,000 fellow Jews settled in the East End in the 1880s and by 1891, according to Margaret Harkness, author of *In Darkest London*, 'there was nothing English about the place, only foreign faces, foreign shops, foreign talk'. At the heart of this new ghetto lay Brick Lane, where everything from kosher butchers, music halls, Jewish publishers, tobacconists, tailors and jewellers flourished. From day one, the Jews had to rely on their entrepreneurial skills to survive. Few sought jobs beyond the ghetto and, although political and religious divisions were rife within the community, people generally clubbed together and helped each other out.

'When my granddad needed a job, he was given one by another Polish Jew 'oo was a barber,' said Gilda, as the soup bowls were removed and replaced with plates of roast lamb, sprouts and boiled potatoes. 'The only problem was that my granddad 'ad never cut 'air before. In Poland 'e'd been a butcher.'

'So what did he do?'

'Well, the barber promised to teach 'im,' continued Gilda. 'But when my granddad turned up on 'is first day of work, he found the barber lying face down dead on the floor of 'is shop. He'd gone and 'ad an 'eart attack!'

Gilda laughed out loud, but the rest of the table had heard the story many times before and ate on in silence.

'After the funeral, the barber's widow said to my granddad, "You'll af to take over the business and we'll be partners." Well, he was 'orrified. He'd never cut an 'ead of 'air in 'is life. But the widow insisted. She said, "You can cut meat, so why not hair?" So he gave it a go. 'course, he was a natural. After that 'e married the widow – my gran – and they 'ad five children. The youngest of them was my Dad. He took over the business and much, much later, I took it over from 'im.'

The plates were removed and replaced with bowls of rhubarb crumble and custard. Gilda ate a spoonful of her helping, daintily wiping away some custard from the corner of her mouth with a napkin. Then she leaned towards me again and signalled for me to come closer as if she was about to impart a great secret.

'I was the first woman 'airdresser in the East End,' she said. 'Doesn't sound like much now, does it? Not when you've got women up in space and becoming prime ministers. But in them days, I was considered a genuine revolutionary, just like that Che Guevara.'

———◆———

November saw the weather grow colder and, with the boiler on the blink and no central heating, and Mr Ali being his usual thrifty self, it became a struggle to keep warm. The attic was draughty and expensive to heat so I remained in the kitchen where I sealed up the gaps in the window frame with silicone gel and made fires in the Victorian fireplace with wood that I scavenged from skips and building sites.

Washing also required initiative on my part. I had to invest in a heating element designed for campers, which took twenty minutes to warm a bucketful of water.

My finances were also in a state of deep freeze. Although I had applied for work at almost every news organisation in London, no offers had yet come my way. Cheap Tesco spaghetti featured heavily in my diet, and I had to stop buying the daily newspapers, reading only what I found abandoned by other passengers on the bus.

By mid-November things were so tight (by now I was living on three pounds a day), I started searching for a menial job. But before the crunch came, I was offered a few overnight shifts as a producer in a TV newsroom. The pay helped keep my head above water, but was not enough to cover a higher rent and deposit. Much as I hated to admit it, it looked as if Anu would be arriving in January to a cold, claustrophobic attic.

───◆───

Solly had grown up on Brick Lane and, until 1989 when he moved to Romford in Essex to be with his son, lived for most of his life in Shoreditch. For him, the East End was now a site of pilgrimage where he came a few times a year to visit his ever-diminishing group of childhood friends, to wander through the old neighbourhood to see what had become of the place, and to have a salt beef bagel, which he liked to eat with plenty of pickle and hot English mustard.

The next time he came to Brick Lane, I met up with him outside the bakery.

It was a cold Saturday morning and Solly was waiting for me on the pavement. He was wrapped up warm, the collar of his winter coat turned against the biting wind, his hat pulled down over the top half of his face. His hands were snug inside a pair of fur-lined leather gloves. Beneath the right leg of his corduroy trousers, which was caught in the top of his sock, I spied a flash of white long johns. A West Ham scarf hung round his neck, and his nose, a great beak of flesh that was pitted like the surface of the moon, protruded beyond the rim of his hat where it was exposed to the elements and blushed Rudolf red.

'Look what I've got,' he said as soon as he saw me approaching from the other side of the street, his voice deep and scratchy.

He opened a plastic bag bulging with bagels which he'd bought to take home with him to Romford.

'I always load up whenever I come down here,' he said, pronouncing 'bagels' just as the word appeared on the signs above the bakeries: 'beigels', with a stress on the 'i'. 'It's the one place left in London where you can get the real thing.'

He handed me one stuffed with cream cheese and smoked salmon. 'I got this one for you. You can eat it while we walk.'

Solly led the way south down Brick Lane.

'There were once brick kilns north of here,' he said. 'The bricks used to build the City after the Great Fire were brought down this way. They say the street got its name because of all the bricks that fell off the carts.'

We passed a couple of gaps in the terraces, which Solly claimed were World War Two bombsites, and reached the old railway bridge. The wind blew stronger here, driving pages from tabloid newspapers along the pavement like tumbleweed in a Wild West town, affording us fleeting glimpses of topless Page Three girls. I worried that it was too cold for my guide and suggested we turn back. But Solly claimed to find the weather invigorating and, as we walked, he spoke enthusiastically about the Brick Lane he had known as a boy, the Brick Lane that had lain at the heart of the old Jewish ghetto.

'I've got more memories of this street than I know what to do with,' he said as we approached the old Truman Brewery. 'Sometimes I have trouble remembering what happened last week. But when it comes to my childhood, I remember every detail as if it were yesterday.'

Solly described what the street had been like on a Friday night at the start of the Sabbath when candles twinkled in the windows and his parents hired local Cockney kids – *Sabbath goys* – to come into their house and do odd jobs like keeping the fires going. He told me about the sweatshop where he was sent to work at the age of fifteen after his parents made him leave school to help provide for the family. He imitated the calls of muffin men. He described gambling dens where cards were played and politics discussed, the Russian Vapour Bathhouse, the Yiddish theatre, and the *kheder* where he and his brothers and sisters were sent every Sunday to study under a stern rabbi.

Solly also told me about some of the more memorable characters who used to be his neighbours. Like the chain-smoking widow who set fire to her mattress and burnt herself to death; the old butcher who people used to say was Jack the Ripper; Mrs Engel, the middle-aged housewife who lived on Frying Pan Alley and robbed Solly of his virginity when he was seventeen; and his father's cousin Benjamin, who had been a sniper in the Russian army and used to win all the prizes on the firing ranges of travelling fairs.

'When Benjamin was a young man, he always had a new girl on his arm,' Solly told me. 'Then he met Hinda and, before he knew it, he was married and a father and a slave. Hinda was a fearsome woman. She never let him out of his sight. "Benjamin do this! Benjamin do that!" At her beck and call night and day: that became his life.

'Gradually it wore him down, killed his spirit. It would have done the same to any man. She was relentless. He died at the age of fifty-three, a tragedy. The doctor said it was from nothing in particular. But we all knew she killed him – as assuredly as if she'd used a knife.'

While Solly had been telling me all this, he had slowed down to a snail's pace. It took us almost twenty minutes to reach the corner of Woodseer Street. Here he stopped and pointed out a terraced house, his home for the first eleven years of his long and varied life.

'We lived on the second floor above a fishmonger's,' he said, pointing up at the window, which now housed a solicitor's firm. 'The stench from downstairs was something awful. It got into everything: into your clothes, your hair, your skin. I used to go to school smelling of it. All the other kids used to call me "Cod boy".'

He stared up at the window, momentarily lost in thought.

'I'll tell you something strange,' he said, leaning towards me as if he didn't want anyone else in the street to hear what he had to say. 'It was horrible living here. Horrendous! It was cramped, boiling in summer, freezing in winter. For years after living here, I couldn't smell fish without feeling sick. But now? How things change! Whenever I pass a fishmonger's I get a nostalgic feeling for the old place. It's as if I want to be back here, sharing a bed with my two brothers and washing in a tin bath in the courtyard at the back of the house.'

He laughed and, with a shrug of his shoulders, led me on to the next block. We were soon standing outside another terraced house where the family moved when he was twelve.

'It was a bigger place – three rooms – but just as grim. The building was infested with armies of cockroaches as big as your fist. They lived in the walls, under the floorboards, in the kitchen, in your shoes. There were millions of bed bugs as well. They were like vampires, sucking at our blood. We used to have to stand the legs of our beds in bowls of paraffin to stop them from crawling up on to the mattress.'

Solly walked on to Princelet Street, pausing to show me a doorway where he had kissed his first girlfriend, a ballerina called Norah Peterson.

'She had beautiful red hair, cheeks dotted with freckles, and nipples the size of walnuts,' he said with a nostalgic sigh. 'I used to write her poetry and walk out with her in Victoria Park. We'd sit on a bench and I'd read it to her.'

'So what happened?' I asked him as we stood staring at the doorway, both of us picturing Norah in our own way.

'I fell in love with her. What can I say? I was young. But it wasn't to be. She was a "*goy*" – non-kosher, if you know what I mean.'

'So your parents didn't approve?'

'Didn't approve!' Solly echoed with a chuckle. 'They went berserk! When he found out, my father gave me a thrashing and sent me to the rabbi to have some sense talked into me. I had to swear that I would never see her again. But of course I did. We decided to run away together. Our plan was to smuggle ourselves on to a ship to America and start a new life in Chicago. But when her family got to know, her father told me that if I came anywhere near Norah again, he'd have me cut into pieces and thrown into the Thames. After that I never saw her again.'

Solly made a face as if to say what's done is done. As we turned back on to Brick Lane, I asked him what his parents had been like.

'They fled from Russia in their twenties and arrived as refugees in the East End. They lived here for the rest of their lives, rarely ever leaving the ghetto. In all that time, they never mixed with non-Jews and never learnt English. By the time I reached my teens, we were like foreigners to one another. They saw themselves as guests in Britain. They believed that once the Messiah came, all the Jews would return to the Promised Land where no one would be able to kick us around. Until then, we should keep our heads down.

'When I got bullied at school or some Cockney kid called me "Jew Boy", they'd always tell me to turn the other cheek. "Don't make trouble," they'd say. But I didn't see it that way. Britain was my home and I wasn't about to let anyone shove me around. So I learnt to box.' Solly put up both fists, and began to punch the air playfully. 'I had a deadly right hook. It came in very handy, let me tell you.'

Solly left home at seventeen and joined the Communist Party. In 1936, he took part in the Battle of Cable Street (when 300,000 social-ists, anti-fascists and a fair number of housewives armed with rolling pins prevented Sir Oswald Mosley's Black Shirts from marching through the East End), and, later, travelled to Spain to fight with the International Brigade. In 1937, he was wounded in the groin in the Jarama Valley and had to give up the fight against fascism. He spent World War Two helping German Jews start new lives in England. In the 1950s, he took a degree in history and became a teacher.

'My job kept me here in the East End,' he said. 'I was one of the few to stay. There was a huge exodus after the war. People changed their names from Rothenberger to Gordon and went to live in Golders Green. In the seventies, the Bangladeshis started to take over. Halal butchers replaced the kosher ones, mosques the synagogues, prayer caps the yarmulkes. Before long, the place had been completely transformed.'

We reached the mosque on the corner of Fournier Street. Architecturally, it was an unremarkable building, a rectangular brick structure that looked like a bank or perhaps a town hall. But Solly regarded it with admiring eyes and crossed over to the far side of the street to get a better view.

'You wouldn't know to look at it but that's one of the most extraordinary buildings in the world,' he said. 'It was built as a church by Huguenot silk weavers in 1743 and since then it's been a synagogue and a mosque. As each big wave of immigrants has settled in the East End, they've made it their own. After the French came the Irish, then the Jews and now the Bangladeshis.'

We stood there watching a couple of greybeards approach the front door and take off their sandals on the doorstep. They were followed inside by a young man in jeans and a T-shirt who took a crumpled prayer cap from his back pocket and placed it on his head.

'You might say that the building doesn't belong to anyone, that it belongs to the street, to Brick Lane. It's the heart of the community – whoever they might be,' said Solly.

He took me round the side of the building on to Fournier Street.

'See that sundial up there?'

I looked up to where he was pointing.

'It's original to the building – put there by the Huguenots. The inscription reads, "*Umbra Sumus*", "We are Shadows" – it's proven a fitting motto, not just for the French but for all the immigrants who have settled here.'

We carried on down Fournier Street. The back of Hawksmoor's Christ Church loomed large over the Georgian town houses built by the Huguenots at a time when Spitalfields was known as Weaver Town. Most were suffering from decades of neglect inflicted on them by generations of migrants and immigrants. But here and there stood a few that had been lovingly renovated by so-called 'New Georgians', many of them architects. With sandblasted brickwork and the original weaver lofts converted into plush, top-floor studios, they looked as good as new.

'If you'd come here in 1700, you'd have heard only French being spoken in the streets – and bird song,' said Solly. 'The Huguenots kept singing birds in ornamental cages and used to hang them in their windows.'

Solly was a great admirer of the Huguenots. French Protestants who fled from persecution at the hands of the Catholics, they arrived in the East End in the late 1600s as refugees (thus introducing the word *réfugié* – one who seeks sanctuary – into the English lexicon). Many were master weavers who revolutionised the indigenous silk industry. In their heyday, they owned 15,000 looms and employed some 30,000 people. This was a time of great prosperity for Spitalfields, when the streets were safe and clean, and society ladies from west London were carried here in their sedans to buy taffeta and brocade and luxurious silk stockings from their favourite tailors.

But it was not to last. The great-grandchildren of the community either drifted away (many of them into Essex) or intermarried with the Cockney community. By the 1830s, when Lancashire cotton and Nottingham lace suddenly flooded the market, the silk industry was already in serious decline and Spitalfields was suffering accordingly. The final blow came in 1860 when peace was made with France and French silk once again became available for import.

'That's been the history of the East End since the beginning,' said Solly. 'Its streets have been irrigated with immigrants for centuries: Chinese and Ethiopian sailors, Flemish brewers, German sugar bakers, Irish labourers, Vietnamese boat people. After the war, you even got the Maltese and Cypriots living in Spitalfields. But they all come and go. Tomorrow you'll wake up and find that Brick Lane's changed once again. I should know! I've watched the world I grew up in vanish before my eyes. Look at it now. You'd never know that fifty years ago it was the heart of a Jewish ghetto.'

Solly was right. There were few reminders of the Jewish presence to be found anywhere in the East End. A couple of synagogues, a graveyard, one or two street names, that's about all there was to show for it.

'There's not even a kosher restaurant left. Blooms on the Whitechapel Road was the last to go. They used to do the best *gedempte* meatballs and jumbo haddock in London. But they closed a few years ago. Now it's a Burger King. Burger King doesn't do kosher.'

We reached the end of Brick Lane and entered Osborn Street where Solly stopped outside a funeral director's shop. Through the glass I could see a row of blank, white gravestones, pre-carved with Stars of David, waiting for names and inscriptions to be added. Solly approached the window and stared in at them. Suddenly he looked sad.

'This is one of the only businesses left that caters for us Jews,' he said. 'We won't be putting much more custom their way.'

————◆————

The impression of the East End that Solly painted was somewhat at odds with the one portrayed by Jack London. Despite the poverty that his family had known, to Solly it was no abyss. It was a nursery, a melting pot, a place of opportunity.

'Look at those Jewish firms like Glaxo, Gestetner – they're house-hold names, multinationals. And they started right here!'

The Jews had settled around Brick Lane, worked hard and then escaped. 'Anyone who tells you different, that they wanted to stay, is deluded or suffering from nostalgia,' he said. 'No one wanted to stay! Anyone who did is the dregs. And that goes for Jews and Cockneys alike.'

He saw the most recent wave of immigrants, the asylum seekers from Africa, Europe and the Middle East, as following a well-established tradition.

'You come here, you struggle and then you move on. That's how it works; that's how it will always work.'

But there was one group of newcomers that did not fit into the scheme of things, at least as far as Solly was concerned. These were the so-called New East Enders, the urban trendies whose world revolved around the old Truman Brewery. They were not immigrants or poor migrants desperate for work, but had moved to the East End voluntarily to live in renovated warehouses and lofts. In doing so, they were pushing up property prices, and Solly was concerned that this would make it harder for immigrants to settle around Brick Lane in the future.

'They don't belong here,' said Solly, dismissively.

As someone who had an aversion to living in such grungy sur-roundings, I found it hard to understand why anyone should want to move there voluntarily. But after I met Tristan, an anti-globalisation activist who lived in an old warehouse in Shoreditch, I realised that, contrary to what Solly and others had to say on the matter, the arrival of the New East Enders was in fact in keeping with the spirit of the East End.

To look at Tristan, you would never have guessed that he grew up in Dulwich and was privately educated at some of the best schools in Britain. His clothes looked like charity shop rejects, although he assured me he had paid reasonable money for them; his hair had not seen a comb or brush for years and was 'styled' in such a way that it looked as if he had cut it himself; and his accent betrayed not a hint of the hundred thousand pounds his father had paid for his education.

'After uni, I worked in the City for a couple of years, but it wasn't my scene,' he told me the first time we met in the bagel bakery, his accent a pseudo-cockney – 'mockney' – drawl like Jamie Oliver's. 'Deep down I knew that I wasn't a yuppy.'

Tristan opted instead for journalism and, after joining an international news agency, worked as a foreign correspondent in the Middle East. From there he moved on to Africa where he travelled to Rwanda and found himself caught up in the middle of the genocide.

'I saw things that no one should ever have to see – images I'll never be able to get out of my head,' he said. 'There was nothing I could do to help. I had to stand by and watch it all happen. When I got back to London, I decided to throw in the towel. I decided I wanted to make a difference and I knew that journalism wasn't the key.'

In 1996, Tristan joined a British charity and spent the next couple of years helping to raise funds for education programmes in the Third World. His work inevitably brought him into contact with the growing anti-globalisation campaign and, after a 'political awakening', he became a committed member of the movement. In 1998 he resigned from the charity and moved to Shoreditch where he ran a website dedicated to bringing down the IMF, the World Bank and G8.

'I chose to live here because there are a lot of like-minded people in the East End: people like me who've got fed up with the way things are. It's also the one part of London that hasn't been ruined. Everywhere else has been taken over by McDonald's or Starbucks. The East End hasn't succumbed to all that blatant commercialism. It's the one place where you can be yourself. It's got this anonymity about it.'

'But I've got tramps pissing on my front door and when people come to see me they get mugged,' I said. (It was true: a few mornings earlier, I had opened the front door to find one of the tramps standing beside it, doing up his zipper; and a friend who had come to visit had been relieved of her handbag on her way back to Liverpool Street.)

Tristan laughed. 'I'll take the tramps and the piss over life in the 'burbs. If I had to go back to live in Dulwich I'd die.'

And yet, much as he identified with the East End, Tristan's was a very different tribe from the so-called indigenous white East Enders of Bethnal Green. Like Solly, such people resented the newcomers almost as much as they resented the immigrants.

I saw this clearly for myself when, a few days after we met, Tristan and I went to eat lunch at a local pie and mash shop.

The reception we received from the women serving at the counter was, at best, frosty, and Tristan's best mockney failed to break the ice. Undaunted, we took our plates of pie and mash and 'liquor', or parsley sauce, and sat down at one of the half a dozen benches ranged along the shop wall. We had to share it with a middle-aged woman who looked as if she'd dyed her hair in the kitchen sink. As we ate, she kept up a conversation with the women behind the counter about all the 'toffy-nosed yuppies moving in'. Such people, she claimed, were driving people like her out.

'Bunch of wankers if you ask me,' intoned a man at another table behind us.

Tristan and I did our best to ignore their jibes. But to make matters worse, I couldn't eat more than a couple of mouthfuls of my pie and mash. It was the most disgusting food I had ever tasted; a bag of flour would have been more palatable. Tristan did not think much of it either. But he was not about to leave his; after all, he'd been the one who'd suggested we go and 'soak up some good old Cockney atmosphere'. So with a grimace, he wolfed down his portion, quickly washed down with a couple of glasses of water.

As we got up to leave, the woman at our table drew attention to the fact that I had hardly touched my food.

'Not good enough for you, then?' she said.

We beat a shamefaced retreat.

Tristan held fortnightly meetings in his warehouse space to which he invited like-minded individuals dedicated to 'curbing the power of multinationals and the evils of globalisation'. When he invited me along to the next one, I decided to attend.

Tristan's building was a few minutes' walk from the top end of Brick Lane. A heavy metal door slid open on to a huge space divided at intervals by concrete supports. Tristan's bedroom was little more than a mattress and a side table in one corner; the bathroom was partitioned off by a couple of Japanese screens; the kitchen was arranged around an old butcher's block; the 'living room' in the middle was arranged with a collection of retro furniture straight out of *2001*.

Some thirty other people attended the meeting, at which they discussed their views and campaign strategy. I disagreed with almost everything they had to say. But I could not help admiring Tristan's spirit. He was passionate but not fanatical about his chosen cause and, in the coming months, I used to drop in on him every now and then.

Through Tristan, I met a number of New East Enders involved in other causes – everything from the movement to cancel Third World debt to the Anti-Nazi League – as well as some of the 'local' artists who were part of the Brit Art scene. It was a young sculptor, originally from Teddington and a 'pioneer' of the new community, who pointed out that east London had long been the abode of political radicals, religious dissidents and artisans, the most famous of them being William Shakespeare.

'In Tudor times players and playwrights were classed as vagrants and had to live outside the City walls. Shakespeare's on record as having been a tax evader,' he said. 'The first Shakespearean theatres, the Curtain and the Theatre, where many of his early plays were performed, including *Romeo and Juliet*, were built in Shoreditch, a five-minute walk from Brick Lane.'

I read later that the East End has also been home to the likes of the herbalist Nicholas Culpepper, and a haven for religious groups such as the Ancient Deists, Ranters, Muggletonians, Anabaptists, as well as the Quakers. It was here in the depths of London's poverty that the London Corresponding Society and the Chartists first met, and the trade union movement found its feet. In 1888 the landmark match-girls' strike took place at the Bryant & May factory in Bow, and the following year, the dockers staged their first industrial action. Sylvia Pankhurst set up the headquarters of the suffragettes in Bethnal Green; and it was in Whitechapel that Lenin held the preliminary meetings of the Fifth Congress of the Russian Democratic Party where Stalin – alias Koba Ivanovich – first met his rival to be, Leon Trotsky.

Peter Ackroyd believes there is a special atmosphere in the East End that works 'to encourage an anti-authoritarian spirit'. But that didn't make the New East Enders any more welcome.

'Scruffy lot,' complained Sadie the next time I had lunch with her and her friends. 'In my day we might 'ave been working class, but we always dressed respectful-like. This lot look like they've been sleeping rough on the street!'

To Gilda they were plain 'daft'.

'Let me tell you a story,' she said. 'One of my oldest friends who lives up Golders Green way 'as a grandson, Jeremiah. Now this Jeremiah just bought one of them fancy new flats in Spitalfields. When 'e moved in, 'e calls 'er up, very excited and proud, to tell 'er 'is news. So she asks 'im, "Jeremiah, 'ow much did you pay?" And 'e tells her, "Two 'undred thousands pounds."

'Well, when she hears this my friend starts to cry and Jeremiah, all confused, says to 'er, "Waas wrong? You should be 'appy for me." But she replies, "You don't understand! I grew up round there, in the 'ell of poverty. For three generations our family worked to get out. When we left we didn't even look back. And now you go and pay two hundred thousand pounds for a one-bedroom flat! Have you lost your mind?"'

3

A Child of the Jago

'Many and misty are the people's notions of the East End; and each is commonly but the distorted shadow of a minor feature.'
Arthur Morrison, *Tales of Mean Streets* (1894)

IT WAS A Tuesday morning in late November and Abdul-Haq, the estate agent, was eating breakfast in the kitchen of his flat in Bethnal Green. He had spent much of the past hour ranting to his wife about a dispute he was having with one of their neighbours when, quite suddenly, he dropped his cereal bowl on the floor and clutched at his chest with both hands, apparently overcome by a searing pain.

His wife, who was standing at the sink doing the washing up, rushed over to his side to try and help him. But beyond calling 999 and explaining the nature of the emergency in her tearful, broken English, there was nothing more she could do.

When the paramedics from the nearby Whitechapel Hospital arrived a few minutes later, they immediately set about trying to save the stricken man's life. But it was already too late. The heart attack had been a massive one. And before long, as his wife looked on, Abdul-Haq slipped away.

In an instant Mrs Abdul-Haq found herself completely alone in the world. She had no children, no relatives to speak of, and no friends. Even the neighbours were strangers to her. There was no one to whom she felt compelled to break the sad news; nobody she could turn to for words of comfort; no one to advise her on what to do next. Abdul-Haq had been her entire world.

And so, once the paramedics had taken away her husband's body, Mrs Abdul-Haq cleaned up the broken cereal bowl and did the one thing she could think of. She left her flat and followed the same route along Bethnal Green Road that she and her husband had taken each morning to his estate agency near the north end of Brick Lane. Once through the door, she sat down behind her desk. She had spent the past twelve years there, making cups of tea and occasionally answering the phone, and it was behind that desk that she felt compelled to sit, grieving and, no doubt, contemplating her future.

I had first set foot in Abdul-Haq's estate agency in October when I had been searching for a place to live in the East End. From the outside, the business looked as if it had long ago gone under. The red paint on the wooden façade was peeling, the shop sign above the window was missing a couple of letters, and the windows were so filthy that it was difficult to make out the faded property details fixed to the pin boards inside.

The shop itself was sparsely furnished with a couple of desks and a few chairs. A gas heater in one corner was permanently turned on full blast, creating an oven-like heat. Customers stepping in from the cold soon found themselves wiping sweat from their brows. The only adornment to the whitewashed walls was a large black and white photograph of the Ayatollah Khomeini, striking his usual sour expression.

Unlike his wife, who greeted anyone coming in through the door with a shy smile, Abdul-Haq's demeanour was no more welcoming than that of his late spiritual leader. He regarded his customers with a deep mistrust, his bushy black eyebrows permanently knitted into a stern frown.

Life had not been kind to Abdul-Haq – at least that's what he had repeatedly told me. An engineer by education, he had emigrated to London from Kenya in 1978 with high hopes of finding a good job, raising a family and providing them with a solid, British education. He brought with him his new bride of seventeen, who had never before left Africa. They settled in Whitechapel near some distant relatives from Mombasa.

Abdul-Haq's idealistic image of England was soon shattered. He had arrived during the Winter of Discontent. Piles of rubbish lay uncollected on the pavements. There were electricity blackouts, daily strikes, bread shortages, mass unemployment.

'One of the first things I noticed when I arrived in Britain was that the trees had no leaves. I remember asking myself, "What kind of country is this where the trees have no leaves?"'

The engineering job Abdul-Haq had expected to land never materialised. Instead he was forced to work as a bus conductor, then as a postman, until eventually he found his way into the property business. To make matters worse, his family never materialised, either.

'Allah,' he said, 'has not blessed me with a son, or even one daughter.'

He was willing to attribute this, his greatest misfortune, to the will of God; the rest he blamed on his neighbours and the Inland Revenue.

'Since the day I arrived in this country, they have been working against me,' he said as he showed me around a flat above a fish and chip shop. 'As a young man in Kenya, I used to dream of travelling to Great Britain. I believed it was a place of poets, of thinkers, of tolerance and understanding and, above all things, equality. I believed it was truly Great. But I have seen that this is not so. Britain is a lie. Racism is ingrained in the conscience of its people. Here, if your skin is dark, you are little better than a dog.'

I asked him why he did not move back to Kenya where, surely, his qualifications would stand him in good stead and he might find acceptance in society.

'Yes. Perhaps one day I will live there again,' he said, vaguely.

But there was something in his voice that told me he had no intention of returning to his birthplace. His pride seemed too great an obstacle.

———◆———

I heard about Abdul-Haq's demise from Mr Ali who in turn had been told by Suleiman, a Turk and owner of a rival leather jacket shop on

Bethnal Green Road. It had been Suleiman and his wife who had discovered Mrs Abdul-Haq slumped over her desk just a few hours after her husband's death. The two of them had persuaded the distraught woman to come and stay with them in Stoke Newington.

It was not until a week or so after the funeral that I saw Mrs Abdul-Haq in the shop again.

It was a Saturday afternoon and she was back sitting behind her desk, her eyes fixed on her husband's empty chair. As usual, the gas heater was on full blast and the faint orange glow of the flames flickered on her cheeks. Streams of tears had left her skin looking blemished, her eyes pink with soreness.

My tapping on the glass of the front door startled her and she looked out at me anxiously, quickly adjusting the black *hijab* that framed her face. Slowly, she came to the door, managing a shy smile and thanking me for my condolences.

'I am all right now,' she said, as she made us some tea and I took a seat in front of her desk.

But there was no hiding her anxiety, nor her sadness, and she soon started to pour out her problems.

'Life is very complicate,' she said, her voice choked with despair.

Her husband, she explained, had left no will, nor any financial provision for her in the event of his death. To make matters worse, all his private papers were locked away in a safe, the combination for which he had taken with him to the grave, along with the password to his computer. Mrs Abdul-Haq had been left without a penny to her name and was now relying on charity to eat.

'Maybe I return Mombasa,' she said. 'Why I stay here? Nothing there is for me – no.'

'Do you have family in Kenya?' I asked her.

'My mother and father dead. No sister. No brother,' she said. 'The family of Abdul-Haq, they tell me – "don't come."'

'So if you return to Kenya, you will be on your own?'

'Yes. Here in East End on my own and in Kenya on my own. Always I am to be on my own,' she said.

I offered to try and help Mrs Abdul-Haq sort out her problems, but she turned down my offer.

'You, I don't know,' she said, displaying the same kind of suspicion that had characterised her husband.

But over the course of the next few weeks, I kept an eye out for her. In the evenings, from my kitchen window, I would watch her close the estate agency and head along Bethnal Green Road towards her home. The sight of her sad face muffled in a *hijab*, her body braced against the wind, affected me deeply. She would disappear into the gloom and I too would feel my heart sink in despair. Some evenings, I'd mentally tick through my address book, realising that there was no one to call or share my own troubles with.

Mrs Abdul-Haq's story was a reminder that, just as Jack London and Hugh Massingham had found, the East End was a world where people could fall between the cracks. Was I one of them?

Only recently my parents had told me that they did not approve of Anu, whom they'd met briefly the year before, and urged me to break off the engagement. I was shattered. I knew I loved Anu, but the rift with Mum and Dad, whom I also loved and had always been close to, coloured my every waking moment. Their disapproval undermined my confidence – not to mention my morale – and their warnings about the difficulties we would face as a couple of mixed ethnic and cultural backgrounds preyed on my mind.

Meanwhile, Anu's parents were being just as difficult. Her father had said that under no circumstances would he ever give his blessing to his daughter marrying a non-Indian. And to add to my misery, my career in journalism was foundering, and I had received several rejection letters from major publishers to whom I had sent my manuscript.

For the first time in my life, I sank into a deep depression. With the December days at their shortest and virtually no natural light in the attic, I found it a struggle to get out of bed in the morning. Often, when I did not have to be on shift in the TV newsroom (where by now I was working on average a couple of days a week), I would lie on my foam mattress, with the slanted roof just a few feet above me, and shudder to think that I might be trapped in Brick Lane for ever.

This was no homecoming.

The only respite came on Sunday mornings when the weekly market rolled on to Brick Lane. Instead of waking to car horns and obscenities, I would open my eyes to the sounds of street vendors, conjuring up images of *My Fair Lady*.

'Lovely peaches, twelve a pound! Come on, girls! Cauliflowers a pound for three! Beautiful toms. A pound-a-bag-a-sprouts! A bag-a-sprouts-a-pound! Come and get 'em!'

Every week, I would look out of my kitchen window to find that the usual traffic had been replaced by rows of trestle tables and barrows manned by boisterous touts with ruddy complexions.

'Today only! The world's first, fully reversible plastic bags! Tested by Laboratoire Garnier in Switzerland! Each with its own lifetime guarantee!'

Washing quickly, I would head downstairs to find the pavement knee-deep in cardboard boxes and the street beyond packed with a throng of East Enders from all walks of life. Bangladeshi women accompanied by their husbands standing in line with Cockney grans pushing wheelie bags; bottle-blonde Bethnal Green mums with bare legs tinted sapphire-blue by the cold rubbing shoulders with rotund Albanian women wrapped in layers of woollens and headscarves.

One of the pitches that lined the street was owned by an elderly Cockney with a crooked back who sold fruit and veg from a barrow. He told me once that his father and his grandfather before him had done business in the exact same spot.

'In them days it was all Jewish round 'ere and the Jews don't work Saturdays. It's got to do with their religion. Thas why the market's 'eld on Sunday,' he said.

The stall next to him sold tinned sardines, unlabelled cartons of brie, goldfish food, Belgian chocolates made in Poland, and packets of imitation Duracell batteries – all perilously close to their sell-by dates. The next was piled high with fake designer luggage and cartons of perfumes with names like 'Canal No. 5'. The one after that was devoted to just one product, a 'miracle tool' that 'cuts through any substance known to man' – or so the vendor flogging them out of a large leather suitcase claimed.

'Brick Lane's the 'arrods of the East End,' a fishmonger selling

jellied eels, winkles and prawns measured by the pint told me. 'There's
not another street market like it left in London. It may not be pretty,
but you'll find anything and everything for sale 'ere. I shouldn't be surprised if you found someone flogging an elephant.'

I liked the market most for its characters. A group of old men who
looked like the cast of *The Ladykillers* always hung around on the
corner of Bacon Street with designer watches up their arms, and gold
chains hanging from hooks sewn into the lining of their trench coats.
'Cartier, Rolex, we've got the lot,' they would whisper to passers-by.
On most Sundays, a teenager with spiky peroxide hair would appear
with a collapsible table that he'd set up on the pavement. On top of
this he'd lay three rubber discs and start to move them round and
round each other like a magician performing a trick. One of the discs
was marked on its underside with a white dot, and it was with intense,
concentrated expressions that the knot of people who invariably
formed around the teenager tried to follow its progress. Every so
often, one of them would reach out and touch one of the pads and,
at the same time, slap down a ten or twenty pound note. Occasionally,
they would pick the pad with the white dot and double their money,
but more often than not, the teenager would scoop up their cash and
add it to the thick wad of notes he clutched in his left hand.

There were a number of genuine Del Boy–Arthur Daley types, too.
Like the bloke who flogged electrical items that could be relied on not
to work for more than a few days; an elderly lady who sold new bicycles and cursed like a sailor; and a man who sold pedigree puppies
which he kept in the pockets of his raincoat. But for the most part,
the market traders were straight out of *EastEnders* and customer cour-
tesy was not always their strong suit.

'Oi! I 'aven't got all fuckin' day!' a woman stallholder shouted at me
one Sunday when I dithered over whether to buy her cans of tomatoes, which had dents in their sides. 'If you wanna browse, go to John
fuckin' Lewis.'

Often, they would make blatantly racist remarks to their ethnic
customers.

'You like-eey look-eey cheep-eey buy-eeey,' I once heard one of
them say to a Chinese.

Still, for all the insults and sarcastic banter, there was no beating the prices on offer and I soon found that I could get a week's supply of food at a fraction of the price charged at the local supermarket. I would buy my meat from a butcher on Bacon Street who flogged steaks by the bagful; and my fruit from a stall on Sclater Street where the juicy Alfonso mangoes cost little more than they did in New Delhi.

There was no doubt in my mind that at times I was profiting from the black economy. As one trader put it: 'A lot of what's being flogged down Brick Lane 'as come off the back of a lorry – and if it 'asn't then it's wandered out the side entrance of a showroom or been taken out the back of a ware'ouse just before someone burned it daan.' The French cheese and sausage I often bought from a man on Cheshire Street was obviously smuggled in through the Channel Tunnel. And the cigarettes I purchased from the Albanians who mingled in the crowd – calling out 'Bensan! Marlboro! Tobacco!' – were duty free.

But there was much else on offer that my conscience would not allow me to buy – like the pair of Leica cameras and lenses housed in a professional titanium case that I was once shown down a side street, or the 'good as new' Epic home theatre speakers that were on 'special offer' at three hundred quid.

I would not touch any of the dozens of 'second hand' bikes that appeared in the market, either. Many of them were fantastically expensive, handmade models with traceable serial numbers, and were sold by kids loitering on the pavements asking suspiciously low prices.

It was one of the more established dealers with dozens of bikes on offer who told me that he could get his hands on any model that I wanted.

'Sometimes it'll take a week or two to track one down, but eventually, I can get my hands on anything.'

As we were talking, a Bangladeshi teenager pulled up on a mountain bike worth at least seven hundred pounds. The dealer gave it a quick inspection and handed the lad a twenty pound note.

'Aren't you worried it might be stolen?' I said.

The dealer shrugged. 'Naa! For all I know, it was 'is Christmas present.'

'That seems unlikely, seeing as Bangladeshis don't celebrate Christmas,' I pointed out.

'Then maybe it was a birthday present,' he replied. 'Bangladeshis 'ave been known to 'ave birthdays, 'aven't they?'

Mr Singh, the local newsagent, referred to Brick Lane as Chor bazaar, or thieves' market. One of the first times I went into his shop soon after arriving, to try and have the newspapers delivered, he warned me to steer clear of the place.

'People are entering from one end and, before reaching the other end, they are finding their wallets, minus credit cards and cash, being offered for sale by one of these disreputable fellows.'

Mr Singh believed that the East End was the lair of bands of dacoits belonging to professional robber castes. It was in their blood to steal and murder, he said.

'You think that it is so far-fetched,' said Mr Singh raising a bushy eyebrow. 'You have much to learn, let me tell you. Hereabouts, people are constantly going missing. Why do you think they are always digging up the roads time after time?'

He leaned forward over his shop counter with the look of the conspiracy theorist about him.

'That is where they are placing the bodies,' he whispered.

This was the most original explanation I'd heard put forward as to why the city's streets were forever being dug up, a mystery Londoners have been puzzling over without success for decades.

'I can see you are not believing me. Few people are understanding. So perhaps you can tell me why my street has been dug up seven times this year alone?'

I suggested mismanagement as the likely cause. But Mr Singh shook his head and produced a number of photographs he had taken – each of them through the gap in his living-room curtains – of the work that had been carried out in his street. They showed conclusively that Murphy's, the building firm, had been involved in six of the seven excavations. It was, he said, all the proof he had needed to take the matter to the police.

'Just, they are looking into the matter,' he said proudly.

I congratulated him on his detective work and quickly changed the subject. Would it be possible to have the newspapers delivered, I asked.

My question provoked a burst of loud laughter – not just from Mr Singh, but also from his wife who was sitting in the room behind the counter, knitting a woolly scarf and apparently listening to our conversation.

'What's so funny?' I asked.

'Really you are a comedian. No one is delivering papers round these parts,' said Mr Singh.

'Why not?'

'For three reasons and three reasons only. Number vun: customers are not paying bills. Just they are making excuses or disappearing and never being heard of again. Number two: delivery boys are not to be trusted. Simply, they are taking the papers and placing them in the dustbin. Thus the delivery of newspapers is not achievable. Number three: few people are reading newspapers hereabouts. The East End people are not educated as a class. Therefore profit margin is not there.'

He shrugged his shoulders and, with a sigh and a flick of a hand, employed my favourite Indian expression: 'Vhat to do?'

***

Despite Mr Singh's warnings I went to the market every Sunday and it was there one morning that I got chatting with a 'local businessman' called Chalky, who was selling boxes of Côtes du Rhône out of the back of a white van.

Officially, Chalky didn't exist – not on paper, at any rate. He wasn't listed in the phone book, or on the electoral roll, and the Inland Revenue had never heard of him. But this 'technicality', as he referred to it, had not prevented him from collecting the dole, renting a council flat, driving on a 'valid' licence, and making occasional use of the National Health Service. Nor had it stopped him from acquiring a passport, which he had put to use on dozens of occasions during his 'operations' to and from France.

Chalky's entire teenage and adult life had been spent dodging and manipulating the system. He had made a career out of living off his wits and staying one step ahead of the law. He put his success down to adhering to what he called 'Chalky's Golden Rules'. These, he claimed, had saved him from the fate of his brothers, both of whom had been 'banged up' for receiving stolen goods.

'Never work for no one else,' he would say, as if imparting profound philosophy, 'and never trust no one 'xcept your Mum – and even then, don't tell 'er nofing she don't need to know. Don't 'ave nofing to do with robbery, pimping or drugs. That goes for weapons and all. And never, ever under any circumstances, shag a copper's Missus.'

Chalky had the added advantage of looking inconspicuous. He was short with white, pasty skin, and in his dowdy anorak and thick glasses, which were held together with sellotape, he looked more like a librarian who had been starved of sunlight than a petty criminal who flouted the law as a matter of principle. But as I got to know Chalky, it struck me as extraordinary that he had never been caught for anything beyond stealing a bike when he was twelve and collecting his grandmother's state pension after she died. Not that he was lacking in guile; on the contrary, Chalky was cunning and intelligent. He had a knack for remembering unusual facts and he could do complicated sums in his head – abilities which, under different circumstances, might have been put to something more productive than winning pub quizzes. But Chalky was also cocksure and a compulsive show-off. He took pleasure in telling everyone how to break or bend the rules, and he would do so in such a condescending manner as to make others feel as if they were, at best, a bit dim.

'Only mugs pay taxes,' Chalky once told me. 'Every now and then, I go down Liverpool Street Station to Ponti's for a bacon sarnie and watch all them toffy-nosed fuckers in their off-the-rack suits comin' and goin'. Robots, the lot of 'em. At their desks by nine, staring for hours at their computer screens. "Yes sir, no sir. Give you a blow job, sir?" Silly cunts.'

Chalky's usual watering hole was the Bethnal Green Arms, which was walking distance from Brick Lane. He was one of a dozen or so regulars who were so well known to the publican that they were allowed to draw their own pints at the bar and on most nights remained locked inside the establishment well after closing time.

In its heyday, the pub had been a haunt of the Kray Twins and various other East End underworld figures and thugs. But since then, its popularity had dwindled, possibly because the décor and ambience dated back to the same period. Thirty years of cigarette smoke had turned the wallpaper a sickly yellow so that it was impossible to tell what colour it had originally been. No light filtered through the windows, which were caked in London dirt. The lamps mounted on the walls glowed only marginally brighter than the tips of the customers' cigarettes.

Chalky and I met there one evening in early December. It was Karaoke night and although the publican was offering a free pint for the best contestant, the only contenders were an Irish drunk who belted out *Danny Boy* regardless of whatever else was being played over the loudspeaker, and a middle-aged tart dressed as lamb. Another regular, who had served as a sailor during the war and was known as 'Nelson', sat on his own at the back of the pub in a cloud of smoke, drinking steadily from his glass. A fresh pool of vomit lay splattered on the carpet between his shoes.

Chalky and I sat at the bar, which was draped in a flag of St George with ENGLAND emblazoned across the red cross. I had persuaded him to have a drink with me on the pretext that I was interested in making a little cash on the side. It wasn't true, but I was curious to know what he might offer me.

'So do you want to know where the serious money's at?' said Chalky as the barman served us two pints of Guinness.

'Yes,' I said. 'I'm broke.'

'Well, I'll tell you.'

He ran the tip of his tongue along the gummed edge of a Rizla that he'd just rolled.

'Fish,' he said.

'Fish?' I repeated, sceptically.

'Yeah. You 'eard. Fish.'

Chalky took a gulp of his Guinness and wiped the cream from his upper lip with the back of his hand. He inclined his head so that it was only a few inches from mine.

'We're not talking about your average cod or 'addock,' he continued. 'We're talking carp. Massive fuckers – up to thirty pounds in
weight.'

'Carp?'

Chalky sat back on his stool, a smug smile on his face, and drained
his glass, banging it down on the bar.

'Your round, I reckon,' he said.

Chalky was expert at finishing his drink just as he was on the verge
of telling you something that he knew you wanted to hear. So I called
the barman over.

Once his glass was full again Chalky started to tell me how the carp-
smuggling business worked. It was, he said, a simple case of supply and
demand. British carp did not usually grow to the large proportions
they did in France. Importing them into the British Isles was illegal;
therefore, British anglers were willing to pay 'mega bucks' for them.

'What do British anglers want with these giant carp?' I asked him.

'What do you think? They stick 'em in a lake or reservoir and then
fish 'em out again,' answered Chalky. 'What can I say? Whatever turns
them on.'

'So how do you go about bringing them into the country?'

'Well, not that yours truly would 'ave anything to do with fish
smuggling, you understand, but let's imagine for a minute that you
were to give it a go,' he replied, ''ow would you go about it? Well, I
reckon the first thing you'd need would be a transit van – a lot like the
one I've got parked outside. Inside that van you'd want a secret com-
partment with a pump to oxygenate the water, and you'd need to
invest in a coupla rods, tackle, bait and all that malarkey. Then you'd
need to drive over to France to a coupla lakes in the north and, in the
middle of the night, catch yourself a few whoppers.'

'What do the French have to say about people stealing their fish?'
I asked.

'Well, there you need to be careful. The old gendarmes can be a bit
of a fly in the old ointment. If they catch you in the act, they'll
impound all the rods and tackle, and maybe even the van. Plus they'll
slap you with a fine.'

'How much?'

'Enough.'

As far as the actual smuggling was concerned, Chalky recommended the Eurostar as opposed to the ferry – 'Customs does searches of vehicles on board the ferry and they don't do none on the train.' He also advised filling the van with cases of wine or beer; that way, if customs searched the vehicles, their attention would be drawn to the booze and not the fish.

'There's about as much chance of being nicked as the Beatles getting back together,' said Chalky. 'Smuggling into Britain's a doddle. Anyone with a bit of nous can get anyfing in. Drugs, fags, people. You name it, everyone's at it. The government's losing billions every year and they've got asylum seekers to worry about. The last thing on their minds are a couple of old carp.'

I asked him what a would-be carp smuggler would do with his catch once he reached the UK.

'You'd need a lock-up and a coupla tanks to keep them in till you can make the delivery. Then you'd put an ad or two in the usual angler magazines and sit back and wait for the old mobile to ring. A big one will net you five 'undred quid.' He paused to let the figure sink in. 'Two grand for two, three days' work at the most. Not a bad little earner. Easy peasy Japanesey.'

'And you – sorry I mean, I – would then sell the wine in the market?'

'Clever boy,' he said, opening a packet of barbecue flavour crisps and cramming a handful of them into his mouth. 'Fifteen quid a case,' he added with a crunch. 'Believe me, at that price they don't 'ang around.'

While Chalky had been telling me all this, his voice had remained only a fraction lower than its usual pitch; now it dropped to just above a whisper. It seemed to me that this was for effect rather than out of necessity, for the drunken Irishman was now belting out *Danny Boy* along to the Barbie song.

'As it 'appens,' he said, 'I know a bloke 'oo can get you a coupla cases of the old vino,' said Chalky. ''e's knocking 'em out at a tenner apiece. Special Christmas offer. Just give us the word and I'll get you sorted. Nice bottle or two of Coat de Roen to wash down the old Turkey and stuffing wouldn't go amiss now, would it?'

I nodded my head in agreement and reached for my wallet.

'Luvly!' said Chalky as he snatched away my two ten pound notes and stuffed them inside an inner pocket of his faded denim jacket. ''oo ever said never mix business with pleasure was a total prat.'

Spending time with Chalky made me realise that Mr Singh's theory about the East End being populated by robber castes was not so far-fetched after all. Many of the area's most infamous gangsters ran family enterprises, and most of Chalky's family had been on the wrong side of the law for at least four or five generations.

'We've done more time than Big Ben,' he once told me.

Chalky's most famous – albeit distant – relative was an arch-criminal called Arthur Harding, who was born in 1866 and became the 'King of Brick Lane'. In later life, he dictated his memoirs to a professor of social history at Oxford and they were published as a book entitled *East End Underworld*. Chalky lent me his copy, in which Harding recalls his childhood days spent stealing wigs off the heads of Jewish women on Brick Lane, his apprenticeship with a gang of 'whizzers', or pickpockets, who disguised themselves as Eton boys, and his eventual graduation to armed robbery and protection rackets. The Brick Lane of his day was a 'hotbed of villainy', where criminals with names like 'China Bob', 'Cocky Flatnose', 'Spud Murphy', 'Biddy the Chiver' and 'Scabby' fought for control of territory.

'Women paraded up and down the street . . . and sold themselves for a few pence,' recalled Harding in one chapter entitled 'The Terrors of Brick Lane'. 'Thieves hung about the corner of the street, waiting . . . In the back alleys there was garotting . . . "stringing someone up" was the slang phrase for it.'

Harding grew up in the Old Nichol, London's most notorious slum, where the death rate was four times higher than anywhere else in London. It lay north of Bethnal Green Road, a stone's throw from where I was living, a teeming warren of alleys and courtyards with not a single church but seventeen pubs. It 'bore an evil reputation'. Even the people of Bethnal Green regarded the area as being 'so disreput-able that they avoided contact with the people who lived' there.

Coincidentally, the Old Nichol was the setting for Arthur Morrison's most famous work, *A Child of the Jago*, which stirred many a conscience within the Victorian establishment when it was published in 1896. The story of young Dicky Perrott and his attempt to 'make good', the novel vividly depicts a world in which neighbours brawled in the streets with broken bottles and women lured drunken men into dark alleys where their husbands would cosh and strip them of anything of value right down to their underwear.

The Jago – the Nichol – was bulldozed shortly after the publication of Morrison's novel and replaced with London's first municipal housing project, the Boundary Estate. This was where Chalky had lived all his life.

'So you might say that I'm a child of the Jago myself,' he said.

Like Arthur Harding and Dicky Perrott, he too had grown up in an environment where crime was the norm. One of his uncles had been a professional fraudster. Another had run a protection racket at the dog track. And his father, who had been in and out of trouble with the law his entire life, had been an eel poacher.

'Thas 'ow I got to know the old fishing business,' Chalky told me when I knew him better. 'When I was young, my old man used to take me down the Thames to lay 'is nets. 'e knew all the best places. 'e used to flog 'em to the pie and mash shops. Once in a while I still go and catch a few myself for old time's sake. But there's no money in it these days. Too much foreign competition. From 'olland, mostly.'

Having grown up and lived in the same neighbourhood all his life, there weren't many people in the area that Chalky didn't know. He was forever being called on his mobile phone by someone wanting to know where they could lay their hands on such-and-such an item, or by someone looking for someone else to sort out such-and-such a problem.

'I'm a walking yella pages,' he would brag.

And yet, true to the Cockney tradition, Chalky was anything but conventional. He despised modern living with its mortgages and credit cards and, unlike many of his childhood friends, he had chosen to remain in the East End because of the anonymity the area afforded him.

'Everyone knows me round 'ere, but if it came to it, they never 'eard of me – know what I mean?' he once said.

Central to Chalky's world was Brick Lane market. He was always to be found there, bargaining, doing deals, keeping his ear to the ground. It was here that he had started his 'career', working on a stall for a man called 'Fingers'.

'Name anything you need – 'onestly need, mind you – and twenty quid says I can find it for ya down the market,' he once challenged me. 'Go on, name something – anyfing.'

I tried to think of something obscure and hard to come by but also something I needed. The thing that came to mind was an English–Hindi dictionary.

'I left mine in India,' I explained. 'I need another one as I'm trying to improve my Hindi.'

'Fair enough,' said Chalky, shaking my hand to seal the bet. 'Tomorrow we'll go down the market and find you one. All right?'

The next day at eight a.m. sharp, Chalky rang the fire alarm doorbell and we headed off down Brick Lane. He had no joy in the main market at the stalls selling books and magazines, so he led me inside the East End's abandoned railway terminus, the Bishopsgate Goods Yard, which lay between Brick Lane and Commercial Road. A maze of damp caves and tunnels that reeked of mildew and echoed with murmured voices, it was packed with stalls selling bric-a-brac, second-hand furniture and surprisingly fine antiques.

Chalky stopped to chat with one man who offered us a pair of Corinthian columns and a couple of mounted animal heads. Further on, a stallholder was selling provincial French furniture and musical instruments, including a cello, which I recognised as being worth thousands of pounds. His stock also included a collection of sequin-studded women's outfits from the 1930s, some African tribal art, a collection of syringes that might well have been used by Dr Frankenstein, and a pair of Damascene daggers with bird-headed handles, which looked as if they belonged inside a case in the Victoria and Albert Museum.

The last place Chalky tried was along the stretch of Bethnal Green Road that skirted the Goods Yard. If anything in the contemporary East End compared with Jack London's description of the Abyss, it was here. Within the shadow of the glass office blocks of the financial district, home to the world's largest foreign exchange market and financial institutions with some $2.2 trillion under management, dozens of figures squatted in the rain along the pavement next to pathetic collections of junk arranged on sections of the paving stones. At one pitch I stopped to make a list of what was on offer. It read:

One chewed toy dog, one broken umbrella, one scruffy copy of *Catch 22*, a coconut shell ashtray, two matching lampshades one burned with a cigarette hole, one chipped Tetley's ashtray, a collection of TV remotes, one keyboard missing the letter B, one clip-on bow tie, one Bic lighter containing enough fuel to light, at most, a couple of cigarettes, one scratched *Muppets Christmas* LP, a half-empty bottle of HP sauce, a brass lion door knocker, a faded black and white postcard of Ben Nevis, a phone in the shape of a banana, a boxful of chipped crockery, a pair of second-hand tennis shoes with string for laces, a VW hub cab.

Chalky searched methodically through piles of junk until he came upon three boxes of books owned by an old man who was sitting on an empty engine oil tin, a plastic bag on his head to keep off the rain. Sure enough, as Chalky rummaged through the books, he brought out a copy of the Collins English–Hindi dictionary and, with his usual smug smile, handed it to me.

'That's twenty quid you owe me,' he said. 'Cough up.'

I looked the book over. It was dog-eared, various pages were missing, someone's name was scrawled on the inside cover. But I was suspicious. Chalky could easily have bought it at a bookshop the day before, bashed it around a bit and then, before coming to meet me, placed it in the box. When I suggested this might be the case, however, he denied it vehemently.

'What do you take me for? Straight up. 'and on 'eart. I never put it there – 'onest.'

'And how am I supposed to trust you?' I asked him.

'If you don't believe me, ask 'im,' replied Chalky, indicating the old man. 'Go on, ask 'im.'

'That's not going to prove anything,' I said.

'All right then, I'll ask 'im.'

Chalky took a step forward and raised his voice to be heard over the din of traffic.

'Oi! Geezer. 'ave you ever seen me before?'

The old man looked up, sucking on his gums. 'What's that?' he asked.

Chalky shouted louder this time. 'I said, 'ave you ever seen me before?'

The old man shook his head and smiled a gap-toothed smile.

'Naa, Chalky,' he croaked. 'Never seen you before in my life!'

4

Christmas Mubarak!

'London demands the continual influx of new blood, whether
for the high or the lower work.'

Walter Besant, *East London* (1901)

B Y MID-DECEMBER, I knew I had to tell Anu the truth.
'Brick Lane's a dump,' I said when I called her in Delhi. 'It's
not the London I knew when I was growing up and it's not the
London where I pictured us living.'

I also warned her that by contrast to the privileged, ex-pat existence of New Delhi (where we lived in a spacious flat with a roof
garden overlooking a sixteenth-century Mughal tomb), life in
London was bleak and tough.

'Perhaps you shouldn't come for a while,' I suggested. 'Give me a
few months and I'll find a nicer place to live. By then the weather will
be better.'

But Anu was loyal and wouldn't be put off. Although none too
pleased at having been lied to, she was steeled in her resolve by our
parents' attitude. She was also worried about my state of mind.

'I don't want to leave you on your own,' she said tenderly. 'We'll
get through this, don't worry.'

Anu reminded me that she had lived in the Bronx for the first few
years of her life.

'Besides, you're the one who used to say that if you can survive
India, you can survive anywhere. Surely roughing it in London can't
be that bad.'

The approach of Christmas brought only a few cosmetic changes to Brick Lane. The bagel bakeries put up some fairy lights, sprayed fake snow on the inside of their windows and started selling mince pies. Plastic holly wreaths, gyrating Santas and last year's surplus plum puddings appeared in the Sunday market. A trendy new art gallery erected a tree made of soldered steel plates, and decorated it with condoms. And one of the local Bangladeshi butchers stocked up on halal turkeys and reindeer meat, which the proprietor seemed to believe was seasonal Christian fare.

Despite the lack of traditional Christmas cheer, however, the thousands of Bangladeshis, Somalis, Afghans and other Muslims living in the East End were in festive mood. That year, the lead-up to Christmas coincided with the holy month of Ramadan (which started at the end of November) and while London's West End was hosting the annual shopping orgy, there was devotion in the air on Brick Lane.

The faithful were fasting from dawn and gathering in each other's homes or in the local eateries at four thirty in the afternoon for *iftar* to break their fast. The mosques were attracting larger than usual crowds at prayer times, and on Fridays the congregation spilled out into the streets. The local *madrasas* were full of children sitting in orderly rows, repeating passages from the Koran in a chorus of squeaky voices; while a number of the normally less pious leather jacket shop owners donned their prayer caps and started carrying rosaries strung with ninety-nine beads, one for each of the names of Allah.

Even Mr Ali was taking his religious duties seriously.

'Fasting's murder, innit,' he admitted to me at the end of the first week, groaning and clutching his stomach. 'All I can think about all day is 'aving a Whopper cheese burger with chips and a Coke.'

Mr Ali's daily strategy for the fast was to rise at four o'clock and stuff himself with an enormous breakfast. In the afternoon, he would sit down to a huge *iftar* meal. And later, before going to bed, he would feast again, usually on a large Turkish doner kebab with extra chilli sauce.

In the years when Ramadan fell in the height of summer (the ninth month in the Islamic calendar, it commences after the sighting of the new moon and is usually a few days earlier each year) and the days stretched from five in the morning to well past ten o'clock at night,

Mr Ali refused to fast. Taking advantage of a loophole in Koranic law that pardons anyone sick or on a journey from participating, he left the country. The last time, it had been to a beach resort in Majorca where he took the wife and kids.

'There's only so much fasting I can take, innit,' he said.

But despite his lack of commitment, Mr Ali often appeared concerned that I should not form an impression of him as being a wayward Muslim. Ramadan was about the community coming together and focusing on non-materialistic matters, he reminded me on a couple of occasions. Abstention helped cleanse the soul.

'Wherever I am during Ramadan, I never touch alcohol,' he assured me. 'It's all about self-discipline, innit.'

Mr Ali never fixed anything in the building until he was cajoled into doing so, and then it was always on the cheap. Only recently, after I had hounded him to repair the main roof, which had started leaking, he had instructed Rafik the Builder to smother a load of wet cement over the portion of tiles that needed replacing. A few hours later it rained and the concrete was washed away, clogging the guttering and causing yet more water to seep into the attic.

But the start of Ramadan brought a sudden change in the man. He adopted a more caring tone with his tenants, was more considerate towards his employees, and swore with less of his usual gusto. When two volunteers from an Islamic charity came knocking on the door appealing for funds to help Chechen refugees in Ingushetia, he gave them a whole pound.

I hoped that his new-found generosity might mean that he could be persuaded into making the much needed repairs to the building. But when I tried to press home my advantage, I was still disappointed. Instead I received an impromptu invitation to join my landlord for *iftar*. It came one afternoon about a week after the start of Ramadan in the form of a shout up the stairs.

'Oi! I'm 'aving a bit of a snack, innit!'

The snack started off as some Syrian dates and soon evolved into an enormous feast of fish curry, spiced rice, chickpeas, pakoras, samosas, and rice pudding, all of which had been prepared by Mrs Ali and her daughters and delivered to the shop.

Mr Ali was a considerate if not overbearing host and, as we sat cross-legged on the floor, he saw to it that whenever a bare patch appeared on my plate, it was quickly covered with more food. As we ate, he kept me entertained with stories about his schooldays in Limehouse where he had been bullied mercilessly by the white kids – 'Every day some bustard called me "Paki"'; about his days working in a Jewish sweatshop in a basement on Princelet Street; and about his 'Missis', who never let him watch cricket on TV because she was addicted to Bangladeshi soap operas beamed in from Dhaka.

I returned upstairs having enjoyed the meal and the company, but feeling as if I had been wrong-footed. Fraternising with Mr Ali was no way to go about persuading him to make repairs to the building. And so, despite his hospitality, I decided to keep him at arm's length.

Mr Ali had other ideas. As far as he was concerned, we were now fast friends and he started to make a habit of coming up to my kitchen in the evenings to sit by the fire and watch my TV. During Ramadan he stuck to tea; but once it was over he turned to the booze I kept in the cupboard above the kitchen sink. So regular did his visits become that I had to start buying cheap rum in place of the good stuff, which I hid under the floorboards.

It was an unlikely friendship that developed between us – more so given that few East End Bangladeshis fraternised with their white neighbours and vice versa – but we found a surprising amount of common ground. Cricket provided an inexhaustible topic of conversation and we often watched internationals together. It also helped that I had been to Bangladesh (I was the only English person Mr Ali had ever met to have done so) and that I was familiar with Islamic culture, something he seemed to find refreshing, even though he was no Koran basher.

'When I was at school in Lime'ouse and our teacher tried to get us to say the Lord's Prayer and I told 'er my people prayed to Allah she says, "Never 'eard of 'im,"' Mr Ali recalled as we sat drinking in my kitchen one evening. 'The white kids used to tell us, "Oi! Why are you lot always bendin' over bashin' your 'eads on the ground? Don't it hurt?"'

During his adult life, Mr Ali had experienced a similar degree of ignorance amongst older white East Enders as well.

'They don't 'ave no respect for our culture, innit.'

One story he told me involved an Essex plumber he had hired a few years earlier to do some work in his home.

'Me and this plumber geezer get talking one day and I tell 'im that I'm taking the family to Mecca. So this plumber, 'e says, "Oh yeah, go there often, do you?" And I says to 'im, "Naa, iss the first time, innit. I'm taking the 'ole family."'

At this point in the conversation the plumber said that his wife had been nagging him to take her to Mecca as well.

'When I 'ea this, yeah, I'm thinking, "What the 'ell's 'e on about? 'e can't go to Mecca, 'e's not Muslim, innit." So I says to 'im, "They won't let you in, mate!" And 'e says, "Thas all right with me. I don't wanna go any'ow. I was planning a night down the boozer with my mates. Bingo does my 'ead in."'

Mr Ali laughed.

'Thas when I realised, yeah, we're talking at like cross purposes, innit. I'm talking about going to Saudi Arabia and 'e's talking about going down the Mecca bingo 'all on the 'ackney Road.'

He laughed again, but then shook his head in despair.

'These people, yeah, they don't know nafing about our culture. Iss just ignorance, innit.'

Mr Ali lived in a three-bedroom terraced house behind the mosque in Whitechapel. He shared it with his wife, their three daughters who were twenty-two, eighteen and fourteen respectively, their eleven-year-old son, Mr Ali senior who was thought to be about seventy, one of Mr Ali's elder sisters who was a widow, and a boy of eleven called Salim whose parents had gone to visit Bangladesh for a couple of months and were yet to return, four and a half years later.

Mr Ali's family, like ninety-nine per cent of the Bangladeshis living in the East End, hailed from the district of Sylhet in the north-east of the country. Amongst the fifty thousand-strong community, there was hardly a person to whom they were not related or didn't know by sight. Just to walk down Brick Lane or the busy Whitechapel Road market with Mr Ali was enough to dispel the oft-repeated Cockney gripe that the East End had lost its neighbourliness. With virtually every step came a wave and a shout from somebody on the other side of the road, or the approach of an old friend with a warm smile and an extended hand.

Whenever he needed something done, there was usually someone in the clan with the required expertise. As well as his builder, Mr Ali's doctor, solicitor and accountant were close relatives. When he needed a travel agent, a glazier, a locksmith or someone who dealt in mobile phones all he had to do was flick through the family Rolodex and find himself an uncle, a nephew or a cousin.

'Let me know and I'll get you anything you want. My sister? 'er 'usband's brother's son's a dentist. 'e's got a place in Poplar. If you want a couple of teeth pulled aat, 'e can get it sorted. I 'ad some of mine out with 'im. 'e's got qualifications, innit.'

Living in such a tight-knit community had its drawbacks, however. Nothing anyone did went unnoticed and Mr Ali rarely had a moment's peace to himself.

'I can't get away from all them cousins, aunties and uncles. They're coming out of the woodwork, innit,' he complained during another rum-drinking, cricket-watching session in my kitchen. 'There's always people turning up from Sylhet. They come in and they says to me, "I'm, like, your auntie's sister's son's nephew. Give us a job, yeah."'

I asked him why so many people came from one single district and not other parts of Bangladesh?

'Thas a big mystery, innit,' he said. 'All I know is where one of us goes, the 'ole village follows.'

In fact, as I discovered through my own reading, the first Sylhetis settled in Britain as early as the mid-1700s. Hired out of Calcutta as ship hands aboard the vessels of the East India Company, some jumped ship when they reached London while others found themselves abandoned in the docks by unscrupulous captains who reneged on their word to provide them with work on the return journey to India.

With no one to care for them, these lascars, as sailors of African and Asian origin were known, had to sleep out in the open where they often succumbed to disease and freezing temperatures. Begging and crime became the only means of survival for many and a good few ended up behind bars (of those some were shipped as convicts to Australia).

By 1842, there were approximately 3,000 lascars arriving in London every year. Those who could afford lodgings were 'herded like cattle – six or eight in a single room or cellar without bedding, or chairs, or tables', or ended up in 'abodes of infamy and vice'. It was not until 1857 that philanthropic Christian consciences were finally stirred and the Strangers' Home for Asiatics, Africans, South Sea Islanders and Others Occasionally Residing in the Metropolis opened its doors. Situated near the docks in Limehouse, it provided cheap, clean lodgings, as well as assistance for those seeking work on ships bound for India.

The coming of the steam ship, with its need of stokers, brought ever greater numbers of lascars to London and, increasingly, in the first half of the twentieth century, they elected to settle in the East End. The Sylhetis were quick to flex their adolescent entrepreneurial muscles, setting up *chai* stands in the docks and some of London's first curry houses. By the end of World War Two, with word filtering back to Sylhet of the fortunes waiting to be made in London, more young men set off for England via Calcutta. Mr Ali's uncle was just one of the thousands who came during that period. He arrived on the banks of the Thames in 1947 – his dream, like that of so many, to work in London for a few years and then return to Bangladesh a wealthy man.

' 'e never went back,' said Mr Ali. ' 'e worked in Jewish sweatshops, innit. And 'e flogged stuff cheap in the street. 'e was seriously poor, yeah. But back in Sylhet, everyone thought 'e was, like, a millionaire, innit. 'cause every month, yeah, 'e'd send money back to 'is family. In them days, a few quid was like a fortune in Sylhet.'

In 1970, with civil war looming in Bangladesh – then East Pakistan – Mr Ali senior decided to send his son to Britain to live with his uncle. He was just fourteen at the time.

'My father says to me one day, "Oi! You're goin' to London, innit." 'e thought it was a good opportunity, yeah. 'e tells me, "Come back in five years and you'll be rich." 'e said I'd get a beautiful wife and we'd build a big 'ouse. That was, like, 'is dream, yeah. But my old man didn't understand what it was like 'ere in the East End. 'e thought you just turned up and people gave you money. Thas the mentality of them Bangladesh people, innit. They think that in Britain the trees grow money.'

Mr Ali was brought to London by another man posing as his father who delivered him to his uncle's door in Spitalfields. His new home was a cramped, rat-infested flat in a crumbling Victorian tenement building. The three small rooms were occupied by seven other Sylheti men. There was no glass in the windows, no heating and no running water. A bucket served as a toilet; food was prepared using a gas stove on the floor. For bedding the men made do with second-hand mattresses taken from the back of the Whitechapel Hospital; Mr Ali's was covered in stains and smelt of disinfectant.

The day after he arrived, Mr Ali began work in a Jewish sweatshop in the basement of an old Huguenot house. It was owned by a certain Mr Saul whom Mr Ali referred to as 'the old Jew'.

''e was a right bustard,' said Mr Ali of his former boss. 'Seven o'clock I'd start work and 'e'd be standing there with 'is watch every morning. If I was late, 'e'd take money off my wages. 'is wife was worse. She was this fat bitch with big boils on 'er face. She was always watching us. If you stopped working for one minute, she'd get at you: "Oi! Back to work! Back to work!" Stupid bitch, innit.'

The conditions in the sweatshop and the tenement building soon took their toll of Mr Ali. A few months after arriving in England, he fell seriously ill and spent the next six months in hospital where he was treated for malnutrition and rickets. Once he was fully recovered, the appropriate authorities saw to it that he was enrolled in a local school. When his uncle tried to make him go back to the sweatshop, he was prosecuted.

'Nobody in my family 'ad ever been to school. My uncle thought it was a waste of time. 'e says, "You're 'ere to work. Books won't 'elp your family, innit." I couldn't read or write. I didn't speak no English.'

In the evenings and on weekends, Mr Ali continued to work in another sweatshop that was owned by a fellow Sylheti. It was this man who took him on as an apprentice, gave him a place to live and ensured that, when he was old enough, Mr Ali was able to set himself up in business. Without the patronage of this 'godfather', my landlord conceded, he would never have made good, although his willingness to work hard had also been a factor in his favour.

'I didn't get nowhere by sitting around watching satellite TV. I've worked 'ard every day of my life. I tell my kids, no one never got nowhere by being lazy. Don't take my word for it, I tell them. The Prophet Muhammad, peace be upon 'im, yeah, 'e said, "Be a worker; don't sit around on your arse, innit."'

Had he ever thought about returning with his family to Bangladesh as his father had once hoped he would, I asked him.

'The Missis wants to go. She tells me, "This place is no good. Le's live in Bangladesh." But I tell 'er, "What am I going to do in that shit 'ole?" Sit arand, yeah. Thas what they do in Bangladesh, you know. Sit arand all day, innit.'

He shook his head from side to side.

'In Bangladesh, yeah, when one person gets a job, everyone else like gives up their job and lives off 'im. They've got this mentality, innit. "I don't af to do nafing; let my brother pay for everyfing." The coupla times I've been back there, yeah, my relatives, yeah, they says to me, "Oi! Mr Ali. Give us some cash!" So I tell 'em, "Fuck off, yeah! Make it yourself!" I'm telling you, them bustards wouldn't last five minutes 'ere. Any'ow, 'er Majesty, yeah, she shouldn't let 'alf of them in.'

———•———

Part of Mr Ali's sweatshop was housed in a crudely constructed extension built on to the back of the building. Its flat, sagging, asphalt-covered roof was accessible from the window on the first-floor landing via a rickety wooden ladder held together by waxed rope. During its more agile years, Sadie's cat had used it to come and go from the house. Now it served as a fire escape, or so Mr Ali liked to pretend.

The roof was covered in junk that had been bleached and warped by the elements: an old mangle, a few bald car tyres, a black and white TV gutted of its insides, a bathtub filled with dark-green algae, a life-size plastic Alsatian that was missing its front legs. There was also a rickety school chair carved with children's graffiti.

Sometimes, when the weather permitted, I would climb out on to the roof and sit on the chair and enjoy a smoke and a cup of coffee.

Occasionally, I would go out there for a nightcap. But being out on the roof was not without its hazards. A section at the far end was rotten and the first time I walked across it, my left foot suddenly disappeared through the asphalt and my shoe ended up on the sweatshop floor. There were also a number of pipes jutting out of the roof that originated in the sweatshop and periodically let out blasts of hot, hissing steam. And then there was the threat posed by the flock of pigeons living in a corrugated iron shed on an adjacent roof, who made frequent formation fly-pasts, targeting anyone sitting below.

Still, the roof could be a surprisingly quiet and relaxing place to be. The rows of drab four- and five-storey terraced houses along Brick Lane and Bethnal Green Road shielded it from the noise of the traffic and, for the most part, from sirens and security alarms. At certain times, it was so quiet that I could hear the call to prayer from the East End mosque on Whitechapel Road, and the clatter of trains as they passed along the underground line from Shoreditch station. Sunday mornings brought the distant sounds of pealing church bells and music-box tunes played by roaming ice-cream vans. From the backs of the curry houses came the smell of Indian cooking and, when the wind was in the right direction, the sweet aroma of fresh bagels from the bakeries.

My neighbour to the left was an ex-dockworker called Harry who owned the pigeons and often reminisced about Winston Churchill's state funeral and how, as his casket was taken down the Thames, the cranes in the docks were bowed before it. Next door to Harry lived a commune of Australian vegans who once tried to 'liberate' Harry's pigeons.

'But being 'oming pigeons, they all flew back,' Harry told me once when we had a chat over the wall that divided Mr Ali's property from his.

My other immediate neighbours were three asylum seekers who lived in a one-room bed-sit that they rented from the Pakistani landlord. They, too, had access to a flat roof at the back of their building and across half of it they had constructed a makeshift greenhouse out of some plastic sheeting. This misshapen yet sturdy structure was heated by way of a washing-machine hose run off a kitchen vent, and three 60-watt light bulbs hooked up to an extension cord. In this environment, the plants were flourishing; indeed so thick was the vegetation that it was impossible to tell from the outside what the asylum seekers were growing.

During my first months on Brick Lane, I never met my green-fingered neighbours. They were not around in the daytime and I caught a glimpse of them only occasionally at night when they came out on to their roof.

I was sure that the eldest of the three was a Pushtun and more than likely an Afghan. He stood at just over six feet tall and had a hooked nose, a bushy black beard and a pair of watery brown eyes that looked almost fake, as if he was wearing tinted contact lenses. He always wore a *salwar kameez*, Caterpillar boots and a thick winter jacket, and he ate large quantities of pistachio nuts, the shells of which littered their roof.

As for the Afghan's friends, Mr Ali was of the opinion that they were Albanians. He had made this deduction based on the fact that, to his eyes, they were 'shifty-looking, innit'. But although their gaunt, unshaven faces, fair looks, dark hair and black leather jackets fitted the bill, they could have been from anywhere in the Balkans.

'They're always smoking and listening to Turkish-sounding music,' said Mr Ali, who reminded me of his past dealings with Albanian tenants.

'Everyone from that part of the world smokes and listens to Turkish-sounding music,' I said.

'Yeah, but I've 'eard them watching football, yeah. And Albanians are football crazy, innit.'

'They could be from Armenia for all you know.'

'Waas the difference? They're all the same.'

My landlord was not the only person on Brick Lane who had formed an unfavourable impression of asylum seekers in general. Sadie said they were ''ooligans' and Mr Singh condemned them as 'leeches sucking off the bodies of law-abiding British taxpayers'. He objected to the presence of the Somalis in particular. They had overrun the local National Health Service surgery, he complained. Nowadays you could not get an appointment to see a doctor for three weeks.

'The East End is becoming like Africa, only.'

Mr Singh was so concerned about all the new asylum seekers arriving in the UK that he was planning to join a political party that promised to make the issue a priority when and if they came to power. He had been persuaded to this course of action by a 'respectable gentleman' in 'a shirt and tie' who had stopped by the shop to explain the said party's policies. Mrs Singh had been so impressed that she had given the canvasser ten pounds.

'They are one British National Party,' said Mr Singh.

'The BNP!' I could hardly believe my ears. 'But they want all immigrants driven out of Britain, Mr Singh.'

'Precisely.'

'But you're an immigrant yourself.'

'Not immigrant! Thirty-three years I am living in Great Britain, paying income tax, voting Labour, listening to Queen's speech on Christmas Day. I am number one British citizen and patriot. Also, like all Sikh peoples, I am working night and day and raising one family of the most respectable order. My son is chartered accountant, graduated and certified. In our family, integrity is there, respectability also. Why should we be compared to all these layabout fellows?'

There were similar grumblings amongst the regulars at the Bethnal Green Arms, where Chinese people were generally referred to as 'Chinks', the French 'Frogs', the Germans 'Krauts', Mediterranean-looking types as 'Dagos', and the token Welshman as 'Taff'. They, too, made clear distinctions between different types of 'farawners'. Significantly, blacks were never talked about in derogatory terms; they seemed to have won a degree of acceptance – more than once I heard it said that they had learnt to 'respect British ways' – and it was not uncommon to see a black person drinking at the bar. Similarly, 'Paul the Greek', the owner of a local minicab firm whose last name no one could pronounce, had also found acceptance – as had the Italian family who owned Pellicci's café on Bethnal Green Road (the owner, Nevio Pellicci, was known to his clientele as Neville).

But when it came to talk of people of South Asian origin and asylum seekers, the language was disturbingly racist.

'Let one lot in and the rest follow,' ranted 'Tel', the most outspoken of the regulars, who had a collapsed lung that prevented him from working but not from smoking forty Silk Cut a day. 'First it was the fuckin' Pakis and now they're coming from all over the fuckin' shop. Countries you 'aven't even fuckin' 'eard of.'

After every other sentence, Tel had to take an extra deep breath, wheezing like a child's squeaky toy.

'Fuck knows why we should af to put up with the likes of them. Tell me that. Why don't they fuck off back to where they came from? Last time I checked, Britain wasn't a fuckin' 'otel. What we want is a big sign up on the White Cliffs of Dover that says, "No Vacancies. Fuck off back to where you come from!"'

Tel's diatribes were generally met with solemn nods from the other men standing around the bar and the occasional mutter of 'thas right'.

'I've been in Dover,' continued Tel, whose complexion grew ruddier with each pint that he poured down his throat. 'All someone 'as to do is jump out of a truck and say "watcha" and they get free fuckin' 'ousing, free fuckin' cash and a blow job from Tony Blair. They're lining up in Calais to get over 'ere. What I say is round 'em all up, fly them over wherever the fuck they're from and kick the fuckers out from a very 'igh fuckin' 'ight.'

Chalky generally kept quiet on matters of race and immigration. One of his grandparents was Irish and his eldest sister had married a Jamaican car dealer. Chalky also played in a football team with a couple of West Indian players and he had once had a long-term relationship with a woman from the Cameroon.

'I fancy a bit of darkie every now and again,' he once told me after I mentioned that my fiancée was of Indian origin.

But he was dead set against letting asylum seekers into Britain – as I discovered one evening when he'd had one too many.

'They'll tell you they're from Kosovo and they're fleeing from Milošović. What a bunch of bollocks! All them ones down the market selling fags and mobiles are from Albania. They're not fleeing from fuck all.'

'I'm sure there must be genuine Kosovar Albanian asylum seekers amongst them,' I said.

'Could be,' he replied. 'But tell me this, 'ow many are we meant to allow in? There's already too many of us. What are we meant to do with millions of them? The line's got to be drawn somewhere. I mean, how would they feel if we all started going over there? They wouldn't put up with it – not for five minutes. I don't see why we should, neiver.'

Such talk was nothing new for the East End. As Jane Cox writes in *London's East End: Life and Traditions*: 'Little has changed since the days when everybody hated the Flemings, the Dutch, the French Huguenots, not to mention the Irish, Scots, Welsh and anyone who spoke "funny" or ate strange food.'

The likes of Tel came from a long line of what Margaret Harkness described as the 'East End loafer'.

'It is amusing to see his British air of superiority,' she wrote of the type in 1889. 'He is looked upon as scum by his own nation, but he feels himself to be an Englishman and able to kick the foreigner back to "his own dear native land" if only Government would believe in "England for the English" and give all foreigners "notice".'

Immigrants arriving in the East End have traditionally faced a barrage of hostility from one quarter or another. The Huguenots were derided as 'a set of rabble' and accused of growing rich at the expense of the poor. The Irish, who were called 'mumpers', or scroungers, were discriminated against for their Catholic faith and restricted from doing all but the most menial jobs. And a century later, the Jews were vilified as 'the very scum of the unhealthiest of the continental nations' and accused of spreading disease.

'The more there goes away, the more there comes to fill in the gaps,' complained a Stepney basket-maker to the Victorian chronicler Henry Mayhew in 1871. 'Last week there come about a thousand from abroad . . . an' here they seem to stick.'

During times of economic hardship, hostility has occasionally turned into violence. The years 1736 and 1780 both saw the Irish targeted by the mob; Whitechapel's German population came under attack in 1914; and more recently, skinheads tried to drive out the Bangladeshis. The East End has been the birthplace of most of Britain's racist groups, including the British League of Brothers and the National Front.

And yet despite the best efforts of these organisations, their campaigns of hatred, whether targeted at Jews, Bangladeshis or today's asylum seekers, have always met with limited success. There has never been a group in the East End – or anywhere else in the UK for that matter – to rival, say, the Ku Klux Klan or even Jean Marie Le Pen's *Front National*. Spitalfields and Whitechapel have never witnessed cross burnings or lynchings. And the breakdown in the social order forecast by the omnipresent prophets of doom in the press has never materialised.

'Whenever the East End's gone through periods of extreme social tension and things have flared up like they did in the 1970s or 1993, the papers have started screaming about the bloodbath to come,' said Jim Boon, one of the regulars at the Owl and the Pussycat on Redchurch Street, where I went for a pint from time to time.

Jim, who was a teacher at a school for children with special needs, had lived in Hoxton for fifteen years. His obsession was the Jack the Ripper mystery, and he was an amateur historian who saw the East End as a fundamentally tolerant place.

'Even at the worst of times, you've never had open warfare with neighbour fighting neighbour or people being dragged from their homes and butchered in the streets. Not like you have in, say, the Balkans, Rwanda or India. In fact, given the poverty, unemployment and lack of education that's existed here for so long, there's been relatively little violence over the centuries. The place has a kind of equilibrium of its own.'

Why did he think this was, I asked him, given the xenophobia that lurked beneath the surface?

'It's been said that the Jews got better treatment here than they did anywhere else in Europe. London's history has a lot to do with it. Even in Roman times the capital was highly cosmopolitan and, apart from the occasional glitch – like the Peasants Revolt when all the Flemings in London were massacred – it's always been a tolerant place. Unlike a lot of cities in Europe and even the US, you've never had laws defining where immigrants should live.'

Jim believed British secularism had also played an important part.

'The fact that your average Cockney has never been much of a churchgoer has been crucial to the stability of the East End,' he said. 'It's made them tolerant of others' beliefs. You might hear Cockneys complaining about how newcomers are stealing their jobs or council houses, but you won't catch them objecting on the grounds of their religious beliefs. This isn't Northern Ireland.'

It struck me that there was probably some truth in this. But much of what I read in the newspapers, where the debate over the 'asylum issue' raged every day, made me wonder if perhaps England was not reaching its immigrant limit. The numbers entering the country were, after all, unprecedented (there were now more foreigners coming to London than New York), and in Newham, the borough to the east of Tower Hamlets, whites were now in the minority.

Did this mean English identity was under threat, as many a pundit in the press was warning? Would immigration cause a breakdown in cultural cohesiveness, as Chalky and Tel believed? Or could the country continue to absorb foreigners? If anywhere could provide an answer it was here in the East End.

In the weeks that passed before I finally met my neighbours, I tried to keep an open mind about them. But it was not always easy. After I spotted the Afghan outside the Whitechapel mosque handing out flyers to passers-by, I began to wonder if perhaps Mr Ali and the others were right about them after all.

But as I soon discovered, my suspicions were unfounded. Far from being a Muslim fundamentalist, the Afghan, Gul Muhammad of Kandahar, hated the Taliban (almost as much as he hated the Russians) and had fled his homeland to avoid fighting in their ranks. Most of his family were now living in a refugee camp outside Peshawar on Pakistan's North-West Frontier along with some two million victims of decades of war.

The flyers I had seen him handing out on the street carried a photograph of his brother, Hamidullah, who, three years earlier, had given a people smuggler some six thousand pounds to take him to the UK. The money had comprised the family's entire savings and had been paid in the hope that Hamidullah would reach Britain and, once he found work, send funds back to Peshawar. But no one had heard from Hamidullah since he had crossed from Iran into Turkey, nearly two years ago. So Gul Muhammad had set out in search of him.

It had taken the Afghan some eight months to reach London, walking, hitching rides, smuggling himself inside trucks, taking what little work was available, and seeking charity from mosques and others along the way. In Iran, he had been arrested and beaten; in Anatolia, he had been attacked by a pack of wild dogs; in Istanbul he had worked in a sweatshop and slept rough on the banks of the Bosphorus.

The journey from Turkey across Europe had been no less harrowing. In Italy he had broken an arm while jumping from a train to avoid arrest. He had been locked up in Spain and, in France, come under attack from the people-smuggling mafia who had tried to prevent him from crossing the Channel after he refused to pay them a fee. His right hand still bore a scar left by the blade of a Kurd during a fight in Sangatte, the camp for refugees outside Calais. But despite everything the Afghan had endured, he had been able to trace his brother's progress only as far as Istanbul. From there the trail had gone cold.

The Afghan's two friends were Kosovar Albanians and were both called Sasa, which they pronounced 'Sasha'. The two men had fled from their home a few days after Serbian paramilitaries had rounded up most of the men and boys in their village and massacred them. Big Sasa, as I called him (he was three inches taller than his friend Little Sasa who was five feet eight), had lost his father and his grandfather. His grandmother had also been murdered, shot in the head as she pleaded for the life of her seventy-two-year-old husband.

Little Sasa had also lost a number of family members during Milošović's ethnic cleansing programme: a grandfather had been shot while firing his old World War Two revolver at the Serbian forces when they rolled into his village; and his younger brother had joined the Kosovo Liberation Army (KLA) and been killed in action.

The two Sasas, who were childhood friends, had escaped death only because they had not been in their village on the day of the massacre. The day before, they had been picked up by the Serb police and thrown in a cell where they were kept for four days with no beds or toilet and only a little food and water to sustain them. Their Serbian captors tortured them for information about the KLA; they were doused in water, electrocuted and the soles of their feet were beaten. Little Sasa had been so badly beaten about the head that he had lost the hearing in his right ear.

By the end of the fourth day, both Sasas had given themselves up for dead. But help then came from an unexpected quarter: one of the Serb prison guards, who had been a childhood friend and neighbour, took pity on them and arranged for their escape. He had done them this favour on one condition – that the two Sasas leave and never return. Kosovo, he told them, was no longer their home. It belonged to the Serbian people.

I learnt all this from Big Sasa, whom I met for the first time a couple of days before Christmas when I climbed down on to the roof and found him sitting on top of the wall that divided our two properties. This was the first time I had seen him in broad daylight and I was struck by how tired he looked. At the age of twenty-six, he was going prematurely grey. Patches had appeared in his hair that looked like splatters of paint. The lines that ran across his forehead and fanned out from the corners of his eyes belonged to the face of a man scarred by a lifetime of toil and anxiety. His cheeks were sunken and sallow, like those of an ailing hospital patient, making his stubble and the dusky bags under his eyes appear darker than they might have done ordinarily. When he drew a cigarette out of its packet, his hands trembled and it took all his concentration and effort to hold the lighter still and keep the tip in the flame.

'Even sometimes to take piss it is the problem,' he told me in his Americanised-Balkans accent. He took a hard drag and held the smoke in his lungs before blowing it up into the air and leaning forward on the wall. The skin underneath his right eye twitched involuntarily and he rubbed at it irritably.

'I think in my head I am fucked up, no,' he said, smiling sardonically and tapping at his temple with his knuckles.

I could tell that it had been a long time since Big Sasa had enjoyed a good laugh; the tension had constrained the features in his face as assuredly as a stroke would have done. Pain and worry had eaten away at his innocence and imbued him with a certain weariness. He was prone to lengthy bouts of silence and often stared off into space absentmindedly. But Big Sasa was a survivor and he was extremely proud. He shrank from sympathy and accepted charity with a reluctance that was not always gracious.

'I am not beggar,' he told me haughtily when I asked him how much he received from the British government every week. 'I collect voucher when there is no work; otherwise I do not take.'

Above all else, Big Sasa hated being mistaken for an Albanian.

'I tell people I am from Kosovo but they don't believe,' he said, with anger in his voice. 'Many Albanian people here in London, they say they are from my country, claim asylum. So British people they think I make lie. But really I prefer to be in my country. I prefer not to be the refugee. Everything is lost to me. My home, my father, all gone. Many of my friend is killed. If I return my country, I will be killed also. So I must be the refugee. This is not my choice. To be the refugee is the worst thing. No one like the refugee. To everyone he is the problem. But I think maybe I am the lucky person because I am alive. This is God's gift to me. If I can do the work, I can make future for myself. Then I will not be the refugee. I will be the human being again.'

Since arriving in London in June, the two Sasas and Gul Muhammad had done just about every menial job imaginable. They had washed cars and dishes, laboured on construction sites, moved heavy furniture, stacked cases in warehouses, cleaned drains, slaughtered chickens, worked in a giant laundry and mopped up sick from nightclub dance floors. Much of the work had been arranged through unscrupulous employment agencies and middlemen for whom their lack of official papers had not been an issue. Other jobs had come their way by hanging around in the streets of Cricklewood, north London, where dozens of asylum seekers and illegal immigrants gathered every morning touting for work.

'We are like whore,' he said. 'We stand on street and the car it pull up and the people they say, "How much?" And we tell, "What you want?" Maybe they say to dig ditch, build wall. Maybe cutting tree.'

The day before, Big Sasa had spent ten hours using a pneumatic drill to dig up a driveway for an Irish builder. He had injured his wrist in the process and it was bandaged. The doctor at the Whitechapel Hospital had told him to rest for a few days, which was why he was at home and not out searching for work. It was his first day off in nearly six months.

I asked him how much he usually earned in a day.

'Twenty, twenty-five pound. One time I get thirty pound from one lady. She is very nice. Usually we do the work eleven, twelve, maybe thirteen hour. Worst pay is coming from foreign people. Every time they pay less, sometime nothing.'

Only recently, a couple of Russians – 'They are the mafia, they have Mercedes-Benz and blonde whore' – had cheated the two Sasas and the Afghan after hiring them to clean out a drug addicts' doss-house in Stratford.

'In all my life, I never see nothing like this,' said Big Sasa. 'There is the shit and piss and needle on floor. I think that perhaps the pig is living in this place. All the furniture and windows they are broken. We spend all day to clean. No food, no rest. When the Russian motherfucker people come, they give us ten pound, total. We tell them, no, this is not right, why you do like this? They tell us get lost or we break leg, maybe worse. So we leave that place. Afterward, my good friend Gul Muhammad, he say Russian people not good. He say they make destruction of his country. He say he enjoy to kill them with AK-47 machine-gun.'

Big Sasa picked up his pack of cigarettes, which lay on top of the wall where he was sitting. It was empty. He had smoked his way through half a packet in the hour that we had been talking. I offered him one of my Marlboro Lights and, after a moment's hesitation, he took one and lit up again.

'Thank you,' he said, regarding me through narrowed eyes.

There was an awkward silence. Then he asked me where I was from. His voice was suspicious.

'London,' I replied.

'You are British person?' He still sounded sceptical.

'Yes.'

He tapped the butt of his cigarette thoughtfully and watched the ash float down to my side of the roof.

'You know, during six month, you are first British person I am speaking,' he said, adding quickly: 'Please, you understand. I do not make the complaint.' He held up his hands defensively. 'I think Britain is good country. Not like France or Italy. Here we can work and there is help from your government. Of course, I am grateful.'

'But the British are not very friendly, right?' I said.

Big Sasa nodded his head. 'Yes.' He seemed relieved to hear me say it. 'Like you say, British people not friendly. This I find confuse – I don't understand. It is true, they give the asylum. But I think perhaps they are not liking foreign people.'

He told me about an incident that had occurred in the local post office a few days earlier. He had been standing in line to send a letter to Albania where many of his family and friends were now stranded in refugee camps, when an old woman had started berating him. 'You're not wanted in Britain,' she screamed. 'You're taking British jobs and British housing and taxpayer's money. Go home!'

'The other people in the post office, they stand there looking, staring to me. They don't say nothing. So I leave that place.'

The Serbs who had murdered half his family and evicted him from his country had introduced Big Sasa to fear and hatred, despair and helplessness. He had come to cherish hope. But as he had stood in the post office on Bethnal Green Road, it was the first time the Kosovar felt shame.

'I do not understand. I am not make no problem for no one,' he said.

Face to face with my neighbour I now felt guilty for the suspicion I had harboured about him and his friends. There can be few things worse, I reflected, than being evicted from your own country, to lose everything that is dear and familiar to you, and then to encounter hostility wherever you go.

The moral obligation to provide a safe haven for such people seemed clear. And despite all the scaremongering by some politicians and sections of the press, there were strong economic incentives for doing so as well. Asylum seekers were not a drain on the economy, as many claimed: far from it, they were adding some £2.5 billion annually to the government's coffers and providing a badly needed workforce. Furthermore, with the average fertility rate in Europe at around 1.5 per woman, Britain could not afford to turn away able-bodied immigrants if its economy was to continue to grow. The only alternative was for the British to start producing larger families again and to stop emigrating at an average rate of 150,000 per year.

But what did all this mean for the social fabric of England? As someone who was about to bring a foreigner into the country, it was something I felt a responsibility to consider. Would I be helping to undermine the very identity of my own culture?

Again, the figures did not support the voices raised against 'the hordes' of immigrants entering Britain. The country was not quite the soft touch it was made out to be. It ranked eighth in Europe in terms of the number of asylum applications per thousand and was kicking out hundreds of asylum applicants every month. According to Migration Watch, immigrants added only 0.25 per cent to the total population each year.

Hearing Big Sasa's stories gave me a sudden reality check. My own problems paled by comparison and I went to bed that night feeling less troubled than I had in months.

When I awoke the next morning, I decided to invite Big Sasa and his friends for Christmas lunch the following day. But my neighbours had already made plans to celebrate Eid Al-Fitr, the festival that follows on the heels of Ramadan, and Big Sasa in turn invited me to join them.

'We make something very special,' he promised.

Christmas Day. I woke early and went to the kitchen window, somehow expecting everything outside to look brighter and cleaner. But the scene was as grey and dreary as ever, the terraced houses and concrete buildings camouflaged against the slate sky, the street lights ringed by shimmering halos in the light drizzle. No Christmas miracle or ghost of past, present or future had cleaned up the litter that lay scattered across the pavements, nor removed the graffiti and tattered billposters on the walls, or the patches of vomit left on the pavements by revellers the night before.

None of this had stopped Brick Lane's tramps from enjoying themselves, however. Their high spirits were being fuelled by a bonanza of lager bought with unusually generous donations given by passers-by.

The regular group had been joined by half a dozen other guest tramps, and together they were standing around a fire lit inside an empty oil drum. All of them were wearing paper crowns and, between the occasional bout of laughing and cursing – 'Merry Christmas, you cunts!' – they blew on plastic whistles, sounding like an ensemble of out of tune wind instruments.

I watched the tramps and people coming and going from the bakeries for a while and then washed and went for a walk round the neighbourhood. At the far end of Brick Lane, the Bangladeshi community was out in full force. Taj Stores was packed with shoppers and on the corner of Woodseer and Spital Streets there was a traffic jam – possibly the only one in the whole of London that day. By noon the curry houses were open and the usual touts stood in their doorways, trying to tempt customers inside with offers of Turkey vindaloo. Worshippers crammed into the Brick Lane mosque – in sharp contrast to Christ Church in Spitalfields where the congregation for the morning service numbered no more than a few dozen. On the pavement outside the Indian sweet shops, people queued to buy *burfi* to take to friends and family for Eid.

When I returned to the top end of Brick Lane, I found that Little Sasa and Gul Muhammad had gone shopping and Big Sasa was preparing lunch on his own. I offered to lend him a hand, but there was only room for one in the kitchen area of the room, so I sat against the inside of the window ledge and kept out of his way.

The bed-sit made my place look palatial. Every inch of the room was being used in some way. A makeshift platform bed constructed from scaffolding that was large enough to accommodate three mattresses took up almost half the space. Beneath it stood a cupboard and a set of drawers, and hinged to the wall was a door, which could be raised and lowered like a drawbridge to serve as a table. The kitchen, too, had been ingeniously designed. A cooker stood inside the fireplace below the chimney that drew away all the steam from the pots boiling on the hob. The sink was cleverly concealed beneath a removable counter. And the remaining pots and pans were suspended in mid-air from a bicycle tyre rim that hung from a pulley fixed to the ceiling.

Gul Muhammad had designed and built all the furniture in the room, as well as the greenhouse on the back roof, using materials taken from skips and building sites.

'Really he is very clever,' said Big Sasa, who showed me the chessboard the Afghan had made out of the top of a biscuit tin with an assortment of nuts and bolts for pieces.

As Big Sasa continued preparing lunch, he told me how he and his friends had arrived in London and stayed at the Finsbury Park mosque. They had not liked it there, he said. It was full of 'fundamental' people who had tried to persuade them to return to their respective countries and fight a *jihad*. After a few weeks they moved to a council estate where they found themselves the targets of repeated racial abuse. Then in June Gul Muhammad met their Pakistani landlord, a fellow Pushtun, who took pity on the Afghan and offered him the bed-sit at a cheap rate.

I had noticed that whenever Big Sasa talked about his Afghan friend it was with awe. I asked him how they had met.

'In Calais,' he replied. 'Gul Muhammad is in big fight with Albania mafia people. We see them one night fighting. We think perhaps they like to kill him so we help.'

Big Sasa had a way of telling his stories in a casual, almost indifferent manner. I always had to ask him to pause, backtrack and fill in the details; invariably, they turned out to be the most salient ones. In this case, I learnt that the Albanian thugs had been armed with knives, and by intervening the two Sasas put themselves in considerable danger. Indeed, had a passing French police car not come to their aid they might have been killed.

After this incident, which saw the Afghan and his two new friends locked up for the night in a cell together, Gul Muhammad swore to remain with the two Sasas until such time as he was able to repay them for the debt he now owed them. It was thanks to him that the two Sasas reached England. For several days the two Kosovars had been trying in vain to sneak on board one of the trucks bound for England that stopped in the port at night. The Afghan suggested a new approach. He led them back south along the highway to a roadside truck stop. There, under cover of darkness, they were able to slip into the back of a cross-Channel lorry, thereby avoiding any further entanglements with the smuggling mafia or the French authorities.

The following morning, the two Sasas and Gul Muhammad stepped out of the back of the trailer into a car park. At first, they could not be certain which country they had been brought to. But the driver of the truck soon made it known to them.

'He tell us "fuck off",' said Big Sasa. 'Then I know we arrive in Britain.'

We waited an hour or so for the others to return.

Gul Muhammad was the first through the door, an imposing presence, both confident and strong. Over his shoulder he carried a brown potato sack, which he dropped to the floor before shaking me by the hand and half crushing my fingers in the process. Little Sasa came running up the stairs behind him, calling out excitedly to Big Sasa and closing the door with a bang. He was out of breath and, between gasps, giggled uncontrollably, saying something in Albanian while pointing at the potato sack.

'I don't believe,' said Big Sasa in English, and as he spoke, he picked up the potato sack and turned it upside down. A plump, black and white feathery carcass tumbled out on to the floorboards. I recognised it immediately as a Canada goose.

'Where did you get that?' I said in astonishment.

'From park,' replied Little Sasa.

'From Victoria Park?'

He nodded his head proudly.

'You killed it?'

'Not me, heem!'

The Afghan smiled and picked up the limp body of the goose; its throat had been cut.

'But you can't go around killing geese in parks,' I protested.

The Afghan shrugged his broad shoulders at my credulity. It was common knowledge that geese were extremely stupid, he said in his broken English. Besides, they taste good.

'But how did you catch it?'

It had been easy, the Afghan assured me. The park had been empty. Was not today some Christian holiday? The goose had been lured out of the boating pond and into some bushes. A piece of bread had been held up above the unwitting creature's head, causing it to stretch out its neck. At that moment Gul Muhammad had struck. In one lightning movement, he had grabbed the bird by the neck and slit its throat with a knife. All the blood had been allowed to drain from its body and the limp carcass had been bundled into the sack. Then Gul Muhammad and Little Sasa had made their getaway down the Regent's Canal.

'Look, this is England. You can't go around killing geese. You'll be arrested,' I insisted.

'No worry, mate,' said Little Sasa. 'We go very quick.'

Gul Muhammad carried the goose out on to the roof where he set about plucking its feathers and removing the offal. I watched him working from the window, hoping that no one in the neighbouring houses would look out and see what he was up to. I was particularly concerned that the Australian vegans might spot him. If they did, I was certain they would not hesitate to call the police. I tried to imagine how I would go about explaining how we came to be in possession of a Canada goose. They were hardly likely to believe that it had fallen out of the sky.

Luckily, Gul Muhammad worked quickly and it wasn't long before the bird had been stripped of its feathers. Little Sasa helped by gathering them up in a black bag, which was later deposited in a dumpster around the corner, along with the head, feet and all other evidence of its existence. The goose was then chopped up and cooked in a big pot along with tomatoes, onions and spices. Most of these ingredients came from the greenhouse where, I learned, the trio were growing a variety of vegetables in a collection of unlikely containers including an old bathtub and a toilet.

Christmas-cum-Eid lunch was served around three in the afternoon. My contribution to the meal included some mince pies and a fruit cake. To the 'table' (we ate sitting cross-legged on the floor) were added the goose *karai*, Afghani pilau and fresh chopped salad from the greenhouse. Everyone agreed that the goose tasted excellent (if a bit tough) and Gul Muhammad spoke about returning to the park and getting hold of another one. But I warned him against poaching any more birds; it was theft and, if caught, he would land himself in trouble. Besides, the geese were not there to be killed and eaten.

'Why?' he asked.

'I don't know. But you can't eat them. That's all there is to it.'

'And goat?' he asked.

'Goats? Where have you seen goats?'

'At farm,' answered Little Sasa.

He meant the Bethnal Green Farm near Shoreditch underground station. It was an attraction for schoolchildren and home to a few scrawny chickens, some sheep, a couple of ponies, and a few old billy goats.

'No killing of goats either,' I said.

The Afghan looked disappointed. He liked the taste of goat, he said. And it had been a long time since he had eaten one.

'You can buy goat at the Bangladeshi butchers,' I pointed out.

'And sheepses' head,' chimed in Big Sasa. 'Next time, I am cooking sheepses' head. Really it is very nice. You will like.'

'*Insha'allah*, God willing,' intoned Gul Muhammad.

Later that evening, after we had all watched *The Great Escape* (Gul Muhammad kept throwing things at the TV whenever the Nazis made an appearance and called out his support for Steve McQueen) and played several rounds of chess (Big Sasa had been weaned on the game and beat me three times, each time in less than a dozen moves), I made my way back next door.

For a while, I stood by the kitchen window, watching people coming and going in the street.

Not long before I went to bed, I noticed Gul Muhammad emerge on to the street. He was carrying something wrapped in tinfoil. He approached one of the tramps and handed it to him. The tramp pulled back the foil to reveal a plate piled with some of the remains of our lunch. He thanked Gul Muhammad and, in return, offered him a swig of lager from his can. But the Afghan, who was strictly teetotal, declined the offer and, wishing him good night, turned and headed back inside.

5

The Incomparable Mrs Suri

'London has always held out hands of toleration, if not of welcome, to the alien.'

Walter Besant, *East London* (1901)

IN THE FORTNIGHT before Anu arrived, I did all I could to make the attic as comfortable as possible. I sanded and varnished the floorboards, put up spotlights and shelving, bought some rugs and a set of drawers, and got rid of the thin foam mattress that I had been sleeping on and replaced it with a new futon (the sloping ceiling was too low to accommodate a proper bed).

I also threw away Mr Ali's fridge, which was leaking coolant on to the floorboards; and in the bathroom, with the help of Gul Muhammad, I rigged some plastic guttering to the ceiling to divert dripping water away from the toilet seat and into the shower.

By the New Year, the place was looking reasonably homely. But for all my efforts, I still shuddered to think what Anu was going to make of it.

In the event, the street did me no favours.

Anu arrived in mid-January on a sombre Sunday afternoon only an hour after the market had closed. Brick Lane was looking its worst. The street was awash with a swill of half-trampled fruit and vegetables, prawn shells, styrofoam cups and crumpled paper bags, mixed in with a jumble of battered cardboard boxes sodden by the morning's rain. Strewn across the pavement a few doors down from Mr Ali's lay the entire contents of someone's flat – clothes, shoes, crockery, mattress and all – thrown out of a second-floor window by a ruthless landlord.

To make matters worse, the tramps had got hold of a couch and placed it on the pavement to the right of the bakeries where they were sitting in a row, shoulder to shoulder, lager cans in hand, watching people coming and going in the street like a family gathered around the TV for the night.

As our airport cab pulled up, one of the tramps approached the nearest lamp-post, dropped his trousers down to his ankles and proceeded to spray a wide arc of piss into the gutter.

Anu sat next to me on the back seat of the taxi, looking out on to the street, an expression of horror on her face.

'*This* is it?' she said in a voice betraying genuine alarm. 'This is where you're living?'

'It's not usually this bad,' I said, gently taking her by the hand. 'The market is only held on Sundays.'

But I could see that my words did nothing to soothe her apprehension and, as we climbed out of the taxi and I unloaded her bags, Anu stood on the pavement regarding the street with consternation.

'This is like a slum,' she said as I paid the driver.

Anu's eyes were fixed on a homeless man in rags who was pushing a supermarket trolley filled with junk down the pavement towards us. As he passed other pedestrians, he looked up at them like a tortoise straining its neck out of its shell and asked them something which elicited hoots of laughter, looks of bafflement, or shrugs. He drew closer and I could hear him mumbling a question to himself over and over again like a secret mantra that contained some hidden meaning. And as he reached the front of Mr Ali's shop, he looked up at Anu with pleading, bloodshot eyes and asked her with desperation in his voice:

'Can you tell me how to get to Sesame Street?'

When I showed Anu around upstairs, she seemed to recognise the effort I had made to improve the place. She particularly appreciated the flowers I had arranged in an old jug in the kitchen, and the photographs of India taken during our travels together, which I had framed and hung on the walls.

She kept a brave face as I showed her around the neighbourhood. But in the next few days, her impression of the East End grew more baleful. On the first morning after she arrived, we walked down

Bethnal Green Road to find the place swarming with police investigating a murder. And the following evening, when we got dressed in our best clothes and waited at the bus stop for the number eight to take us into the West End for a night out, a local prostitute approached and warned Anu to get off her patch.

At night Anu had trouble sleeping and, like me, found it hard to wake up in the morning. She was irritated by the freezing temperatures in the bathroom, the ringing of the fire alarm doorbell, and the mice, which had survived all my efforts to exterminate them. She also took a dislike to Mr Ali, who walked into the attic one morning unannounced as she was getting dressed.

I could tell that, in those first days, she was trying her hardest to keep a grip on herself, desperate for our relationship to work. But it was an uphill struggle. She knew that my parents wanted her gone and she had no friends or family of her own to welcome her and offer their support.

'I feel like the girl in *A Little Princess* who had to leave India and live in England and hated it,' she told me after a few days when she finally broke down in a flood of tears.

The similarity between Anu's circumstances and those that confront young Sarah in Frances Hodgson Burnett's classic tale – their love of India, the sudden move to a cold London attic – were admittedly striking. But Anu was no little princess. She was the product of a tumultuous childhood that had begun in New York's notorious Bronx and taken her to a motel beside a freeway in Tennessee. Roughing it was in her vocabulary.

Her father was an Indian of strict religious beliefs, unable to relate to his American daughter. His conservative outlook and suspicion of Western ideas meant that his concept of discipline was out of tune with the culture in which he had chosen to raise his children. Beyond a certain age, Anu was not allowed to wear skirts or make-up – 'Don't do fashion!' he would tell her – and she was discouraged from reading fiction, which she was passionate about. Anu's mother was similarly unsympathetic to her daughter's interests, and as Anu reached adulthood, there was talk of an arranged marriage to a suitable boy from the Kshatriya caste.

Anu's life took a different direction when she met an American boy and they went out on a couple of illicit but innocent dates. When her father found out, his reaction was characteristically extreme: Anu was thrown out of the house and cut off financially, and she had to put herself through university. After she graduated, she left for Delhi to work as a freelance journalist and to discover India and its culture – as distinct from the Indian expatriate scene – for herself.

When I first met Anu in Delhi, she was writing for a news agency earning one rupee per word, living in a small flat without air-conditioning and loving every minute of it. India had brought out her natural enthusiasm for life and when we started working together and travelling to different parts of the country, I quickly fell in love with her.

Within a year I decided to ask her to be my wife. On Christmas Eve, I hired a private dining room at the Oberoi Hotel and took her there blindfolded. She didn't hesitate to say yes. But our engagement prompted the question of where we were going to live and, as my three-year contract with the Associated Press was coming to an end, I decided that I wanted to return to England. Anu was not at all keen on the idea. She had been in India for only three years and, at twenty-five, she wasn't ready to leave.

It took a considerable amount of persuasion – and a certain amount of bullying – to convince her otherwise. She would like London, I assured her, and being there would be good for her career.

Although fiercely independent, Anu had trusted me against her better judgement. So far, I had let her down badly and cracks were beginning to appear in her faith in me – in us. Given that I myself was not in a positive state of mind, the cracks soon began to open.

I would be lying if I said that our first few months in London were happy ones. There were arguments, tears, many hours spent in the gloom of the attic in the grip of despair.

Looking back, I'm not sure how our relationship survived. Perhaps it was love that kept us together. Perhaps it was the fear of failure in the face of our parents' opposition. Perhaps it was a recognition that our problems were not half as serious as those faced by others nearby.

Anu didn't quite know what to make of Banglatown. On the surface, there was much about it that appeared familiar and to which she was naturally attracted. She liked shopping at Taj Stores, where she could buy every ingredient she needed to cook Indian food – as well as ripe Alfonso mangoes and pistachio *kulfi*. In the video stores, she found many of her favourite Bollywood classics for rent. And she soon discovered a local beauty parlour catering to South Asian women where she could have her bushy Punjabi eyebrows expertly threaded.

But she quickly realised that whereas in Delhi she had felt at home amongst the population, to the East End Bangladeshis she was as much an outsider as I was. During visits to the beauty parlour she found the women either shy, distant or simply unable to communicate in either English, Hindi or Urdu. Brick Lane's curry houses also proved something of a mirage. They looked Indian, smelt Indian and even claimed to be Indian. 'But this isn't Indian food as I know it,' she said, looking at the menu of the restaurant where I took her a week or two after she arrived.

'Why are "papads" called "popadums"?' she asked. 'And why are they serving food in buckets?'

'What do you mean?'

'Here on the menu it lists a number of "baltis",' she laughed. 'In Hindi a "balti" is a bucket. If you ordered one in a restaurant in India, they'd probably bring you the washing up.'

Anu also pointed out that technically there was no such thing as 'curry' – except in the Punjab where it was a dish comprising dumplings in spiced buttermilk – and Chicken Tikka Masaala was not authentic, either.

To be fair to Brick Lane's chefs, they were hardly catering to the discerning Indian. 'Indian' food as it is known in Britain is a hybrid cuisine cooked by Bangladeshis pandering to a British palate. Most dishes are smothered in a thick, paste-based sauce vaguely reminiscent of the Mughali style with plenty of cayenne thrown in to achieve the requisite eye-watering results.

Or so I explained to Anu. But being in the restaurant only made her pine for India even more, and made London seem all the more foreign and strange.

As close as she came to packing her bags and heading back to Delhi, Anu soldiered on and started applying for jobs. Criss-crossing London, she went to many an interview, making use of all the connections I could muster. Her prospects looked strong; as a multi-skilled journalist with an ethnic background, it seemed only a question of time before an opportunity presented itself. But as she came into contact with potential employers and we started to socialise outside of the East End, Anu began to gain a sense of the cultural divide between England and America. 'The only thing the two countries seem to have in common is the language and even there I have my doubts,' she once said.

For one thing, Anu had never heard of Scousers before. And when she went for a trial day at a British TV news organisation and had to work for a particularly grumpy one, she couldn't understand a word he said. This was unfortunate as the Liverpudlian was the person in charge of taking on new recruits and Anu did not improve her chances of landing a job by asking him which part of Australia he came from.

She also made the classic mistakes typical of Americans new to Britain, such as asking for pants in Marks & Spencer and being shown to the underwear section; and trying to buy a 'fanny pack' only to be laughed at by the shop assistants. But more crucially, Anu found that English social conventions differed greatly from those of the US. Or rather, she was used to America where people talk straight.

'What does it take to break the ice with the Brits? A power drill?' she asked me when we were on our way back to Brick Lane one evening from a stuffy soirée in Islington. 'It's like trying to talk to a bunch of spies. They're so guarded!'

She was right: the people we had met had been a pretty aloof bunch. In fact, the evening had been spectacularly boring.

'I'm sorry I took you,' I said. 'From now on we'll avoid Islington soirées.'

Anu fidgeted in her seat on the top deck of the bus as it made its way back towards the East End; I could tell that she had something else to say.

'What is it?' I prompted her.

'It's . . . it's not just about tonight,' she said. 'Wherever I go in

London, I find everyone's aloof. Even people who are friendly stay at a distance. It's like there's this line in the sand and you'd better not cross it. No one wants to hang out. Heaven forbid that you should ask anyone over for a meal. It's like telling them that someone just died. They start wringing their hands, looking down on the floor and mumbling incoherently. What's wrong with them?'

I took a deep breath. Anu had been my constant interpreter and counsellor in India; now that our roles were reversed, I knew that I should show the same level of patience.

'The English generally keep people at arm's length until they get to know them,' I explained. 'They recoil in the face of foreigners who are too forthright and they're especially wary of Americans because they know how up-front they can be.'

Anu seemed to take this on board, so I continued:

'England's not like North Carolina where they throw a barbecue for anyone who moves into the neighbourhood. There's an expression here: "Good fences make good neighbours." '

'It's strange being on the tube,' she said. 'Everyone keeps so quiet and no one looks at anyone else.'

'It's considered bad form to talk in a loud voice in public,' I went on. 'And you'll find that no one ever complains – or not hard enough to get anything changed. Even when the entire rail network comes to a grinding halt and tens of thousands of people can't get home after work, there'll be lots of moans but none of them will do anything in serious protest. The ability to "muddle through" is seen as a great attribute. And if you happen to step on someone's toes in the street, don't be surprised if they apologise.'

Anu looked at me quizzically and shook her head from side to side.

'You Brits are weird,' she said.

On the morning of the first Sunday in February, the phone rang on the dot of seven o'clock. The terse, bossy tone of an Indian woman's voice on the other end brought me to my senses faster than usual.

'I vant Anu Anand!'

For a moment I thought it was a call from India. But the line was too clear and I could hear the theme tune to *EastEnders* playing on a TV in the background.

'Anu isn't here,' I said although she was lying next to me, now half asleep and with a pillow drawn over her head.

'Where is she?' the voice demanded. 'Tell her to come to telephone!'

'Who is this?' I replied, injecting as much anger into my voice as I could manage so early in the morning.

For a moment I could hear the woman on the other end speaking in Hindi to someone else in the room with her. Finally she replied in English:

'I am Mrs Suri from Upton Park. I am her auntie calling.'

'Well, Mrs Suri, Anu's not here at the moment and it's very early, so can you call back later,' I said, stopping myself from adding, 'preferably in the next life.'

But my words were ignored and, after a long gap in which I could hear more Hindi being spoken, Mrs Suri tutted disapprovingly, muttered something unintelligible and then hung up the phone.

'Who was that?' asked Anu dreamily, turning over towards me.

'Some auntie called Mrs Suri,' I said.

'Mrs Suri,' she murmured. 'Who the hell is Mrs Suri?'

We did not have to wait long to find out. Mrs Suri called again an hour later.

This time I didn't make the mistake of picking up the phone, and she got the answering machine instead. For the next thirty seconds or so, she bawled 'hello' down the line over and over again, until, mercifully, the tape ran out and she was cut off.

But two minutes later, Mrs Suri called again – and again. Only on her fourth attempt did she finally leave a message.

'For your information, I am Mrs Suri of Upton Park, east London,' she began. 'Saturday following I am arranging one tea party at my residence in your honour. Please come promptly at four o'clock. I am sending proper invitation by Royal Mail first class postal service. Indian dress is required.'

Anu sat up in bed and was looking at the answering machine with an expression that suggested she had smelt something putrid.

'My mother's behind this,' she said, as Mrs Suri finished speaking. 'How else could this auntie have got my number?'

'Perhaps someone we know in India gave it to her,' I suggested.

Anu brushed aside my suggestion.

'No. She's a spy. A member of the ISIA.'

'The what?'

'The International Sisterhood of Indian Aunties.'

The ISIA was what Anu jokingly called the network of Indian women who live in ex-pat communities around the world, maintaining links with one another.

'To the outsider the ISIA appears innocent enough,' she continued. 'It organises *kitty* parties, Bollywood dance shows and Diwali celebrations. But behind the scenes its members work to ensure that their sons and daughters aren't corrupted by Western ways and that, crucially, they marry their own kind. My mother's a long-standing member of the movement. In fact, she's station chief of the Orlando, Florida, branch.'

Assuming Mrs Suri was indeed the East End ISIA operative, her mission would be to gather information on Anu's activities and send regular dispatches back to Florida. She might also attempt to introduce Anu to some hand-picked Indian 'boys' of the appropriate genetic pedigree, preferably with good prospects in medicine. In other words, Mrs Suri's innocent-sounding tea party was a trap.

'I've been through this before,' said Anu. 'She'll give me the usual lecture on how I shouldn't be a burden to my parents and how I should get married to a nice Punjabi boy, settle down and have children. I'll be expected to sit there, listening to her, nodding my head respectfully and saying, "Yes, all-knowing auntie. You're absolutely right. I'm an idiot. Please sort out my life for me before it's too late!"'

It sounded excruciating.

'So what are you going to do?' I asked.

'Ignore her message and go underground.'

Anu was well practised in the art of covert anti-auntie tactics. She bought herself a caller ID display so that she was able to screen incoming calls; and when Mrs Suri's letter arrived the next morning, she marked it 'UNKNOWN AT THIS ADDRESS' and popped it back in the post.

By Friday evening, she had successfully managed to avoid any communication with the relentless Mrs Suri, who, by now, was calling three or four times a day and leaving increasingly frustrated messages. But then, at around six in the evening, the fire alarm doorbell rang and Anu made the mistake of answering the front door. Five minutes later, she returned upstairs to the kitchen holding a letter. It was from Mrs Suri.

'I feel like I've been served a subpoena,' she said, showing all the signs of defeat.

'What happened?'

'She sent her son to track me down.'

Anu collapsed into a chair, her shoulders slouched forward. She reread the letter and folded it in half.

'This Mrs Suri is one smart auntie,' she said.

I placed a mug of freshly made tea on the table before her and sat down in another chair beside the fireplace. 'What are you going to do?' I asked her.

Anu didn't reply. Steam rose off the surface of her tea and drifted up past her face.

'Maybe I should go,' she said, sounding undecided. 'Her son seemed nice. He was telling me that our families are related on my father's side. They're from Rawalpindi, which is where my grandfather lived before Partition. It might be nice to get to know them, to have people I can turn to. Besides, the food is bound to be good. If there's one thing aunties are known for, it's delicious, homemade cooking.'

***

The next day, when Anu set out for Upton Park in Newham, she promised to be back by six o'clock.

By seven there was still no sign of her and I began to worry that she had been press-ganged into an arranged marriage with a dentist.

But when she appeared at around eight, Anu assured me that she had stayed of her own free will.

'It turns out that half of Mrs Suri's family are from the same village as my Dad. So we're family,' she said as we went upstairs.

Anu dropped her purse on to the floor, slumped into one of the beanbags we had recently bought and proceeded to tell me all about Mrs Suri.

'You have to admire her in a way,' said Anu. 'She arrived in England when she was seventeen not speaking a word of English. Her husband died ten years later. She's raised four children on her own. And she runs her own catering business.'

Anu described Mrs Suri as the Queen Bee of Aunties.

'Her house is like a mini court,' she continued. 'She sits in a large armchair, surrounded by all the other aunties from the neighbourhood who drop in for tea and fried pakoras and they sit around and gossip. While I was there, people were coming and going all day.'

'So did she give you the third degree?'

Anu rolled her eyes. 'Yes, my mother and Mrs Suri must have talked for hours because she knew my entire life story,' she said. 'My mother even sent her some photographs of me.' Anu's brow darkened. 'The studio ones,' she added, an edge to her voice.

I knew the photographs she meant; I had come across them once among her things in New Delhi and made the mistake of laughing out loud. They had been taken some five years earlier, at the insistence of her mother, who had made Anu put on a gaudy sari and pose in front of a selection of fake backdrops like the Taj Mahal and a Swiss Alpine vista. Copies had then been distributed to half the families in Jackson, Tennessee (where the family had been living at the time), in the hope of finding Anu a suitable mate.

'My mother also faxed over a copy of her version of my CV. I've seen it before. It makes no mention of my career in journalism. Instead my skills are listed as cooking, sewing, driving and, most crucially, Bollywood dancing. In case you didn't know,' she added sarcastically, 'that's the key ingredient to a successful marriage in the modern age.'

Mrs Suri had already set the matchmaking wheels in motion. Three candidates had been shortlisted, each with shining prospects and varied interests. The number one choice was well on his way to becoming assistant manager at the local branch of Barclays Bank. He also had a GCSE Media Studies under his belt.

'Compatibility must be there,' Mrs Suri had told Anu over tea in her living room as she sat under the piercing gaze of the posse of Indian aunties gathered to inspect her. 'Not to worry about a thing. We'll have you fixed up in no time at all.'

I smiled to myself at the thought of someone trying to arm-twist Anu into an arranged marriage.

'So what happened?' I asked.

'I told the aunties that I had no intention of meeting any "boys" and that I was engaged.'

The word 'engaged' was carried around the room from auntie to auntie, and translated into Hindi and Punjabi for those with a poor grasp of English.

'Engaged!' Mrs Suri had repeated amidst a collective outbreak of tut-tutting. 'Your mummy-ji said nothing of this.'

'She doesn't know.'

'Doesn't know!' Mrs Suri had exclaimed in unison with half the room. 'He is this British boy?'

'British *man*. Yes.'

'But if your mummy and papa's blessing is not there, then engagement is null and void!'

The other aunties had all nodded in agreement and taken it in turns to exercise their assumed right as members of the older generation to warn Anu against marrying a member of that unworthiest of species, the white British male.

'It was the usual stuff,' Anu went on – 'like, "Our cultures are differing too much." And, "They are not sharing our values."'

'That sounds awful. Why did you stick around?'

'Luckily, I was rescued by Mrs Suri's son, Anil, the one who delivered the invitation to the door yesterday. He took me to the back of the house where all the kids were hanging out in the kitchen.'

Anu spent the rest of her visit chatting with Anil and his friends, and, as she had hoped, eating delicious Indian food.

'Are you going to see them again?' I asked warily.

'I'm not sure,' she said, but her expression softened. 'I had a lot of fun with the kids and later, when all the stupid aunties left, Mrs Suri told me more about her life. When she's not being bossy, she can be very funny and likes to sing songs and play games.'

Anu showed me the food the family had given her to take away, all of it packed in tupperware containers. It looked and smelt delicious and I got a plate from the kitchen and tucked in.

'I'm glad I went,' continued Anu. 'But they're all trying so desperately to be Indian. Being there reminded me why I escaped from that world. It's all so incestuous and small-minded. I can't stand the way the aunties and uncles work against their children gaining too much independence. They want them to be successful but not to learn to think for themselves. If you don't break away like I did, they end up controlling your life.'

Anil may have saved Anu from the immediate clutches of the Upton Park mafia, but Mrs Suri was not so easily shaken off. Unbeknown to us, she placed an advertisement in the classified section of a British Asian newspaper inviting suitors interested in 'a young, bright girl with wheatish complexion and US passport' to send their applications to Upton Park. Details of suitable candidates were then forwarded to Brick Lane.

The first of Mrs Suri's manila envelopes to arrive contained the CV of a young man called Ravi. He listed among his interests, 'having a good time', but also claimed to have a 'serious side' and sometimes watched the news on TV. Ravi attached a photograph of himself standing in front of the Hippodrome nightclub in Leicester Square wearing a cheap suit, a tie with an extremely thick knot, and a great deal of gel in his hair.

He telephoned a couple of days later to find out if his packet had arrived and to ask Anu out to 'one of them fancy restaurants down the West End'. He also suggested that in the not too distant future, she might like to meet his parents in Ealing.

'I'm sure that would be nice,' replied Anu. 'But you don't have a PhD and I could never marry anyone without one.'

That was the last she heard from Ravi. But he must have reported back to Mrs Suri because soon afterwards she called to say that she had located a university professor who was forty-two, unmarried and still living with his mother.

'Frankly speaking, he is not the best-looking fellow – but he is a Pisces and owns one Alfa Romeo,' she said.

———◆———

Things started looking up for Anu at the end of February when she was offered a job as a producer of radio news at the BBC World Service. There she fell in with an international crowd drawn from every continent save Antarctica: Americans, Arabs, Australians, Canadians, a Caribbean, a German, a Russian married to a Frenchman, Indians, an Iranian, some Pakistanis, a couple of Mauritanians, and a Spaniard with a Lebanese boyfriend soon ranked amongst her circle.

Their common knowledge and use of English aside, Anu's new-found friends had one thing in common: they were all ex-pats or immigrants living in London and, to one degree or another, Britain was an enigma to them. As such, they would gather after work in the bars or cafés near Bush House and puzzle over their experiences.

Often, when they were stumped by something 'a Brit' had said or done, they would turn to me for advice and I would have to field questions like: 'Please explain, what is gobsmacked?' and 'What does "he's barking" mean?'

At other times, they would raise more complex issues such as why it is that one Brit can greet another with the words, 'All right, you old bastard?' and it doesn't result in a punch-up; and how it can be that a Scot can live in Great Britain and object to being called English; or someone can be Irish, live in the United Kingdom and pride them-selves on being British.

Inevitably, I spent a good deal of time trying to explain the class system, the intricacies of the constitutional monarchy, and the basic rules of cricket – as well as bringing newly-arrived Americans like Anu up to speed on why soccer is called football, public schools are private, orange squash is not a vegetable, and meatballs served in a gravy are called 'faggots'.

Questions about British irony were harder to field.

Anu's fiery Russian friend was particularly confused as to why anyone should say 'nice weather we're having' when it was pouring with rain.

As ex-pats the world over are inclined to do, some of Anu's friends also liked to pick apart the culture they were living in and I often had to listen to their pet complaints.

'English Culture is Dead', was a common theme. As the Russian put it, 'All you have left are cream teas and Beefeaters.'

It was generally agreed that English people are slouchy and badly dressed, terrible communicators, emotionally repressed, don't work together, still behave as if they have an empire and/or haven't got over losing their empire, drink too much, are stiff, and don't have much of a sense of humour. But the most common charge levelled was that they were cold and distant.

Perhaps unsurprisingly, such conversations succeeded in getting my back up and I often found myself defending the English character to Anu. I also made a point of introducing her to several family friends who had lived in London for decades and were able to provide a more considered perspective.

Amongst them was Sally, my godmother, who had grown up in Rhodesia, emigrated to England in 1962 and lived in East Finchley. As well as being a great Anglophile, she was a fan of Louis' tearoom and patisserie on Heath Street in Hampstead and it was there that I invited her to meet Anu for the first time one Sunday afternoon.

'I started coming here when it opened,' she said as the three of us were led to our table by a young East European waitress. 'When Louis the owner arrived in London from Hungary he didn't have a penny to his name. Now he drives a Rolls-Royce.'

Sally took a seat at the table, glaring hungrily at the selection of cakes that were being served to the people at the next table.

'The only problem with this place is that everything is so delicious it's almost impossible to decide what to have,' she said mischievously. 'I'm always tempted to order one of everything!'

But she didn't. 'Doctor's orders,' she said, opting for a fruit tartlet and a cup of Earl Grey tea and settling back into the comfortable seat.

'Now I want to hear all about you,' she said to Anu in a well-meaning way that was not at all intrusive. 'Tarquin didn't mention you were quite so beautiful. And that's such a lovely shawl. An exquisite design! Do tell me where you bought it?'

Sally and Anu talked about shawls for a while and then about India and Africa. But inevitably the conversation turned to our parents and their reaction to our engagement and, given that Sally was a psycho-therapist and a sympathetic listener, we were soon pouring out our hearts to her.

'Oh you poor dear,' she said to Anu, with a kindly smile when we were finished. 'The last thing you need when you're trying to adjust to a new culture is everyone telling you you're not wanted and that you're not going to make it. It's such a hard thing swapping cultures. I should know, I did it myself.'

Sally, who was in her late sixties, had been a journalist and had spent some thirty years on Fleet Street before retraining as a therapist.

'When I first came here, Britain was in a very bad way,' she said. 'It was bankrupt, set in its ways, disillusioned after the loss of the Empire. I found the English to be closed books, so I didn't bother much with them outside of work. I had lots of foreign friends instead; they were my community.'

Sally stirred some milk into her tea and placed the spoon on her saucer.

'But over time something strange happened. Without intending to, I began to change. I noticed it during my first visit back to South Africa when everyone said I sounded so English. At the same time, something else began to occur. Gradually, I found that the English were accepting me. It was as if I'd discovered their secret password. But I think what really happened was less mysterious, that I'd learned to give off the right signals.'

'But why are they so guarded, so stand-offish?' asked Anu.

'It's part of their defences,' she said. 'The English know that if they're too friendly and make it too easy for others, they might get the horrible idea that they can remain foreign.'

She patted Anu's hand where it lay on the table.

'Don't worry,' said Sally. 'It will all work out in the end. Promise.'

After tea, the three of us went for a walk on Hampstead Heath. Anu and Sally chatted away and I could tell that they had taken a shine to one another. It was such a relief at last to have the support of someone I cared about. And I was pleased when in the coming weeks Anu adopted Sally as a surrogate auntie, whom she could visit independently of me for a dose of what my godmother affectionately referred to as 'Granny Therapy'.

———◆———

February gave way to March and Mrs Suri's manila envelopes became rarer until, finally, they stopped arriving altogether.

I had hoped that perhaps she'd given up, that she'd finally realised that Anu would never change her mind. But not long afterwards she telephoned again, this time with an unexpected proposal.

'She wants to meet you,' said Anu, when the two of them had finished speaking.

I jumped up from my chair in the kitchen where I had been reading the papers and enjoying a quiet cup of coffee.

'What? You can't be serious!'

Anu rested on the edge of the windowsill and shrugged.

'She says she's family and that it's her duty. Which really means that she's talked with my mother and been asked to find out more about you.'

I paced back and forth in front of the cooker and sink.

'Well, tell her I've gone away – to Afghanistan,' I said. 'Or better still, that I'm deep in the Peruvian jungle and won't be back for months.'

Anu stepped over to the kitchen table, picked up my mug of coffee and took a sip.

'I could do that except, well, I told her we'd kind of . . . go for tea tomorrow.'

'Tomorrow!'

'Yes, at four o'clock.'

I shook my head like a stubborn child. 'Absolutely no way am I going to have tea with Mrs Suri,' I said, prodding the air with my right index finger in time with the sound of each consonant. 'I'd rather shoot myself.'

Anu's gaze dropped to the floorboards.

'Look,' she said, her voice suddenly soothing. 'You don't have any choice. If you don't go, she'll report back to my mother that you didn't want to meet her family and that will only make things worse with my parents.' She paused, and then added gloomily. 'I'm afraid there's no escaping Mrs Suri.'

At three thirty the next day, I found myself standing outside Upton Park underground station, in Newham to the east of Tower Hamlets, with a box of Belgian chocolates tucked under my arm and a nervous knot in my stomach.

Anu led the way down Green Street, the area's main thoroughfare, past a pie and mash shop that served as the lone reminder of Upton Park's all-but-vanished Cockney culture and into what she had dubbed Punjabi Town. This was another mini-South Asia in the East End, except that there were fewer Bangladeshis to be found here and the street was lined with shops and businesses owned by Pakistani and Indian Punjabis. It was the closest London came to a Chandigarh bazaar.

Only a few hundred yards from the West Ham football stadium, wedding jewellery shops sold chandelier-style earrings and necklaces fit for maharanees, and sari boutiques offered poor imitations of the latest sequin-studded fashions from Bombay and Karachi. Kebabries with ovens producing freshly baked *naan* were dotted in amongst halal butchers with Urdu stencilled across their windows. Further on, there were *bhel-poori* snack bars, traders selling Lahori *kulfi* and crushed sugar cane juice, a Pakistani KFC – Khan Fried Chicken – and a *paan* shop, Anand's, where the proprietor kept a collage of photographs pinned behind the counter of Indian film stars who had visited his establishment. Hawkers worked the pavements flogging everything from fake Gucci leather bags to battery-operated dolls of the turbaned Bhangra singer Daler Mehndi. Inside the pub on the corner of Plashet Road Sikh men sat drinking pints of bitter.

We pushed our way through crowds of shoppers, passing dozens of short, rotund Punjabi aunties. It was not always easy to tell the Indians and Pakistanis apart. Often, the only giveaway was a headscarf or a *bindi*. Otherwise they wore a standard uniform of long Punjabi suits, chunky gold rings, thick-knit cardigans and woollen socks which bulged through the toe rings of their open sandals.

Many of these aunties were gathered in groups of twos and threes along the pavement, exchanging pleasantries and gossip, and showing off the spoils of the morning's shopping. Others crowded around the windows of the jewellery shops, admiring the displays of sparkly rings and bangles, and fantasising about the day when they would dress up their daughters like princesses and watch them circle the holy flame or be joined in matrimony over the Koran.

I had seen thousands of such women in towns and cities across the subcontinent; the gardens and market of my old neighbourhood in Delhi had been full of them in the afternoons. Mothers, grand-mothers, great-grandmothers, and what Anu called 'Aunties in Waiting' – young brides being initiated into the long-established ways of the sorority and prepared for a lifetime of childbearing, home-making and husband-tending.

But further down Green Street we passed a more Westernised crowd – young British Asian girls in trendy garb who radiated a con-fidence so evidently lacking in their elders. We noticed them chatting on their mobile phones, emerging from newsagents with glossy women's magazines tucked under their arms, relaxing in snack bars with their friends, shopping for jeans in the discount clothes stores. And when we heard them speaking in their strong Estuary accents, they left us in no doubt where they had been brought up.

'Thas well wicked!' I heard one teenage girl say to another as we stood behind them at a zebra crossing.

'Yeah,' replied her friend. 'It's, like, awesome, eenit.'

We soon turned into one of the rows of side streets lined with turn-of-the-century terraced two-up-two-downs. Mrs Suri's house was discernible from the others thanks to the enormous Ganesh idol that sat in her front window, encircled by a ring of pulsating Christmas lights. A low wall, a wrought-iron gate and a front yard three feet deep separated the house from the pavement. Within this space lay dozens of pairs of shoes – high heels, flip-flops, black leather slip-ons, trainers, children's sandals, a pair of bedroom slippers. Apparently Mrs Suri had other guests.

Anu and I took off our shoes and stepped in through the open door. Inside, the house reverberated with the sounds of excited children screaming as they chased one another up and down the stairs. A posse of aunties worked in the kitchen at the back of the house chopping vegetables, blending garlic and ginger, and pounding *roti* dough. From upstairs, the sound of feet thudding on the ceiling rivalled the beat of Asian Dub playing on a stereo. A din of voices suggested that most of Mrs Suri's other guests were gathered in the living room.

An especially wide auntie carrying a platter of samosas was standing in the doorway to the living room with her back to us, unwittingly blocking our way. We waited in the corridor for a minute or two for her to move. As we did so, I caught glimpses over her shoulder of the room beyond.

A long settee upholstered in red velvet and gold braid, and covered in plastic sheeting to protect the synthetic fabric beneath, stood against the far wall. Half a dozen elderly aunties sat along its length, drinking tea, eating snacks and talking amongst themselves. Above them hung a faded photograph of a gaunt, young Indian man with wiry hair and a wisp of a moustache dressed in a suit that dated the picture to the 1970s; next to this, in a larger frame, hung a bright, colourful portrait of an elderly auntie with an enormous red *bindi* on her forehead that looked like the bull's eye of an archery target.

A dozen or so more aunties sat about on the floor, two of them kneeling before a *puja* shrine positioned next to the Ganesh idol, from where incense smoke wafted up towards the ceiling. Four or five toddlers crawled or stumbled across the floor. Near the door, slumped in a chair, sat an elderly gentleman – the token male in the room – who was fast asleep, with his head cocked back and his mouth agape.

Soon the obstacle to our progress moved out of the doorway and we stepped into the living room. Mrs Suri lounged in a wide armchair at the back of the room, munching on fried pakoras dipped in chilli sauce and talking into a cordless telephone. Even by auntie standards, she was a garish dresser. Her purple and green Punjabi suit clashed with the electric orange *chuni* that was draped over her shoulders, and she was dripping in shiny golden jewellery and bunches of bangles, which clinked together each time she moved an arm. The overall effect was made all the more striking by the rich hues of her make-up, the dollop of mascara in the corners of her eyes and the daffodil-coloured wallpaper behind her. A diet heavy in ghee had given her a double chin and thick fingers, which bulged around her rings like puff pastry.

'Come in, *beta*,' she called out to Anu as she hung up the phone. 'I want you next to me.'

The sea of aunties and toddlers on the floor parted and a pathway appeared across the carpet to where Mrs Suri sat. Anu led the way and I followed cautiously behind. Our hostess remained seated as she took Anu's hands in her own.

'Looking *so* nice today,' said Mrs Suri. 'So this is *him*, uh?' She shot me a contemptuous look, her eyes narrow and suspicious.

'Yes, this is Tarquin,' replied Anu, who seemed uncharacteristically timid.

I pressed the palms of my hands and fingertips together and said, '*Namaste*,' and then handed Mrs Suri the chocolates. She took the box and, without giving them so much as a look, placed them on the floor next to her armchair.

'So he's knowing some Hindi, is it?' she said to Anu, sounding weary rather than impressed. 'Well, sit down, uh. Be com-for-taa-ble.'

On cue, two aunties vacated the end of the settee closest to Mrs Suri and we took their places. I felt myself sink deep into the cushions until my thighs pointed up at a forty-five degree angle and my back was perfectly perpendicular. The auntie to my right pressed in against me, as did Anu to my left, and gradually, the combined pressure caused my trousers to tighten around my groin and my thighs to squeeze together like two parts of a vice. I wanted desperately to reach down and tug my trousers loose or better still to get up and sit somewhere else. But before I could move, a young auntie-in-waiting entered the room with a tray and handed me a cup of tea and a dessert plate of Indian sweetmeats.

The eyes of every auntie in the room were now fixed on me. I could tell that they wanted to see what I would make of the sweetmeats, which are rarely popular with non-Indians. So, as I popped one into my mouth and the taste of sour cheese assaulted my taste buds, I smiled with satisfaction and made an appreciative noise. A general murmur of approval passed through the room.

'So he is liking our Indian *burfi*, is it?' said Mrs Suri, who had yet to address me directly.

'They're his favourite,' said Anu cheerily, knowing full well that I couldn't stand them. 'We used to eat them in Delhi all the time.'

I saw this as my opportunity to say something about my experiences in India, which seemed my best chance of breaking the ice. But as I began to speak, Mrs Suri cut me off abruptly and started telling Anu about a nephew of her sister's husband's cousin who was studying journalism and was bound to do well at the BBC if only Anu would make the necessary introductions on his behalf. After that, she switched to the topic of her son, Kunal, who was studying engineering in Houston, Texas, and was top of his class. And then she went on about her daughter, Preety, who had married a regional sales manager for a soft drinks firm.

'Nowadays they are living in one four-bedroom house in Leicester with all modern fittings and two-car garage.'

My attention shifted to the activity in the hallway. A new batch of aunties and their children had arrived carrying pots of food and boxes of sweets. Suddenly the sound of Mrs Suri's voice was drowned out by the noise of the new arrivals entering the living room, saying hello to friends and neighbours and settling down on the floor. More trays of teacups were brought from the kitchen along with yet more plates of pakoras and samosas, and laughter and conversation filled the room.

Sitting there, watching all the activity – the children cosseted and brooded over, the aunties catching up on news and gossip – I felt a warmth for their sense of community. It was something to admire, something valuable that my family had lost.

And yet Mrs Suri's hostility grated on me. To me, her attitude towards British culture was hypocritical. It flew in the face of the individualism that had allowed her to prosper in the UK in the first place. As much as I was for immigrants settling in the UK, I saw integration as imperative. After all, if I raised my own children in India as staunch Brits, eating fish and chips, saluting the Queen and warning them not to become too Indian, I would rightly be ostracised.

My thoughts were interrupted by Mrs Suri, who had finished

telling Anu everything there was to know about her son-in-law and now wanted my full attention.

'You will please listen to me now,' she said, sitting up in her chair and fixing me with her beady eyes. 'With regard to the marriage proposal of Miss Anu, it is proper that you should first ask the permission of her Mummy and Papa.'

I took a deep breath, reminding myself of the promise I had made to Anu not to lock horns with Mrs Suri.

'Yes, you're absolutely right –'

'You must go to Orlando without delay,' she interrupted. 'Otherwise marriage is out of the question.'

She sat back in her armchair and glowered at me.

'Yes we will go. But –'

'There is no but,' said Mrs Suri. 'It is decided!'

She rummaged through a drawer in the table beside her and produced a piece of paper and a pen.

'Next thing,' she said. 'You must write down your date, place and exact time of birth.'

My cup, saucer and plate were whisked away and the paper and pen handed to me.

'Why do you need this information?' I asked, cautiously.

'Because the swami-ji of Miss Anu's Mummy will be making predictions for the future,' she replied. 'We will ask him if marriage between you and Miss Anu is auspicious. In our religion we are believing in such things.'

I glanced at Anu who signalled for me to do as Mrs Suri asked, so I wrote down the information she had requested and handed back the paper.

'Anything else?' I asked.

'Now we will wait to see what Swami-ji says. Perhaps in one or two weeks we will know. This is leaving only one other matter. I must tell you that it is not proper for two people to be living together without marriage. It would be better if Miss Anu was living in my house. In this way everything will be above board. This is her Mummy and Papa's wishes also. I am sure if you marry it will only bring the two of you pain. But we will let Swami-ji decide.'

We had to sit there for another forty-five minutes, while Mrs Suri lectured me on why journalism is not a good profession and how I would be better served giving up my 'hobby' and doing something more 'respectable'.

It was one thing to be told that I was from a good-for-nothing race and that my marriage was certain to end in disaster. But I took exception to being slandered as a professional loser and felt my anger rising.

Anu noticed my growing irritation and made our excuses. I got off the couch, said my goodbyes and hobbled out of the room and the house.

Before long, we were ensconced in a nearby pub, recovering from our ordeal with a couple of double Scotches and enjoying a good laugh.

'Now you see why I had to get away from it all back in North Carolina,' said Anu. 'It's okay in small doses, but she actually thinks I'd move in with her!'

Anu stared into her glass and went quiet. I could see conflicting emotions play across her face.

'What is it?' I asked, putting my hand over hers.

'I'm so confused. In India, I had family – cousins I could talk to, friends to go out with. I knew everyone – the taxi drivers, the tea boys, the women at the beauty parlour. It's the one place where people accepted me as Indian *and* American and I felt I really *belonged*.'

I sighed, realising the profound sense of loss Anu felt.

Wiping away tears, she took my hand.

'I do understand your point that we couldn't live there for ever. It's not your home . . . and we can't be sure of work. I just wish I could find a place like India where I feel at ease.'

'Me too,' I said, draining the last of my Scotch and wondering where that place might be.

6

The University of the Poor

'This London Ghetto of ours is a region where, amid uncleanliness and squalor, the rose of romance blows yet a little longer in the raw air of English reality; a world that hides beneath its stony and unlovely surface an inner world of dreams, fantastic and poetic.'

Israel Zangwill, *Children of the Ghetto* (1892)

M R ALI SEEMED to Anu to fit the stereotypical profile of the lazy, macho, sexist, South Asian male who did everything on the cheap, and although he had his good sides and by now I accounted him a friend, to her he was a natural enemy. From long years of experience, Anu had learnt to exercise a policy of zero tolerance towards such men and entered into a running battle with him to make improvements to the property. Her approach was to humiliate him in public, preferably in front of his business associates.

'There is our esteemed landlord, the man who is so greedy that he refuses to provide a toilet seat for his tenants!' I once heard her say when she spotted Mr Ali standing on the pavement, chatting with the Pakistani owner of the leather jacket shop next door. 'He is so greedy that he refuses to fix the boiler so that another man's daughter must wash in freezing water!'

During more than twenty years of marriage, Mr Ali had been conditioned to quail in the face of an irate and determined woman. Within weeks of Anu's arrival, the shower was fixed, the boiler was replaced (albeit with a second-hand model that later exploded) and the bathroom roof was repaired. But when it came to dealing with the mice, Mr Ali refused to lift a finger to help.

'They were 'ere when I bought the place, innit,' he said.

Anu decided to take matters into her own hands and to present Mr Ali with the bill. All-out war was declared and she set about trying to kill the mice with a determination that put my previous efforts to shame. Increasingly sophisticated traps were bought and loaded with ever more tantalising titbits to lure her prey to their doom. Soon, the attic floor became a minefield that had to be traversed with extreme caution.

And yet despite her best efforts Anu woke every morning to find the traps empty and the bait either devoured or ignored.

'These are smart mice,' she said.

I agreed. They were wily, Cockney mice. 'They know every trick in the book,' I said. 'Perhaps we should call in the professionals.'

But Anu was not ready to concede defeat.

'I'll find a way of getting them,' she said. 'This isn't over yet.'

The solution came unexpectedly when, one Sunday in March, we took a morning stroll through Shoreditch and stepped into the Clerk's House bookshop in front of the church. To one side of the till lay a large tabby cat with grey and black markings, white socks and a white blotch across her chin and nose. She was lying on a velvet cushion a couple of feet from a fan heater that was blowing hot air against her fur.

I paid the cat little attention and began to search through the shop's selection of books about the East End. And then something fortuitous happened: Anu, who had always told me that she was a dog lover and disliked cats, knelt down and stroked her.

This was the moment Her Furriness had been waiting for. Daintily, she lifted her front paws and drew Anu's hands down towards her neck. Anu began to scratch and the cat arched her head and stretched out her body, yawning contentedly.

This was the bookshop owner's cue.

'That poor cat needs a home,' he said. 'She was abandoned by her owner and so I took her in. But sadly I have two cats of my own so she has to stay here in the bookshop at night. Poor thing gets very lonely . . .'

The cat rolled over on to her back, inviting Anu to rub her large tummy.

'What's her name?' asked Anu.

'Jesse.'

One look at the loving expression on Anu's face told me that she was smitten. The cat seemed to sense this as well and, when we left the bookshop, followed Anu to the door and jumped up into the window. From this vantage point, she watched us as we made our way down Shoreditch High Street. Anu looked back at her several times and sighed.

'I think we should get that cat,' she said. 'What do you think?'

I had to tread carefully; I knew that Anu was lonely. But I didn't want the responsibility of taking on a pet and I knew that Mr Ali, who hated Sadie's cat, would not approve. Besides, with all the traffic on Brick Lane, the animal was bound to come to grief.

'I don't think it's a very good idea,' I said gently. 'We don't have anywhere to put a litter tray and the cat looks pregnant. For all we know she's going to have kittens and that's why no one wants her.'

'But she's sweet and she likes me,' said Anu.

'The last thing we need is a pet,' I said. 'We've got enough problems as it is.'

Anu went quiet after that. If I hadn't known her better, I might have imagined that I had won the argument.

———— ◆ ————

Anu's arrival had left little spare room in the already cramped attic and I had been forced to get rid of the desk where I had been revising my book. For a while, I tried working in the kitchen. But with the constant interruptions from Sadie (who was forever shouting up the stairs, asking me to pop out to fetch her something), Mr Ali (who still came up looking for a drink whenever Anu wasn't around), and Anu (who liked to listen to Bollywood film music when she was feeling nostalgic for India), it was impossible to concentrate. So I began scouting around the neighbourhood for a sanctuary.

I found it in the form of the Whitechapel Library, which stood next to the entrance to Aldgate East underground station on Whitechapel Road at the far end of Brick Lane.

At first the library did not strike me as being anything out of the ordinary. Compared to some of the other libraries I had used in wealthier London neighbourhoods like Richmond, it was run-down and outdated. Its entrance was easy to miss – an unremarkable doorway next to the wide, sandstone entrance to its famous neighbour, the Whitechapel Art Gallery. The corridor leading inside was lined with noticeboards plastered with flyers advertising everything from evening classes and poetry readings, to warnings to drug users about the dangers of sharing needles. Just inside the main room stood an oval desk and behind this the librarians who talked in half whispers like priests in confessionals.

Desks and chairs were arranged between rows of shelves for the members of the public to use. A cluster of magazine racks stood next to a stand for English and foreign language newspapers, along with a photocopier, an OUT OF ORDER sign sellotaped to its hood.

It was not the most inspiring place to write. The lighting was dim, the air was stale, the walls were grimy with dirt. But apart from the occasional sneeze and the sudden clatter of a microfiche film spinning on its wheel, it was welcomingly quiet compared to Brick Lane, and so I started going there almost every day.

It was Sadie who made me realise what an extraordinary place the Whitechapel Library was.

'Oh, ain't it marvellous!' she said one day when I mentioned that I had spent the afternoon in the reading room. 'All those books and all of them free. I remember the first time I went there. I was about fifteen. Dad took me. 'e told me I could choose one book and I was to read it. He said, "Opportunities like this I never had when I was young. Grasp them while you can!" You see, 'e wanted me to be educated. In them days, education was the key to escaping from the ghetto.'

Sadie and I were sitting at her table. It was lunchtime and, typically, after hearing the sound of my foot on the stair, she had insisted that I join her for a bowl of chicken noodle soup.

'There was so many books to choose from. 'undreds and 'undreds. It took me ages to decide on one. Eventually I picked *Robinson Crusoe.*'

She pronounced the last two words in a dreamy voice as if she was talking about a long lost lover.

'I'd never 'ad a book before. *Robinson Crusoe* was my first. For weeks, I took it with me wherever I went and kept it safe like a baby. Inseparable we were. I must 'ave read it a dozen times. Then one day Dad said it 'ad to go back. Well, I was devastated, wasn't I? No way was I going to let go of that book. So I hid it. Said I'd lost it. Well, 'e was furious. Said we'd af to pay for it. So I 'ad to own up.'

Sadie chuckled to herself and took a spoonful of soup, some of which dribbled down her chin.

'Then Dad explains that if I take it back I can 'ave another one. Another one! I couldn't believe me luck. So off I went down the Whitechapel Road and this time I brought 'ome *Oliver Twist* by Charles Dickens. 'ard work it was. Long words I'd never 'eard of. But them characters were marvellous! The Artful Dodger and Fagin. I still love *Oliver Twist*. You could say it's my favourite.'

Sadie's father had also loved and cherished the library and spent long hours there reading the newspapers as the cataclysmic events of the early twentieth century unfolded.

'In Poland they 'ad nofing. No rights, no books, no education, nofing. My Mum was illiterate. But my Dad, 'e'd learned to read from a rabbi who'd taught 'im. So to 'im the Whitechapel Library was a very special place. Of course, he didn't speak no English. But they 'ad 'undreds of books in Yiddish and newspapers and all. So 'e used to go there and read whenever 'e got a chance. It meant a lot to 'im the library. 'e used to say it was a treasure-trove – a treasure-trove of knowledge.'

I learned later that the library was known to the East End Jews as the 'University of the Poor'. Many a Jewish teenager forced to leave school in their early teens to work in the sweatshops or hawk goods on the streets spent their free time educating themselves in the reading room. There, amongst the stacks, they were able to escape into the limitless world of fiction or immerse themselves in philosophy. From the library's bibliographic loins sprang writers, social activists and intellectuals, including the poet Isaac Rosenberg and the playwright Bernard Kops, who would sit in the reading room eating sardine sandwiches while brooding over Chekhov and Tolstoy.

I soon came to recognise the eccentric regulars who frequented the library. The handful of sad old men in grimy trench coats whose attendance peaked on days when it was raining outside and filled the library with their musty odours. The woman with a thin beard who pored over world atlases, running her fingers along the contours of continents and international borders, as if she yearned to travel to distant lands. The Goth who wore a net vest that revealed his pierced nipples beneath, and studied dense scientific textbooks, writing out impossibly complicated equations in long hand. And the grizzled black man who wore a bowler hat and spent countless hours reading thick volumes of *Keesing's Weekly Diary of World Events*.

The majority of those who made use of the library were immigrants and the majority of these were Bangladeshis. There were days when they filled the place to capacity, and when there were no more chairs to sit on, they squatted on the floors and leant against the stacks. Some came to search the classified sections for jobs; others to research opportunities in higher education or to do their homework. For teenage lovebirds, the library was a respectable rendezvous in which to conduct an innocent courtship away from the prying eyes of conservative parents and tongue-wagging neighbours. There were also those who came to borrow books.

The collection reflected the multiracial make-up of the local population. Just as a proportion of the shelves had once been stocked with volumes in Yiddish, they now groaned with titles in Bengali, Urdu, Gujarati and Somali. The librarians were from various ethnic backgrounds and it was their job to keep a stock of the classics by Rabindranath Tagore and Kazi Nazrul Islam, and modern literature by the likes of Kazi Abdul Wadud.

'In our country there are no libraries and few people can afford to buy books,' one of the Bangladeshi librarians told me one day. 'You would be amazed how far people come to use the library. They come from across London, from Bradford and Manchester. Only the other day, a man from Edinburgh came looking for a copy of *Bidrohi*. Sometimes demand is so high, we have to stock half a dozen copies of the same title. And when the books are returned to us, I can tell that they have been read over and over again.'

'Are they always returned?' I asked him.

'Oh yes,' he said. 'People have a lot of respect for the library. They realise what a special place it is. Only recently, we got a book posted back to us from Saudi Arabia. It was postmarked Mecca. The borrower had gone on *hajj* and died. But his wife, who was with him, sent the book back to us.'

Another regular at the library was a British Bangladeshi called Naziz.

Naziz was an incessant reader who was rarely to be seen without a book in his hand – invariably a book borrowed from the Whitechapel Library. He would read on the bus, while standing on a street corner waiting for a friend, during the commercials in the cinema before the main presentation, while he ate, and often as he walked down the street. If waterproof books had existed, he would have read in the shower, too.

When I first met Naziz, he was devouring chunky Russian novels at a rate of one a week. Later he turned his attention to Nagub Mahfouz's *Cairo Trilogy*. Then he sank his teeth into *A Suitable Boy*.

'I only read fiction,' he told me during one of our first conversations. 'I've had my fill of reality growing up in the East End.'

Naziz came to the library on his days off and in the afternoons after he finished work. He was not shy or retiring; at twenty-five he had a rare confidence about him. But his demeanour suggested that he wished to remain inconspicuous and, as such, his favoured spot in the library was tucked away in the foreign languages section with his back to the rest of the reading room.

He spent most of his time swotting for his Open University degree and, as his subject was English literature, which required hours of reading, studying for him was no chore. He saw a degree as his ticket out of the East End. The idea of working in a bookshop appealed to him. But ultimately his dream was to become a writer, and he dedicated at least an hour every day to working on his own prose, the subject and format of which he refused to discuss with anyone.

I could always tell when Naziz was writing his own material. First, he would put away his textbooks, papers and pens in his satchel and take out a pad of yellow A4 paper. Then he would step over to the dustbin in the corner and meticulously sharpen a pencil to a fine point, pressing it into the flesh of his fore thumb to ensure that it was sharp enough. Next he would sit down at his desk, lean forward and curl his arm around the pad of paper. And then, slowly but surely, his pencil would begin to form words across the page, pausing at the end of each line as Naziz read back the last sentence to himself.

If anyone came near him while he was writing, his left arm would tighten its embrace and the pencil would hover over the page until the coast was clear.

Being fellow smokers, Naziz and I occasionally found ourselves out on the pavement in front of the library at the same time. He always brought a book with him to read while he smoked, and whenever I said hello to him, the most I ever received in return was a solemn nod. It was only after I stepped on to an underground train one evening and found Naziz sitting in the seat opposite me that the ice was finally broken.

'I come down here a lot in the winter,' he told me as our train headed into the West End and we began to chat. 'You can go round on the Circle Line as many times as you want. All for the price of one fare.'

'You mean you come here to read?' I asked him.

'Yeah. It probably seems strange to someone like you,' he said. 'But it's warm and quiet down here. Not like at home. I can't get five minutes to concentrate. But down here ...' He looked around the carriage, which was almost empty, and smiled. 'Down here you can escape from everyone.'

Naziz didn't like to talk about himself much, but over the next few weeks, as we forged a friendship, I gradually put together the pieces of his life.

He had grown up on one of the most notorious sink estates in Shadwell, the second eldest of four children born of immigrant Bangladeshi parents. His father was a much older man – Naziz referred to him as 'the Old Man' – and had married Naziz's mother when she was only sixteen. She was his second wife. The first had committed suicide six months after arriving in London.

'They didn't even meet before they got married. Her family put her on a plane and she met the Old Man for the first time when she arrived at Heathrow,' Naziz told me during one of our conversations in a local workers' café where we would sometimes go for a mug of tea. 'She was about sixteen and had to live in a shit flat in the damp on her own with this strange man she'd never met before. She got what they used to call "Paki Syndrome". Basically she was depressed. So were most Bangladeshi women who came to live here in those days. A lot of them were given electric shock therapy, but of course it didn't help.

'On top of everything else, she had to deal with all the hostility from the English people on the estate,' he continued. 'They wanted the Bangladeshis out. So they put shit through their letterboxes, hung pig heads on front doors, set fire to people's flats, that sort of thing. She couldn't take it, so she hanged herself.'

But that was only half the story. Several weeks later, when I knew Naziz better, he admitted to me that his father's behaviour had contributed to the unfortunate girl's death.

'He never let her out of the house on her own and never let her see anyone,' he said. 'She had to cook, iron, tidy up, that was it. It was worse than a prison because in prison you know why you're there, you know why you're being punished and that one day you'll get out. For her the only way to freedom was to kill herself.'

I asked him how he knew all this, given that he was talking about events that had taken place before his birth.

'Because it was the same for my Mum,' he said. 'She's been through the same thing. Twenty-six years of hell with that bastard.'

While Naziz was growing up, the only book that Naziz's father allowed in the flat was a copy of the Koran.

'He can't read Arabic – or Bengali for that matter,' Naziz told me one day in the café. 'But he believes that the Koran is the only book a Muslim should keep in the house. He's always discouraged us from reading anything else. He says other books corrupt the mind and put bad thoughts into people's heads.'

'So what did you do when you were going to school?'

'We used to have to hide our textbooks with the neighbours before we came home. Otherwise he would tear them up or burn them.'

The Old Man had tried his hardest to prevent his children from going to school. At the age of twelve, he sent Naziz to work in a

Hackney sweatshop that manufactured handbags. For three months, Naziz worked ten-hour shifts, six days a week, earning less than a pound an hour. Every penny went to Naziz's father. Eventually, when the school authorities and the police came round to the family's council flat to demand an explanation as to why Naziz was no longer attending school, the Old Man told them that he had sent his son to Bangladesh to live with relatives in Sylhet.

'They started criminal proceedings against him and he had to send me back to school. He blamed me for it and he never let me do my homework. He's always said that education was a waste of time.'

With no one to encourage him to study or attend school, Naziz and his brother, Rana, who was a year older, began hanging out with the other boys on the Shadwell estate where they grew up. Before long, they had joined a street gang and found themselves embroiled in a life of crime.

'We were into everything,' admitted Naziz, shamefacedly. 'For a long time, I was the smallest in the gang and a good climber, so I used to be the one to go up buildings and over rooftops and in through the windows. We did houses and flats all over the East End. We'd break into cars and nick stereos and anything else we could find. Sometimes we'd rob people in the street as well. We'd nick their handbags and wallets and use their credit cards. I was also into shoplifting in a big way. I was very good at it. In fact, shoplifting became such a habit for me that I rarely paid for anything. If I wanted some smokes or something to eat I'd always find a way to steal it.

'Being a member of a gang is a dangerous occupation because there are always fights with other gangs. It's like a war zone out there. Someone's always muscling in on someone else's territory or taking revenge for someone else getting beaten up. The fights arc vicious; everyone turns up armed with knives, baseball bats, machetes, iron pipes – even Samurai swords. Someone always ends up in hospital. They get a knife in the gut or a snooker cue across the face. I saw one of my mates get his arm cut down to the bone. Another got a huge scar down the side of his face. He'll have it for the rest of his life.'

It was during one of these showdowns that Naziz was knifed in the chest. He spent several days in intensive care with a punctured lung and, the moment he was released from hospital, he was arrested for assault and sentenced to eighteen months in prison.

'The day they locked me up was the scariest of my life. Far scarier than any of the fights I'd been involved in,' said Naziz. 'Suddenly I didn't have all my mates around me to reassure me. There was no one to help me. I was on my own. I felt very small and ashamed. I realised that I was a nothing.'

For the first few months of his sentence, Naziz felt as if he were falling apart. Every day was a struggle to keep going. But then he discovered the prison library and made friends with the librarian who encouraged him to read.

'He gave me a copy of *Animal Farm*,' said Naziz. 'I couldn't put it down. It was the first book I'd ever read properly from cover to cover. As soon as I finished, I turned to the beginning and started reading it all over again. The words spoke to me in a way that nothing had ever spoken to me before. After that, I read other books and they all spoke to me in different ways. Literature became my life-raft. It got me through prison and opened up new worlds to me. Without it, I'm not sure I would have survived in there.'

Naziz emerged from prison just short of his twentieth birthday a changed man. He enrolled in night classes at a local college and spent two years cramming for his GCSE and A-level exams. After that, he started on his degree. He was living still with his parents (I was only to discover why much later) and supported himself by working an early shift at the Billingsgate Fish Market. He also generated a small, undeclared income by helping East End Bangladeshis whose English was weak to fill in forms and interpret letters from the council.

'At the moment I'm writing love letters for this bloke who's after this girl in Dhaka,' he said. 'She's really gorgeous and educated and from a good family. He wants to marry her. The problem is he's living on benefit and he's as thick as shit. I've been coming up with all this poetic stuff and I've got her believing that he's a medical student and that he's passionate about Shakespeare. She writes back these beautiful letters. She's studying English at Dhaka University and she loves to read. The other day she sent a photograph of herself and I took it.'

He showed me the photograph from his wallet. He was right. She was very beautiful. Naziz was justifiably smitten.

'What's her name?' I asked him.

'Leila,' he said, staring dreamily at her picture.

———◆———

Shadwell was the birthplace of Thomas Jefferson's mother, Jane Randolph, whose family emigrated to the United States when she was a child (the farm in Virginia where she grew up was named after the East End district her family had left behind). At the time the Randolphs lived in Shadwell, it was a pleasant, self-contained town on the Thames. Renowned as 'one of the great nurseries of navigation and breeders of seamen in England', its population was made up of shipbuilders, riggers, anchorsmiths, ropemakers, mariners and many a famous sea captain. From Tudor times, as Britain's navy expanded and prospered, so too did Shadwell. It was from this stretch of Thames shoreline that many of Britain's greatest explorers of the sixteenth century, including William and Stephen Borough, Sir Martin Frobisher, Sir Walter Raleigh, as well as – later – James Cook, set sail. Those who returned did so with news of mysterious, far-off lands, cargoes of rare spices and silks – and the occasional load of Spanish gold.

As sea-borne trade flourished and the empire began to take shape, London developed into the busiest port in the world. Vessels of all sizes plied its waters, their masts – and later funnels – gliding above the rooftops of bonded warehouses and inns packed with sea dogs recounting daring tales of their adventures on the high seas. As recently as 1930, the docks employed 100,000 men and handled 3.5 million tons of cargo a year.

But today the Thames slumbers in retirement, reduced to carrying light traffic – tourist craft down to Greenwich and barges laden with household rubbish heading for Essex landfills. Shadwell's glorious past has faded, too. The original town was knocked down in the 1800s to make way for the docks; and in the decades after the Blitz, the docks wilted and died, taking with them most of the local industry. Thousands of jobs were lost and much of the riverside community moved on. Shadwell was reduced to a portion of the nondescript, urban sprawl lodged between the office blocks of the City and Canary Wharf on the Isle of Dogs.

The tall obelisk at the centre of the Canary Wharf development now towers over Shadwell's narrow streets, a shiny apparition of steel and glass that has risen like a Djinn from the ashes of the docks, with promises of prosperity for the communities that fall within its shadow. Millions of square feet of office and retail space have been constructed, employing up to sixty thousand people. Acres of new plush housing schemes have been built, too, with vistas of the Thames. But the benefit to the East End community has been negligible. Big business has been put first. Most of the jobs created by multinationals drawn to the area by tantalising tax incentives have been awarded to outsiders. Bankers, lawyers, accountants and other professionals have taken up residence in the new luxury apartments, purchasing them for exorbitant prices well beyond the means of the average East Ender. Docklands has developed into a segregated society with the so-called yuppies locked in their gated communities replete with Conran restaurants, and the old Cockneys and immigrants making do on their crumbling estates, which remain some of the most deprived and dangerous in the United Kingdom.

'The only people I know who work there are cleaners and they're on minimum wage,' said Naziz as we emerged from Shadwell underground station one afternoon on the way to his home. 'They move in from the surrounding estates after dark and leave as the sun comes up.'

Naziz turned left outside the station. A circling seagull cawed overhead as if searching for the cranes and masts of the past and eventually settled on a TV aerial above a block of council flats.

'If you talk to people round here – local people: white, black, whatever – you'll find a lot of resentment towards the Docklands development,' said Naziz as we continued down the street. 'They see hundreds of millions of pounds being spent and they wonder why there are no improvements on the estates. Why there's not even a decent community centre. Why the council does nothing to improve things.'

It was a dull afternoon in late March – weeks after I had met Naziz – and this was the first time he had invited me to his home. Having guests or friends over for dinner was not something he was usually able to do. But the Old Man was away.

'He's taken Rana to Bangladesh to find him a wife,' said Naziz.

During previous conversations, Naziz had told me about his older brother, who was now leader of the street gang the two of them had joined as teenagers. He was also the main heroin dealer on the estate and himself an addict.

Amongst young British Bangladeshi males, his case was by no means unique. The streets of the East End were awash with heroin, or smack, which was no longer the exclusive junk of emaciated squatters with puncture marks running the length of their arms. Although as addictive as ever, new improved heroin came in an easy-to-smoke brown resin at a vastly reduced price. Ten pounds was enough to keep any new user in a state of blissful ecstasy for up to twenty-four hours. Heroin's metamorphosis into a readily available, user-friendly narcotic had made slaves of thousands of teenagers ignorant of its potent and destructive properties. In the East End, smack was now easier to come by than marijuana. Consequently, many drug-abusing blacks and whites had turned away from crack in favour of heroin. But its greatest success had been in snaring an entirely new user group amongst whom drugs have always been traditionally taboo: the Bangladeshis.

'British Bangladeshi males are the fastest growing user group of heroin in the UK,' a social worker at a council-funded rehabilitation centre had told me. 'It's brought into the country by the Turks and the Kurds, but significantly, in the last few years, the Bangladeshis have taken over from the Irish as the dealers. They control nearly all the distribution in the East End.'

The Bangladeshis in the UK ranked lower than any other group by measurement of educational disadvantage and social exclusion, he pointed out. The unemployment level amongst young Bangladeshi males was more than double the national average.

'The estates round here are seedbeds for the propagation of smack,' he'd added. 'I've seen addicts as young as ten and eleven. Nowadays when the ice-cream vans come round the neighbourhood, the kids don't come running outside any more. They spend all their money on smack instead.'

The social worker's words echoed in my mind as Naziz led me under a railway bridge that carried the Docklands Light Railway overhead. The clatter of a train passing along the tracks reverberated against the dank brick walls, drowning out the swish of car tyres cutting through shallow pools of water. On the pavement at the far end of the bridge stood a MURDER police sign. It appealed for anyone who had seen a man being pushed under a Docklands Light Railway train to come forward. Naziz stopped to read the sign and walked on, shaking his head despondently.

'The bloke who was pushed on to the tracks lost a leg and died,' said Naziz. 'I heard through a mate that the three who did it were local boys.'

'Bangladeshis?' I asked.

He nodded. 'Yeah, from round here. My mate said they did it for kicks. Apparently when the bloke went under the train, they stood on the platform laughing.'

Shortly after, we passed a gang of teenage boys who were hanging around the street doing nothing in particular except kicking a can, chatting on their mobile phones, showing off to one another, chewing gum, trying their best to look tough. All of them wore the same uniform: leather and denim jackets, jeans, and black shiny shoes. Their haircuts were typical: sides shaved, tops slathered in gel. Their cheeks were covered in pimples – a sure sign of heroin abuse, according to Naziz.

'That's how I used to be,' he said with a sigh after we'd passed the gang. 'Bored out of my skull and looking for trouble. The biggest problem is there's no one to discipline them. Their mothers can't do it because their role in the family has been marginalised, and the fathers won't do it because they're out of touch with my generation. Nowadays they'll mug their own kind – even aunties – which would have been unheard of during the skinhead days of the seventies.'

The Bangladeshi community, Naziz said, was not equipped to deal with the heroin crisis. Few parents wanted to admit publicly that their children were addicts and, consequently, there was little public awareness about the growing problem. For his part, the Old Man was convinced that his son was possessed by an evil spirit. Initially, his answer had been to take Rana to the mosque and ask the local *imam* to exorcise him. The *imam*, a semi-literate village *mullah*, had chained Rana to a bed and given him only water and bread to eat for a week. Ultimately, Naziz's father had taken his son to the local hospital. But the doctors had suggested that the young man be placed in a drug rehabilitation programme.

'The Old Man didn't trust the rehab programme,' Naziz went on. 'He thought they would try to convert him to Christianity or something crazy like that. So he decided to take him to Bangladesh to see a village doctor, a quack.'

'And he's going to get married while he's there?'

'That's right. The Old Man thinks that he'll become responsible and hard working if he's got a wife.'

'Surely he'll have trouble finding a wife, though – being a heroin addict.'

Naziz laughed. 'You must be joking. He's a "*Londhoni*".'

'A what?'

'It's a play on words. "*Dhoni*" means rich. It's what the Sylhetis call us Bangladeshis living in London. They think we're all rich and live like kings.'

We soon reached the edge of the estate where Naziz lived. A row of rectangular blocks eight storeys high sat like giant filing cabinets surrounded by a sea of tarmac. Concrete walkways with laundry and rugs draped over their sides provided access to rows of identical doors painted a uniform yellow. Bars lined the windows and razor wire festooned the tops of walls, completing the impression of a prison.

We approached the easternmost block with its six-foot 'A' painted on its side, past three burnt-out cars that looked as if they had been strafed by Israeli gunships on the Gaza Strip. There were no trees on the estate and no windbreaks either, so that mini-tornadoes formed spontaneously, whipping up plastic bags high into the air and driving tin cans along the ground.

Half a dozen kids were playing soccer in the car park, their goal three chalk lines scoured on a brick wall. Two younger children were jumping up and down on an old mattress. A fat man walking a dog stopped to allow his pet to piss against the tyres of a parked car.

At the entrance to Naziz's block, we found the lift out of order and started up the stairs. All the way up, the walls were covered in graffiti and taggers' slogans: 'WOULD YOU LIVE HERE?'; 'FUCK PRESCOTT!' Cigarette stubs and the odd needle littered the steps. The smell of disinfectant and urine was nauseating. At each level I had to lean out over the side of the building for a gulp of fresh air and then hold my breath until we reached the next level.

We followed the walkway, past a young girl rolling marbles down the gutter, past a little boy with ice-cream stains around his mouth who was smashing a toy against the concrete floor.

Naziz's front door was fitted with a fireproof letterbox.

'Home sweet home,' he said, ringing the buzzer and waiting a minute with his ear to the door before opening it. The aroma of boiled rice and toasted cardamom seeds invited us into the tiny hallway, which was welcomingly warm. From behind one of three doors came the sounds of cooking and the drone of Sunrise Radio. Naziz knocked on the door and called out a few words in Sylheti, which were answered by a woman's voice.

'My Mum,' he said, before leading me into the family's living room.

It was a small room, ten feet square and not an inch more, with a low ceiling that had been stained yellow when water leaked through from upstairs. There was little furniture, just an old foam couch, a couple of stools and a pile of bedrolls. A gas heater positioned against one wall hissed and spat like a cobra; near to it rested the Old Man's copy of the Koran on a carved wooden stand. A side table in one corner bore in its varnish the tell-tale marks of where a TV had once stood.

'Rana flogged it,' said Naziz. 'Now we don't have a TV.'

All the family's other electrical appliances were gone as well. The VCR, the microwave, the blender that Naziz had bought his mother for her birthday. The only thing left was an old, worthless radio.

Naziz invited me to sit down, but I walked over to the window to take in the view. Through the filthy windowpane I could see the City sitting on the horizon with the Lloyds building and the NatWest Tower crowded by lumps of concrete and steel, looking like so many crooked teeth. In between lay the jumble of architecture that is the East End, the legacy of the combined efforts of the Luftwaffe (who designated it TARGET AREA A) and so-called city planners. New developments abut council estates, which loom over terraced streets, which in turn press in against warehouses and factories. Chimneys, church spires and construction cranes peek out amongst the mêlée. Railway lines and four-lane highways slice across the dull landscape, which mirrors a charmless sky.

I turned round to find that Naziz had closed the living-room door behind us and pulled back a section of the carpet to reveal a vent. He unscrewed the lid and lifted it off, laying it to one side. For a moment, his hand disappeared beneath the floor and he brought out a chocolate box.

'I want to show you something,' he said.

Naziz took the box over to the settee, sat down, and lifted off the lid. Inside lay a second-hand book bedded in cotton wool. Naziz carefully picked it out of the box as if he were handling something dangerous and turned it over to inspect it, running a finger down the spine. The binding was frayed around the edges but in good condition. I read the title out loud.

'*The Grapes of Wrath*.'

He smiled. 'It's a first edition,' he said, keeping his voice down. 'I had it valued. It's worth about four thousand pounds.'

'Where did you get it?'

'I found it in a jumble sale on the Isle of Dogs.'

'How much did you pay?'

'One pound,' he said proudly.

Naziz handed me the book and I carefully opened the cover and turned a few pages.

'It's our ticket out of here – mine and my Mum's,' said Naziz. 'Before too long I'm going to sell it and I'm going to use the money to help her escape from the Old Man.'

Just then, Naziz looked up suddenly; he had heard the kitchen door open and he snatched the book from me, returning it to its box. He pushed the box down the vent, replaced the grate, pulled over the carpet and sat on the floor with his back to the gas heater. The living-room door opened and Naziz's mother entered the room carrying a tray of teacups and a bowl of spicy Bombay mix. She was a petite woman who wore a *hijab* tightly drawn around her face. Keeping her eyes carefully averted from mine, she placed the tray on a side table, exchanged a few whispered words with her son, and quickly withdrew from the room.

Naziz watched her leave and handed me a cup of tea.

'She doesn't know about the book,' he said. 'I haven't told her because she might blurt it out to the Old Man. He has a way of sniffing out her secrets. She's scared of him. If he knew the book was there, he'd destroy it for sure.'

I sipped my tea while Naziz called out to his mother. Her reply evidently frustrated him and he stood up and left the room. When he returned a few minutes later he did so with his mother in tow.

'She's not used to mixing with strangers and she doesn't get out much,' explained Naziz. 'I don't want her to be afraid of the outside world. But sometimes she doesn't help herself. She's very stubborn.'

Naziz's mother sat on a stool by the gas fire, while Naziz talked to her in Sylheti. I could tell from the tone of the conversation that he was trying to persuade her to do something that she was reluctant to try. But he persisted and started talking to her in English.

'How are you today?' he asked, pronouncing each word as he might have done to a foreigner.

His mother looked frightened, her eyes darting round the room. Her hands were trembling.

Naziz repeated the question, slower this time and she nodded as if to say she understood.

'Yes. Thank you. I am fine,' she said in a thick South Asian accent, her words stilted like a child reciting poetry.

Naziz smiled.

'OK, next question,' he said. 'What is your name?'

She thought for a moment. 'My – name – is – Rachida,' she said.

Naziz nodded. 'Very good. You speak very good English.'

'Yes,' she replied, and the two of them laughed together.

Naziz had been teaching his mother English in secret for the past two years. Classes were held when the Old Man was out, and nothing was ever written down.

'She was very reluctant to try anything new at first,' said Naziz as we ate the food that his mother had made. 'But now she's very enthusiastic about learning.'

Watching the two of them together during the meal, I realised that Naziz had remained at home to protect his mother. Not from domestic violence, but something just as damaging: the continual erosion of her self-esteem.

'He's always telling her that she's no good, that she's useless. I just want her to be able to live away from him,' he said.

To this end, Naziz and his mother had met in secret with a divorce lawyer. Their plan was to leave the estate together once Naziz had finished his degree and could work full time to support the two of them.

'Where are you planning to live?' I asked him.

'She wants to be by the sea . . .'

A hint of reticence in his voice suggested that he was not altogether happy with the idea.

'And what about you?' I asked him.

'I'm not sure. I've never seen the sea,' replied Naziz.

———◆———

I spent the evening with Naziz and his mother and, promising that I would organise a day trip to the seaside in the next few weeks, I returned to Brick Lane.

Upstairs in the attic I found Jesse, the cat from the bookshop, curled up at the foot of the futon. Anu, aided by a cat-loving friend with three of her own, had sprung her from the Clerk's House bookshop.

At first I didn't think much of Puss, as she became known (Anu didn't like her given name; it reminded her of Republican Congressman Jesse Helms). She spent most of her time asleep, more often than not on one of my clean shirts. She shed seemingly endless amounts of hair. And she ate surprisingly large quantities of food (including Anu's spicy curried chicken if she could lay her paws on it).

The presence of the mice did not seem to concern Puss in the least and, behind Anu's back, I chided her as a useless creature who did nothing for her keep. But about a week after she moved in, some primal force stirred within her and, in the middle of the night, she suddenly sprang into action. For several hours, she tore across the attic like a thing possessed. Through a haze of sleep, I caught glimpses of her scrambling across the floorboards, leaping over obstacles, and crouching in hunter mode, her wide eyes glistening an iridescent green in the shaft of light cast from the hallway.

When we woke in the morning, it was to the sight of Puss standing over half a dozen mutilated mice carcasses. The rodents had finally met their match.

As of that moment, Puss went up in my estimation. I bought her a can of tuna by way of reward and she was stroked, petted and praised. Gratefully, she polished off the treat and then, after giving her paws a thorough licking, curled up on the futon and went to sleep.

Sitting there in the attic, watching her large tummy rising and falling in time with her breathing, I thought of the story of Dick Whittington, five times Lord Mayor of London. He, too, lived in an attic while down on his luck and was plagued by mice – until, that is, a cat came to his rescue.

Later – or so the story goes – the same cat went on to make Whittington a wealthy man.

Perhaps Puss would bring us similar good fortune.

7

Whitechapelistan

'As I walked through Petticoat Lane I thought that if [London] had a sunny climate this part of Whitechapel would become one of the most famous showplaces of the world. Here you have the East without its lepers, without small-pox . . . [a] scene of rich and amusing variety which, were it only a few thousand expensive miles from London, under a blue sky, would attract the attention of the artist and the traveller.'

H. V. Morton, *The Heart of London* (1925)

IT'S BEEN MY experience living in a number of big cities that it's easy to miss what's right under your nose. You can spend months in a particular neighbourhood and, just as you think you've got to know it, you turn a corner and suddenly come across something new or unexpected.

But in the case of the Columbia Flower Market, all the clues to its existence were right there in front of me. For months, every Sunday morning I saw people emerging from the warren of streets north of Brick Lane with trays of nasturtiums and red begonias or giant bamboos and bunches of freshly cut flowers. I just never bothered pursuing them to the source.

Not so Anu.

On the Sunday morning in early March when she first spotted people carrying plants down the street, she lost no time in following the scent. And after asking for directions from a man struggling across Bethnal Green Road with an enormous banana plant, she led the way through the council estates north of Brick Lane.

Emerging on to Columbia Road we came across a scene that left

Anu, a passionate gardener, almost speechless with excitement. Lodged between the rows of old costermongers' homes, warehouses and a Victorian primary school with windows as tall as a cathedral's, lay a riot of blooms, bouquets and blossoms arranged along two rows of tightly packed stalls, creating what looked like a dense, tropical forest.

''oo wants my 'airy palms?'

'Bizzy Lizzies a five-a!'

'Come on, girls! Laavely daffs! Only a pand a bunch!'

With the patter of Cockney traders calling out to the crowd, Anu lost no time in plunging in amongst them, pushing past pitches where everyday apple trees, heathers and cowslips competed for space with Sri Lankan orchids, New Zealand oleander bushes and Appalachian rhododendrons. Making her way from stall to stall, she paused to examine different types of roses and asked for the prices of Himalayan daphnes, Japanese azaleas and South African violets. She came across elegant white calla lilies, too – as well as red bottle-brush trees I'd seen growing in north-east India, fragrant gardenias native to China and yellow Spanish brooms. She discovered a stall that specialised in cactuses and dry alpine plants, another that stocked sweetly scented jasmine and magnolia, and at the far end of the street, a pitch where lemon, orange and olive trees swayed in the breeze.

Listening to Anu chatting with the traders, I was impressed by the depth of her horticultural knowledge. But conversely, she was staggered by the number of plants that she had never come across before (many of them the booty of Empire, diligently collected by British botanists from the far reaches of the globe), and was excited to learn more.

'What's that?' she asked one trader, indicating a clump of bright, magenta-pink flowers.

'Thas a *Li-ch-nus coor-on-aaria*, luv.'

'And that one there?' She pointed to a tall plant with several striking three-foot-long yellow flower spikes.

'*Leeg-oo-laariaa*, darlin'. 'ardy perennial. Comes rand once a year – just like Christmas.'

Anu came away that first Sunday with a few houseplants for the kitchen, a tray of marigolds and a bunch of cut flowers with exotic blooms that looked like the beaks of toucans. Later that morning we went back a second time for some window boxes and compost.

With Columbia Road a five-minute walk from Brick Lane, Anu became addicted to the market. Over the next couple of weeks, she enlisted my help in clearing away the junk from the back roof above Mr Ali's sweatshop so that she could turn it into a terrace garden. We got rid of the old tyres, the life-size plastic Alsatian that was missing its front legs, the ancient clothes mangle and several rusty drums containing suspect chemicals that probably should have been disposed of by UN inspectors in protective clothing. We kept anything that we thought might be useful, like a few scaffolding planks (I laid some of them across the weak sections of the roof), a chimney pot and an old bathtub.

It was almost spring by the time the roof was ready, and with the weather showing signs of improvement, Anu went on a spending spree. Her skills in the art of bargain hunting and price negotiating had been honed in the bazaars of New Delhi and she always insisted on getting to the market early. This meant that from March onwards, on Sunday mornings, I could count on being hustled out of bed by seven thirty.

Anu quickly came to know where the best buys were to be found and which stalls offered the hardiest plants. Her favourite pitch was run by a grumpy old geezer in a trilby and braces whose face was the texture of pummelled putty. His banter and cheeky Cockney patter attracted the crowd as effectively as his knock-down prices.

'Dahlias! Bootiful! Just look at them buds. A winner every time. The Queen 'erself loves 'em – or so she told me once. Popular with all them snobs daan the Chelsea Flower Show and all. Dahlias! 'omebase knocks 'em out at two quid each! I'm letting 'em go at six quid the lot. Thas six quid for a box of yer lovely dahlias!'

Hands clutching five and ten pound notes would shoot up in the air while the old man's helpers distributed his stock.

'Over there, over there and over there!' he'd bellow. 'Everyone's a winner! Lovely jubbley!'

The first time Anu discovered the old man's pitch, she bought several trays of Paris daisies, some purple hyacinths, and half a dozen fuschia-coloured verbenas, all for less than fifteen pounds.

'That's such a bargain!' she said excitedly, as she retreated from the mêlée. 'Let's carry all this home and then come back for more!'

By mid-April, Anu had turned Mr Ali's roof into a little oasis. The terracotta pots she bought at the One Pound Store on Bethnal Green Road were filled with nasturtiums, pansies, violas and roses. Sweetpeas grew from the chimney pot. The planks of scaffolding, some of which I had nailed together to make a six-foot square trough, housed a miniature herb garden where rosemary, thyme, basil and curry plants were starting to flourish. Two passion fruit vines grew over a skylight, and tendrils of honeysuckle curled around the bottom of a trellis attached to the wall. Half an oak barrel that Anu had found discarded down a side street in Holborn and, with great dedication, carted back to Brick Lane on the number eight bus, provided a home for a jasmine already in flower. The bathtub served as a flowerbed for giant daisies and rows of lavender and sage. Gro-bags promised a crop of tomatoes, lettuces and broccoli. A giant buddleia grew in a large plastic tub.

Despite my role as a Sunday morning plant mule, I had no complaints. We now had somewhere to enjoy the odd glimpse of sunshine and the occasional rainbow that formed over the rooftops after spring showers. The greenery, blooms and blossoms helped soften the surrounding backdrop of pigeon-fouled brickwork, wrought-iron fire escapes and protruding piping, and went some way to masking unwholesome urban smells.

More importantly, the roof garden provided Anu with a welcome distraction as she struggled to adapt to living in London and dealt with the acute bouts of loneliness that afflicted her normally resilient spirit.

'Hardly a day goes by when I don't wake up and think, "What am I doing here?"' she told me once during this period. 'I've never felt so anonymous. I often wonder, if I disappeared tomorrow, would anyone but you notice?'

I tried my hardest to be supportive. But I did not always appreciate what Anu was going through and would often try to chivvy her along by telling her that things could be worse, which was of course the last thing she wanted to hear.

In my defence, I was still struggling too. The difficulties with my parents continued to dampen my spirits. And although by now I was getting more work at the newsroom and Anu was earning a decent wage, we were not yet in a strong enough financial position to leave Brick Lane.

◆━━◆━━◆

Mr Ali had granted us permission to make use of the roof, but he was never one to give away something for nothing. I knew it would only be a matter of time before he demanded compensation – perhaps an increase in the rent, or further help composing carefully and often cunningly worded correspondence to the council, the Ministry of Labour or the Health and Safety Executive, all of whom were biting at his heels.

But when he came up to the kitchen one evening shortly after Easter and started complaining about the mounting costs of his eldest daughter's wedding, I failed to see what was coming.

'I'm 'avin' a nightmare,' he began, slugging back the rum and Coke I'd fixed for him and then pushing his empty glass towards me for a refill. 'Iss the Missis. She's gone mental. Every day she's spendin' and spendin' and spendin'. She's like a spendin' 'olic, innit.'

Mr Ali described how his wife and daughter, Rohana, together with a posse of aunties, had been roaming the streets of Upton Park, Wembley, Southall and the West End on a month-long spending spree.

'Every night, yeah, I get 'ome and there's shopping bags everywhere. Jewellery, saris, shoes, fuck knows what else. Iss all over the place! There's, like, no space to sit daan, innit! I says to the Missis, "Keep it up and I'm gonna go bankrupt, and when I 'ave an 'eart attack, the mosque'll 'ave ta pay for the burial." But the Missis, she don't care. She says, "Cough up, yeah." And all night she's goin' on in my ear 'ole and she won't shut up till I 'and over the cash.'

As the father of the bride, it was Mr Ali's responsibility to foot the bill for the entire wedding. And given that his wife was determined to keep up with the Joneses – or rather the Abduls and Miahs – it was costing him a fortune. So far, she had booked a local hall that accommodated three hundred people, a top DJ, a local restaurant to cook all the food, and a wedding planner to provide the appropriate ethnic decorations and flowers.

'The Missis, yeah, she wants all this Bollywood bollocks, innit. Lights, camera, action!' He threw his hands up in despair. 'The video geezer's costing seven 'undred quid alone. And for what? Stand arand for a coupla 'ours, point a camera at a few people. Any idiot can do that.'

He drained his glass again and poured the next one himself.

'Speaking of which, you've got a video camera, innit,' he said.

'Yes . . .' I replied, cautiously.

''cause I was thinking, mate, you could, like, film the wedding for us, yeah. In return for use of the roof. Consider it a favour. One mate to anover, innit. At the most, it'll take a coupla 'ours . . .'

———•✦•———

My video camera and I had seen lots of action. I'd used it to capture river pirates on tape in the Sundarbans, the swampy delta of the Ganges and Brahmaputra; and in Kabul to document the Taliban take-over of the city from the forces of Ahmed Shah Massoud. I had taken it with me on more than one visit to Kashmir; and to Meghalaya, 'the abode of clouds', where I had watched the monsoon rains break upon the hills of Cherapunjee.

Had anyone told me that one day I would be using it to film a Bangladeshi wedding in London's East End as a favour to my landlord, I probably would have snorted in disbelief. But as I stood on the pavement outside Bow register office, I realised that the scene unfolding before me was no less exotic – and certainly no less unlikely – than anything I had watched through the viewfinder in the subcontinent.

Only a few minutes earlier, Mr Ali's immediate family had pulled up in a New York-style, chauffeur-driven stretch limousine with tinted windows. And as I trained my camera on the passenger door, my landlord had stepped out, dressed in a brown three-piece suit of a style worn by Alec Guinness as George Smiley.

'Don't miss nafing, yeah. Otherwise the Missis'll 'ave my nuts in a vice, innit,' he'd told me.

A chauffeur dressed in a black suit and cap had held open the door and the rest of Mr Ali's family had followed. The limo was large, but I couldn't quite believe the number of people inside. They kept coming, like clowns from a Volkswagen at the circus. Mr Ali's nieces emerged first, each in the latest imitation Bollywood disco gear: gold stilettos, flared and sequined trousers with halter tops and long scarves; their hair ironed into long and silky tresses, their cheeks and eyebrows burnished to a high gloss, and pouty lips layered with wet, pastel lipstick. Nail extensions and whitened teeth flashed as they greeted other family members and friends, chewing gum all the while.

Next came Mr Ali's eighteen-year-old daughter Razia in a *lehnga*, with a long Cinderella-like skirt and matching blouse, and the youngest, Fatima, aged fourteen, more modestly dressed in a *salwar kameez* and the only one of the three to wear a *hijab*. Then came three teenage boys all with cropped hair, white shirts hanging out over black trousers, and shiny black shoes with big buckles. After them, several aunties emerged, all wearing traditional silk saris, thick bifocals and a bit of dark lipstick. A few toddlers followed in mini sarongs and kurtas. And then, at long last, came the bride.

Rohana was a petite girl, twenty-two years old, with pretty eyes and dark skin that had been mercilessly lightened with 'Fair & Lovely' cream and then highlighted with crimson blush. She wore what has become standard wedding gear amongst South Asians living abroad, no matter what their regional traditions – a dark red *lehnga*, criss-crossed in gold ribbon and sequins, and chunky South Indian gold jewellery hanging like pendulums from ears, neck and wrists. A gold-rimmed veil covered her face, showing only lips painted the standard maroon. The angle of her head suggested that her eyes were appropriately and shyly downcast.

Now, as Mr Ali and his family waited on the pavement for the groom, who was late, to arrive and for another marriage taking place inside the register office to end, I worked diligently to make sure that I had footage of everyone and tried to guess who was who.

Mr Ali's father was there; he was frail and, judging by the way everyone kept shouting in his ear, almost completely deaf. I guessed that the middle-aged woman upon whom the old man was leaning so heavily was his daughter, a childless widow who lived with Mr Ali and his immediate family in Whitechapel. I recognised Salim, the young boy Mr Ali had unofficially adopted after his parents had returned to Bangladesh four and a half years earlier; talking to him was my landlord's younger brother Shafi, who now lived in Cardiff and had a strong Welsh accent; and behind him stood one of Mr Ali's cousins, Shaz, who came by the shop every once in a while. A self-made man who was in the office supply business, he wore shiny Italian suits.

I was able to identify the infamous 'Missis' as well. Not because she stood out in any way from the dozen or so other aunties gathered on the pavement (contrary to my expectations she was short and distinctly unglamorous), but because of the abrupt, bossy tone that she took with Mr Ali, and his unmistakable subservience to her.

Soon, the groom, Jamil, arrived in a brand new 7 series BMW that he drove himself. A tall, handsome twenty-nine year old who was confidence personified, he wore a black *sherwani* that was a fusion of Western and Indian fashions. Mr Ali clearly adored Jamil. He had described him to me as a 'modern geezer', and now my landlord gave his future son-in-law a fond hug and, amidst smiles and laughter, a hearty clap on the back. Jamil received an equally enthusiastic greeting from the other male members of Mr and Mrs Ali's families as well. He cracked jokes and teased the youngsters, picking up the smallest and giving them hugs, making the most of being in the spotlight. Clearly he was a man's man. But Jamil knew where his bread was buttered. As he greeted the women of the family, he displayed a more deferential side to his nature, charming them with humility and flattery, which brought approving smiles to their faces.

The groom's parents were Mr Ali's kind of East End Sylhetis, too. He had known the father, who was in the import–export business, for over thirty years; the wife, famed for her cooking and the proud mother of four sons, was a distant cousin. Mr Ali had given his unreserved consent to the marriage – that is, after Mrs Ali and Jarnil's mother had cooked up the plan over tea. From the start, the young couple had been keen on the idea as well, and during their three-month engagement they'd gone out together on several dates. Their union was now being touted as a 'love marriage'.

'They're so into each other, innit,' I overheard one of Mr Ali's nieces say to another.

'Yeah. I 'eard 'e took 'er to a Kylie concert.'

But Jamil's family also had what Mr Ali had referred to as a 'dark side'. One of Jamil's brothers and several of his cousins were, as my landlord put it, 'nutters'. By this he meant that they were highly conservative Muslims who were part of a movement that condoned acts of terrorism and sought to radicalise the Bangladeshi community and, ultimately, Islamify Britain.

'They're Koran bashers, innit,' Mr Ali had told me the day before. 'They want Whitechapel to become, like, Whitechapelistan. Always, yeah, they're 'assling people in the street, saying, "Oi! Go daan the mosque!" Or "You're not a good Muslim, innit!" Basically they're bustards! I mean, waas it got to do with them? Islam iss a personal fing, yeah. Tell me where's it say in the 'oly Koran, "I got a beard so I can go rand sticking my nose in where iss not wanted!"'

Mr Ali had been concerned that this element within Jamil's family would ruin the day. At a number of local weddings in recent years, such radicals had insisted that male and female guests be separated, and that during receptions there be no singing and dancing, not even in traditional Sylheti mode. But as I panned the video camera through the crowd of family and guests, who now numbered nearly a hundred, I saw that the radicals were only a tiny minority. Easily identifiable thanks to their beards and skullcaps and dour demeanours, there were no more than half a dozen of them and, together with five women in black *niqabs*, they stood aloof from the main body of the party.

Mr Ali had told me specifically not to film them.

'I don't want no trouble,' he'd said.

But the photographer – and perhaps the mischief-maker – inside me could not help myself, and so I aimed my camera in their direction and started recording. For a minute or so they didn't notice. And then one of them – I only found out later it was Jamil's youngest

brother, Shirajul – walked over to where I stood and blocked the lens
with the palm of his hand.

'Don't film our Muslim sisters,' he hissed in a strong Estuary accent.
'Iss not permitted in our culture. Allah 'as forbidden it.'

It was perhaps fortunate that we only had to wait another few minutes
before we were allowed to move inside the register office. I quickly
took up position at the front of the hall where the ceremony was due
to be held and refrained from pointing my camera in the direction of
the radicals who sat on a row of chairs at the back.

The civil ceremony itself was no different from ones I had attended
in the past, except that throughout the proceedings the bride kept her
veil drawn down over her face and her head bowed toward the
ground. When she spoke, it was in a nervous whisper and the regis-
trar had to ask her to speak up. Similarly, when it came to exchanging rings, Rohana did not so much as glance at Jamil, and when the
couple were declared husband and wife, they did not kiss.

They chose not to walk down the aisle together hand in hand
either, and once we were back out in the street, no one threw con-
fetti or posed for pictures. Instead, all the family and guests piled back
into their cars and, with the over-stuffed limousine leading the way –
and a couple of Mr Ali's nephews standing with their heads sticking
out of the sunroof window, calling out to girls in the street – headed
to Mr Ali's house in Whitechapel.

This was the first time I had visited my landlord's home. It lay down
a tightly packed street, a stone's throw from Whitechapel Hospital,
one of a row of terraced houses that mirrored an identical row of terraced houses opposite. The street itself was unremarkable and depress-
ingly monotonous, with two rows of cars parked along the pavements
and a vandalised phone booth on one corner.

On a normal day, Mr Ali's house would not have stood out from
the others. It had the same net curtains in the windows, the same
front door, the same red brickwork. But it had been dressed up for
the festivities and now looked like a cross between Santa's grotto and
a backdrop for a Bollywood dance sequence. Lengths of pulsating
Christmas lights hung from the guttering down the front of the

building, garlands of plastic mango leaves and peacock feathers adorned the windows, and an archway made of multicoloured cloth with tinfoil borders had been constructed around the door.

The arrival of the limousine brought some of the neighbours out on to their doorsteps and others to their windows. And as Mr Ali's family once again disgorged themselves from the vehicle, the children of the neighbourhood stood around it, running their dirty fingers along its sleek lines and putting their faces up to the tinted windows in a vain effort to glimpse the plush interior.

I filmed the bride being led into the house and the arrival of the groom and his family, and then followed everyone inside.

The Alis' home would have been cramped at the best of times. A narrow corridor wallpapered with rural scenes of Bangladesh led past the sitting room, which was packed with people juggling paper plates of *chaat*, and plastic cups of Fanta. I caught a glimpse of a clock with a photograph of the Prophet's Mosque in Medina on its face, a couch upholstered in red velvet with gold tassels, a fake oriental rug covered in protective plastic matting. Children brushed past me and ran up the stairs where a number of girls sat playing with Barbie dolls. I passed another doorway that led into the kitchen where a group of aunties were engaged in a frenzy of chopping and cooking while samosas sizzled in an enormous wok of spitting oil and steam bellowed from a giant pot of rice. With the fumes of fried spices caught in the back of my throat, I reached the end of the corridor and an outside door that led into a backyard penned in by high walls.

It was a crush there as well. I had to squeeze past the other guests to reach the far side of the yard where a trestle table groaned with food and drink and Mr Ali's adopted son, Salim, who was now wearing a Calvin Klein baseball cap, stood on a small stage manning a sound system that blared *desi* pop. I took some footage of everyone enjoying themselves and then helped myself to a plateful of *biriyani*. Several members of the family made me feel at home, insisting that I eat more and asking me whether I was enjoying myself. Rohana, who had shed her *lehnga* along with her shy demeanour and put on a silk *salwar kameez*, told me how glad she was that I was doing the wedding video.

'Dad says you're, like, a top video director,' she said. 'Thas well wicked, innit. So which videos 'ave you done? 'ave you ever met Robbie? Oooh! Do you reckon you could get 'is aut-agraph for us?'

Before I could answer any of her questions, she was whisked away by her father to meet a member of the family, and after that – with everyone else clustered into small groups organised according to age, sex and family – I was left on my own. For a while I took refuge behind my video camera, but I started to feel out of place and thought about leaving. It was only the arrival of dessert that prevented me from going – that, and a chance meeting with a Calcutta anthropologist at the buffet table where he was helping himself to a large bowlful of *kheer*, rice pudding.

Little did I know that, in the months to come, this man would change the way I perceived not only the East End, but England itself.

Aktar hailed from West Bengal, which considers itself the intellectual capital of the subcontinent, if not the world. As an intellectual himself and a voracious reader, there was little that Aktar did not seem to know, and he was not in the least reluctant to share his knowledge with anyone who cared to listen – and often with those who did not – a habit born of more years of university lecturing than he cared to remember. However, his wealth of knowledge came at a price. Anyone caught in his web had first to endure a lengthy homily on the genius of Bengali culture, peppered with quotes from Tagore.

That he was a Communist went without saying; there can hardly be a Calcuttan intellectual who is not. And likewise, by definition, he was an anti-imperialist and regarded the actions of the Honourable Company and the Raj with disdain. Robert Clive and Co. were to Aktar 'common thugs' and he shared Edward Said's views on orientalism. The troubles facing the present-day state of West Bengal and Bangladesh had little to do with the Socialist politics of post-independence India and could be laid fairly and squarely at the door of Empire.

'In the case of Sylhet, you British destroyed the local textile indus-try, flooding the market with British manufactured cloth,' he said. 'The place has never recovered, so you only have yourselves to blame for making economic refugees of half the population.'

And yet, Aktar still held the British in high regard. Indeed, as a product of the Indian public school system, which apes the English model, he had been raised on a diet of Shakespeare, cricket and toad in the hole. Simply put, he was an Anglophile.

'Are you aware that Laurence Olivier's eldest son is also named Tarquin?' he asked me in an accent that was more Eton than Calcutta when I introduced myself.

Aktar's awe of British literature and academia had brought him to England for the first time as a young man in 1961. It had been a pilgrimage of sorts, a journey that he made partly overland, partly by sea, in order to visit those great seats of learning, Oxford and Cambridge, as well as London University, where Tagore studied, and Stratford-upon-Avon. It had also taken him to Canterbury and York and to Batemans, the home of Rudyard Kipling.

'I could not help but admire the civility of the country and its people,' he told me after we had eaten our dessert and stood in the corner of the Alis' backyard. 'In his youth, Gandhi referred to England as "the land of philosophers and poets" and, to me, this description rang true.'

Forty years later, the idealistic young man who had walked halfway across Asia Minor to reach Europe, had grown old and the idealism he had felt for India in the 1960s as it shrugged off its imperialist yoke had been replaced by cynicism. He had grown weary of academia, too, and after his wife had died the year before, Aktar had taken to the road again. Rather than travelling by air – 'I have never been in an aeroplane and am not about to change the habit of a lifetime' – he had set off for Europe by bus along the Grand Trunk Road. His journey had taken him through Pakistan and the Middle East where he had spent several months in Mecca, Medina and Jerusalem, and then on to Istanbul – 'the Suleymaniye!' – and through the Balkans. Finally, in February, he had crossed from Calais to Dover.

'I do not mind admitting that the first glimpse of the white cliffs brought a lump to my throat,' he said. 'I have always considered England my second home – intellectually speaking of course.'

Modern-day London had come as a shock. Being naturally prejudiced against Americans – he called the Yanks 'pretenders' – he abhorred the influence of so-called 'McCulture', which he saw as having permeated 'virtually every aspect of British life'. He was also appalled by how commercialised the capital had become: 'You are assaulted by it at every turn.' And he frowned upon what he viewed as the 'erosion of the moral and spiritual fibre' of the country.

'It strikes me that Western liberalism encourages a great many activities and attitudes which, from an anthropological perspective, may be termed primitive.'

But there was much that had sparked his interest as well, not least London's burgeoning immigrant population.

'If, forty years ago, anyone had predicted that by the turn of the century there would be sixty thousand Sylhetis living in east London and that a ward of Tower Hamlets would be known as "Banglatown", I doubt I would have believed them. It is extraordinary to think that the British, having ruled over such a powerful empire, have allowed so many of their former subjects to settle here. To the Victorians, the presence of so many immigrants would have been unthinkable. They would have seen it as nothing short of a defeat.'

Aktar believed the British were suffering from collective guilt.

'You people never really had your heart in being rulers,' he said. 'It strikes me that, having caused such havoc and disruption around the world, you are trying to make amends to those you formerly suppressed.'

The transformation of Britain so fascinated Aktar that he had come out of retirement to study the Bangladeshi population of the East End.

'East is East and West is West and never the twain shall meet – or so said Kipling. And yet quite the reverse is happening here in London,' said Aktar.

If anyone was equipped to crack the insular Sylheti community, it was him. Being a Bengali anthropologist and a Muslim provided him with an inside edge, and he also had the advantage of having spent time in Sylhet where, in the 1970s, he had studied the district's Sufic traditions and folklore, which had been introduced by a Yemeni *Pir*, named Shah Jalal.

'He and his followers introduced a moderate form of Islam that blended with Hinduism to create a tolerant culture,' he said. 'The Arab influence also imbued the Sylhetis with a restlessness that sets them apart from other Bangladeshis. Their folk tales tell of a promised land where golden leaves drop from the trees. It lies – or so they say – beyond seven seas and thirteen rivers, and the journey to reach it is arduous and long.'

In the 1970s, he had met a number of Sylhetis who had set off in search of the promised land, working as lascars aboard British vessels. In the past few months, he had tracked down some of their relatives now living in London. Amongst them was the Missis' great-uncle, who went to sea in the 1930s and settled in Whitechapel.

'So in other words you're here at the wedding on the job,' I said.

Aktar nodded. 'An anthropologist's work is never done,' he replied. 'Especially when there is so much excellent *kheer* on offer.'

Given Mr Ali's track record, it shouldn't have been a great surprise to learn that the day's events were but a prelude to a series of celebrations still to come and that I had been duped.

'What do you mean, this isn't the wedding?' I said to my landlord when the party started to wind down mid-afternoon and I decided to leave. 'I saw them get married.'

'That was the civil wedding, innit,' he said. 'To us Muslim people, yeah, that don't mean nafing. The proper wedding's two weeks from now, guvna. And in between, there's, like, all these lunches and dinners and fuck knows what else.'

'But you said that I would only have to film for a couple of hours,' I protested.

'Thas right. A coupla 'ours 'ere, a coupla 'ours there.'

He gave me a matey clap on the back and thanked me for coming.

'Look at it this way, yeah, I'm doin' you, like, a massive favour, innit. After this, you can like set yourself up as a wedding video geezer. I'll give you a blinding recommendation. There's serious money in it, mate.'

I left the house with Aktar, who had an appointment at five o'clock near Brick Lane.

'As part of my research I am interviewing a group of teenage girls who have voluntarily adopted the *hijab*. You are welcome to join me – provided of course that they raise no objection.'

I didn't exactly jump at the opportunity to go with him; although I found much of what Aktar had to say interesting, his long, one-sided disquisitions were getting tedious. But even as I made my excuses, it was clear he wanted company.

'It is a pleasure to meet a bright young Englishman who enjoys stimulating conversation,' he said.

With an hour to kill before the interview, we decided to walk through the back streets. Aktar suffered from arthritis of the knees which was being exacerbated by the London damp, so we made slow progress. It did not help that he was carrying a heavy leather satchel stuffed with books and papers that poked out like Christmas presents from the top of a stocking. Nor that he kept bumping into friends and acquaintances in the street whom he engaged in long conversations.

'You seem to know a lot of people around here,' I commented impatiently after standing on the pavement for ten minutes while Aktar stopped to chat with a shopkeeper about the quality of his papayas.

'Sylhetis have enormous extended families. Traditionally they have always lived close to one another. Banglatown is like a village. Everyone is either related or they know one another.'

We passed down Greatorex Street and turned left on Chicksand. Council blocks populated almost exclusively by Bangladeshis lined the way. The laundry that hung drying over the side of the balconies was mostly ethnic in design and colour, the local government signs that dotted the walls and railings – 'CLIMB-PROOF PAINT'; 'NO BALL GAMES' – were in both English and Bengali. In the car parks that separated the blocks, four or five Bangladeshi teenagers crowded round a new sports car in which the owner sat, revving the engine while techno pumped from his speakers.

On the corner of Spelman Street in front of a row of terraces squatted an old Bangladeshi man on his haunches. The cigarette he was smoking, he held cupped in his hands, drawing the smoke through his thumbs and exhaling through his nose. Behind him, an open door revealed a room packed with rows of boys aged ten or eleven, all wearing prayer caps and sitting cross-legged on the floor. An *imam* – erect, stern, bearded – stood before them reciting verses from the Koran, which the boys repeated in unison, their heads bowed in deference, their squeaky voices spilling out into the street.

It was a scene that I had come across many times before in various parts of the Islamic world where basic religious instruction is provided in every village and neighbourhood just as it has been for centuries. From experience, I knew that such classes are generally held in a similar spirit to that of Sunday School and that, despite Western stereotypes, they are not breeding grounds of fundamentalism. But I had also visited a number of *madrasas* in the Afghan refugee camps on Pakistan's North-West Frontier in which the young Pushtuns who became the Taliban had been indoctrinated. And as we stood in the doorway observing the class for a few minutes, I could not help regarding it with some unease.

I noticed a similar reaction in Aktar. Deep furrows appeared on his forehead.

'From what I have read, a certain proportion of every immigrant group that has settled in the East End has turned to fundamentalism, the Jews included. It is only to be expected,' he said as we turned away from the door and continued down Chicksand Street. 'Nonetheless, it is worrying to see young minds being influenced by these so-called "imams". They are mostly narrow-thinking men who are theologically illiterate and preach an intolerant approach to Islam that is utterly at odds with the Bengali tradition of love, understanding and compassion.'

He compared many of the *imams* to be found in the East End to the blind men in the tale of the Elephant in the Dark.

'Coming across an elephant for the first time, each reaches out and touches a different part of the animal and each in turn concludes that it is something different,' said Aktar. 'One man feels the trunk and concludes that it is a large snake; another runs his hands over the ears and concludes that it is a giant fan, and so on and so forth.'

In short, Aktar saw the *imams* as 'charlatans'. Most, he said, came from rural backgrounds and had no appreciation of foreign cultures, let alone an understanding of the complexities of modern city life in the West.

'They are essentially Muslim evangelists steeped in ideals fostered by fundamentalist schools of thought,' he continued. 'They teach repetition rather than knowledge and understanding and they feed on discontent and insecurity. In so doing, they reduce Islam to a mere cult.'

He believed that the Bangladeshi community should send such religious 'scholars' packing and instead employ *imams* who had grown up in the West and could better relate to their flock. But many Sylheti parents saw the mullah mafia as a necessary counterweight to what they perceived as the corrupting influence of Western culture on their sons and daughters.

'They have invited into their communities these village idiots who are telling the young people that they do not belong here, and that they will never be accepted. It is dangerous rhetoric, although admittedly appealing to those who feel disenfranchised.'

I mentioned the groom's brother, Shirajul, and how he had objected to me filming his 'Muslim sisters' outside the register office that morning. Aktar had seen the incident for himself and knew Shirajul, whom he had interviewed the week before.

'By Sylheti standards he has enjoyed a privileged upbringing. He has received a good education and his parents have provided him with a high standard of living. But sadly, he has been drawn into what he refers to as the "brotherhood" and we may term "the Islamist cult". Consequently, he has decided that he is a victim. He will tell you that as a Muslim he is misunderstood and that Western culture is decadent and corrupt. To my mind, however, he is a spoilt child.'

Before long we reached our destination, a modern townhouse just off Brick Lane. The door was opened by a girl of seventeen who wore a black *jilbab*, an all-enveloping black garment, a black *hijab* and black gloves. The combination made her red lipstick look brighter than it might otherwise have appeared.

'*Salaam aleikum*,' she said with a confident smile, placing her hand over her heart.

'*Aleikum salaam*,' replied Aktar.

The two exchanged a few words in Bangla. The girl nodded her head in agreement.

'Yeah! Of course he can come in,' she said in English as she held open the door.

We stepped inside and were directed down the hallway into a sitting room where six other teenage girls sat on a couch and two armchairs. Four of them wore *hijabs* and a fusion of Western and Eastern fashion, with jean jackets over black *salwar kameez*. The remaining two wore more colourful *salwar kameez*, but nothing over their heads. All of them stood when we entered the room and exchanged salaams.

'This is Monwara, Begum, Samia, Razia, Amina and Rox,' said the girl who'd answered the door. 'I'm Maleka,' she added.

Aktar sat down in one of the armchairs and I was provided with a stool that was placed next to him. We were served tea and cashew nuts and, with the girls sitting in front of us, Aktar took out a bulging notebook from his leather satchel.

'You said you wanted to ask us some questions,' said Maleka. 'So here we are. Go for it.'

A thorough inquisitor, Aktar spent the next hour and a half asking the girls about every aspect of their lives, taking down the details in his tiny handwriting with monastic precision. Fortunately for me, the discussion – which predictably centred on Islam – was conducted in English, although Aktar posed a number of his initial questions in Bangla.

Maleka proved the most vocal of the seven. She described herself as a 'revert' who had adopted the *hijab* a couple of years earlier when she realised that it was 'the will of Allah'.

'It's not a question of how *we* want to dress, it's a question of what *He* wants,' she explained. 'Islam means submission to the will of Allah and that's what I'm doing, submitting.'

She now prayed five times a day, went to the mosque every Friday without fail, studied the Koran and the Hadith, and fasted during Ramadan.

'I'm very different to my Mum,' she said. 'She's never read the Koran and when she was growing up, she wasn't taught anything about Islam. All she knew how to do was say her prayers and she'd fast. I've had to teach her a lot of things. But she still refuses to wear the *hijab*; usually she just wears a scarf over her head like they do in the villages. She couldn't believe it when I started wearing the *hijab*. She used to say it was like I was enslaving myself. But it's helped me find out who I am.'

'And who is that?' asked Aktar.

'I'm a Muslim. I may be British, too. But I'm a Muslim first. I'll always be a Muslim first.'

Maleka's co-*hijab* wearers agreed. Covering their heads had 'liberated' them.

'With this on,' said Samia, fifteen, 'no one gives us any grief.'

Begum told us about her elder sister who was in her thirties. She had not grown up wearing the *hijab* and had never been allowed out of the house.

'My parents never trusted her. They never let her go out with her friends. She was always hanging around at home. They were always worried that if she went out, people would say she was going around with boys. When she was twenty-two, my parents married her to a guy from Bangladesh. He's a really backwards bloke.'

Aktar asked her if she would agree to an arranged marriage.

'No way!' she shouted, her response causing a ripple of laughter to pass through the room.

'None of us would,' said another.

'It's not Islamic,' added Monwara. 'It doesn't say anywhere in the Koran that marriages should be arranged. That's village thinking.'

Marriage could wait; their first priority was establishing careers. Monwara wanted to be a pharmacist, Begum a doctor, Samia a teacher, and Razia, who was studying political science, a politician.

'We dedicate a lot of our time to campaigning,' said the latter.

Only recently they had taken part in a Liberate Palestine march; before that, a protest outside the Indian embassy against alleged human rights abuses in Kashmir. All five of them identified with the Islamic *Umma*.

'Muslims are being persecuted round the world,' said Maleka. 'Look at what's been going on in Kosovo. Muslims are being ethnically cleansed and the West does nothing about it. Why? 'cause they're Muslims.'

'So you see yourself as part of a pan-Islamic community?' said Aktar.

'Yeah, very much so. In that respect, we're very different from our parents. They're not interested in what's going on in the rest of the world. My Mum didn't even know where Bosnia was till I told her.'

And what about day-to-day life? Were they free to go about Banglatown on their own?

'There are certain things we don't do,' said Begum. 'We don't go to nightclubs and pubs. That would be un-Islamic. But basically we do whatever we like. A lot of people don't realise that Islam gives women more freedom than any other religion. The media has this stereotypical image of women in Muslim countries always being repressed, but it's not accurate.'

Listening to the conversation, I began to wonder if they were all quite as devout as Maleka claimed. If the *hijab* assured their independence, had some of them adopted it just to keep the community and a prying family off their backs?

Aktar put just that question to Razia, the quietest of the girls in the *hijabs*. She stammered nervously in response until Maleka interrupted yet again.

'All of us here wear the *hijab* because as Muslim women it's our duty to do so.'

But there was one voice of dissent in the room. It came from one of the two girls who were not wearing a *hijab*. This was Maleka's younger sister, Amina, who was sixteen years old.

'There's a lot of pressure nowadays for people my age to conform. You walk down Brick Lane and guys our age come up to us and say you should cover your head, you should respect your parents, all that sort of thing. They say we're disobeying the *Shariat*. But I won't wear a *hijab* because I don't want anyone telling me what to do. They can piss off as far as I'm concerned,' she said.

Her last words were drowned out by Maleka and a couple of the others. But Amina held her ground.

'This is a free country,' she shouted. 'I can do what I want.'

'You don't get it,' countered Maleka. 'It's got nothing to do with democracy or freedom of speech. It's Allah's will. You can't deny it. We are all Allah's creatures.'

As the argument continued, I could not help wondering what Maleka and her coterie would make of Taliban Afghanistan. I thought back on an interview I had conducted in Kabul with a woman doctor who had been barred from working and ordered to stay at home by the much-feared religious police. She had described herself to me as a 'prisoner' who had been stripped of her most basic human rights. Her *burka* had become the 'bars' of her jail.

By contrast, these East End girls lived in a culture that guaranteed them the freedom to dress and behave in a manner of their own choosing. Ironically it was in the West that they had found a balance between liberty and religious observance. And yet I could not help feeling that Maleka and her friends took this freedom for granted and that, had they been living in certain parts of the Islamic world, it would be liberalisation and not the *hijab* they would be campaigning for.

But it was not my place to say anything. Besides, I had made a promise to Aktar to keep quiet while he conducted his interviews. And when he eventually finished and we left the house, he thanked me for keeping my side of the bargain.

'It is undoubtedly a contentious issue, but one that we should not rush to pass judgement on,' he said. 'The fact that these girls have decided to cover their heads is not such a bad thing. It has given them an identity that has helped bring them out into the world. And the more they are accepted, the less they will feel the need to draw attention to themselves.'

At six p.m. on April 25th, Anu and I were sitting out on the roof reading the Saturday newspapers when we heard a sudden, loud thud from the direction of Spitalfields. The noise caused the pigeons perched on the guttering and chimney pots to take to the air amidst a great flapping of wings. Anu and I paid it scant attention. By now, we had grown used to hearing all manner of noises coming from the neighbouring streets, and we kept our heads buried in the papers. Not even the ensuing sirens in the distance stirred our interest.

In fact, it was not until almost an hour later that we discovered – via a concerned friend in another part of London who was listening to the radio – that a bomb had gone off on Brick Lane.

Perhaps foolishly, our first reaction was to rush outside to see what was happening. At the top end of the street everything appeared normal. But as we followed the sound of sirens down past the old Truman Brewery, we found the street cordoned off. Crime scene tape stretched across the junction with Hanbury Street. Police officers stood guard, keeping back a crowd of onlookers and anxious residents clamouring to be allowed through. Behind them, the façades of the buildings were ablaze with a disco effect of whirring emergency lights cast by a fleet of police cars, ambulances and fire engines. A long pall of smoke rose over the rooftops.

The police manning the cordon could only confirm that a bomb had detonated and that, mercifully, it had caused only minor injuries. They did not know whether anyone had claimed responsibility for the blast. But the talk amongst the crowd was of the racist group Combat 18. It was this shadowy organisation that had claimed responsibility for planting a device in Brixton the previous week in which thirty-nine people had been injured. With Brick Lane now a victim, it appeared that London's immigrant communities were the target.

'Them racialist bustards, yeah, they don't want us 'ere, innit,' said Mr Ali, when we met him later standing outside his shop, chatting with a couple of other leather jacket shop owners about the bomb.

Naturally our landlord was nervous. He had left home and come over to the shop to check that it was still in one piece. Now he said he was in need of a drink. I poured him one up in the kitchen and he gripped the glass of rum and Coke with trembling hands. The day's events had brought back painful memories of the racist attacks of the 1970s and 1993, and the thought that his community might be under siege again filled him with dread.

'Sometimes, yeah, I wonder if we'll ever be, like, accepted, innit.'

Mr Ali stayed for another drink and then said he was going to visit the mosque. It was the first time he had prayed for a while, he admitted.

Over the next few days, the national newspapers were filled with speculation about the bombs and who lay behind them. There was no shortage of doom-mongering. Some commentators warned that the attacks could spark a race war; others spoke of the inherent racism running through British society.

'Bombs will continue to go off because a climate is long established – by Mosley, by Powell and by Thatcher – a climate that gives respectability and licence to those people who perpetrate these acts,' wrote Dr Imruh Bakari in the *Independent*.

Professor Jorgen Nielsen, director of the Centre for Christian–Muslim Relations, was quoted as saying: 'After years in which the Muslim community has grown in self-confidence and begun to feel they are being listened to, it's thrown everything back to the kind of discourse they were used to before the Rushdie affair.'

Members of the Anti-Defamation League and Socialist Workers Party soon turned up on Brick Lane echoing such views and handing out leaflets extolling the virtues of Marxism. 'Get the skinheads off Brick Lane!' they shouted through megaphones.

But there were no skinheads on Brick Lane and, the racket made by the protesters aside, the street quickly returned to normal. The Indian restaurants remained open and continued to do a roaring trade (except Café Naz, which took the full brunt of the explosion); the faithful came and went from the mosque; families shopped at Taj Stores. By Tuesday morning, even Mr Ali was sounding defiant.

'I've lived 'ere nearly thirty years. No bustard's gonna push me out, yeah. Over my dead body, innit. We've gotta stick together.'

He said that the wedding of his daughter would go ahead the following Saturday, as planned.

I managed to get out of filming the events preceding the big day, including the *mehndi* party. Much to Mr Ali's chagrin, he had to hire a professional wedding cameraman. But with Anu working as my assistant, carrying lights and the microphone, I filmed the wedding itself and we were both glad not to have missed it.

There were more stretch limousines, Rohana wore a spectacularly glitzy designer *lehnga*, the reception was held in a hall where the bride and groom sat on thrones upholstered in red velvet on top of a stage that looked like a Las Vegas version of the Taj Mahal, and an enormous buffet was served to hundreds of guests. After dinner, everyone apart from the few determined radicals danced to a live band that played traditional Sylheti folk music, and then to the sounds of Bollywood and Bhangra remixes.

Anu and I stayed until midnight and then returned home. Before going to sleep, I turned on the radio to catch up on the news. The bulletin spoke of another bomb that had exploded, in a gay pub in Soho, killing three and injuring sixty others. The device had been packed with nails, like the bombs in Brixton and Brick Lane.

Later that morning, the police made an arrest. The lone suspect, David Copeland, was later found guilty of planting the three devices. A former member of the BNP, he had left the organisation to pursue a more violent form of action. During his trial, it emerged that he had planned to detonate his second bomb in the middle of Brick Lane market, but came to the East End a day early.

'It was lucky for us that he was like an idiot, innit,' said Mr Ali, when I saw him later. 'But like I always say, Brick Lane's a rough place, yeah. You never know what could 'appen 'ere next.'

8

A Rainy Day

'Pass through [Brick Lane] . . . a hundred times, and nothing . . . will it betray to you of its hidden secrets.'
John Henry Mackay, *The Anarchists* (1891)

SADIE SHOULD HAVE had Mr Begleiter put down long before he finally succumbed to old age that spring. During his last few weeks, the cat had hardly moved from his cushion and when he did, his long drawn-out yeowling betrayed the agony of his arthritis. But Sadie refused to take him to the vet.

'Advice I don't need!' she bawled at me when I broached the subject. 'What are you, a rabbi?'

'I just think it would be more humane to have him put to sleep,' I said.

''oomane 'e says! 'ow can killing 'im be 'oomane?'

I thought about slipping Mr Begleiter some poison on a titbit, something that would put an end to him quickly and painlessly; and I thought about calling the RSPCA and explaining the situation and asking for their advice. But before I got around to doing any of these things, the cat died.

The precise time of Mr Begleiter's death is not something that will ever be known. It could have occurred at any point within a twenty-four hour period between the Wednesday morning when I last saw him alive and the Thursday afternoon when I brought Sadie her shopping and found him lying lifeless on his cushion.

The only thing I can be certain of is this: I was the first to realise that the cat was dead (a prod to his stomach when Sadie's back was turned proved my suspicion). But to my shame, I took the coward's way out and pretended that I hadn't noticed.

It was three or four hours before Sadie discovered the truth for herself, and when, that evening, she broke the sad news to me, I did my best to act surprised.

'That's terrible,' I said, secretly relieved that the poor cat was finally out of its misery. 'Would you like me to call the vet?'

'The vet! What do we need a vet for?' she demanded. 'Idiots, the lot of them!'

'The vet will know what to do with the body,' I protested.

'No vet!' she screeched. 'I don't need no bleedin' vet!'

At Sadie's insistence, Mr Begleiter spent the night in her fridge-freezer. The next day, when I came to take him out, he looked like a prehistoric animal that had been preserved in glacial ice.

'Put him in a plastic bag,' instructed Sadie, who had woken early that morning and called me in to lend a hand. 'Then take him down-stairs and give him to Ron.'

Ron, the cab driver, was parked outside Mr Ali's shop. Judging by his expression when I approached him carrying the bag, I could tell that he had expected Mr Begleiter to be alive.

'When she said she wanted him dropped awf, I thought she meant at the vet's,' he complained.

Ron peaked inside the bag.

'Awww!' he exclaimed, taking a quick step backwards and turning up his nose. 'Thas not right, is it? No, no, no. Thas not right at all!'

I stood on the pavement, unsure of what to say or do. Sadie was watching us from the window. Ron looked up at her and smiled awkwardly, muttering under his breath, 'The old dear's cracked.'

I asked Ron whether he would not take the cat as a favour and, after a moment's consideration, he agreed with a sigh.

'Normally I wouldn't do this, you understand,' he said. 'But seeing as it's Mrs Co'en . . .' He paused. 'I suppose I 'aven't got much of a choice, 'ave I?'

He opened the boot of his BMW and I laid the cat inside.

'Where have you got to take him?' I asked Ron.

'She's given me an address in Islington to drop 'im awf at. Thas all I know.'

He slammed down the boot.

'I'd better get a move on. I don't want 'im thawing out. 'e'll smell up my mow-ta.'

Mr Begleiter was returned to Sadie a couple of weeks later by special delivery, stuffed and preserved in a curled up position. She placed him on his old pillow in the corner of her main room, and soon fell back into her habit of talking to him.

'My Mendel was an Arsenal supporta. Wasn't 'e, Mr Begleiter? Never missed a match when the Gunners were at 'ome.'

But Sadie never recovered from the loss of her cat, and her health, which had started to deteriorate during the past couple of months, took a turn for the worse. She spent the next fortnight confined to her room, being visited by Solly, Ethel and Gilda, who brought her flowers, chocolates, cards and the occasional bottle of gin. Sadie was usually glad to see them, even if her appreciation was sometimes difficult to recognise. But the helpers who came to look after her – the meals on wheels delivery man and the Croatian woman who cleaned and did the laundry – usually got shouted at for their trouble, as did Sadie's doctor whose name was Pike.

'Idiot!' she would call him after he'd made one of his visits. 'Tells me I should be in an 'ome. What do I want with an 'ome for? Bleedin' nurses fussing over me all the time. 'e doesn't know nothing, that Dr Pike. And 'e's ugly. Isn't 'e, Mr Begleiter? I've seen better-looking corpses I 'ave. Why can't they send me an 'andsome doctor? Like that George Clooney. Ooooh! What I wouldn't do for the likes of George Clooney!'

Dr Pike put Sadie on a cocktail of pills, told her to rest and, despite all the abuse he had to endure, visited his patient every other day. But by the middle of May, after she started having trouble holding down her food, she was moved to Whitechapel Hospital.

Privately Dr Pike told me that Sadie had cancer and that he did not expect her to live more than a few months.

Sadie was kept in Whitechapel Hospital in a ward with a dozen other patients. She enjoyed little privacy, save for a curtain that she insisted on having drawn around her bed every morning before she put on her make-up. She was on friendly terms with the woman in the bed to her right – 'She's part Jewish on 'er Dad's side which almost makes 'er one of us' – but she took an intense dislike to the man in the bed to the left who watched snooker on the communal TV mounted on the wall, often preventing Sadie from seeing *EastEnders*.

''oo wants to watch snooker?' she hissed loudly the first time I paid her a visit in the hospital. 'Boring, thas what it is. Real men watch football. Snooker's for poofters.'

Sadie didn't have anything good to say about the hospital, either. She hated the place and wanted desperately to return to Brick Lane.

'Filthy it is in 'ere. Germs everywhere! They keep it like this deliberately so you die off quick. Don't want you taking up a bed. Beds are at a premium. I 'ad a friend 'oo came in 'ere with a leg infection and she ended up in the morgue! Keeping the population down, thas what they're doing. Dr Pike's the ringleader. Mark my words, 'e's going to do me in. Just mark my words!'

I went regularly to visit Sadie in hospital and would often read to her from *Oliver Twist*.

As the time passed, her temperament mellowed somewhat. Even her hostility towards her snooker-watching neighbour waned and she complained less about her arch-enemy, Dr Pike. But still her mood varied from day to day. At times, she could be fatalistic and talked about how she was looking forward to being reunited with her husband in the 'afterlife'. At other times, she seemed to be filled with regret and would reprimand herself for all her self-perceived faults and failings.

'I was a bad wife and that's the truth,' she sobbed one day as I sat by her bed. 'I was a bad mother and all! I could do nothing right. Nothing. I was a bleedin' disaster.'

This was the first time I had ever heard Sadie mention that she was a mother; I asked her how many children she had had.

'Just one. A boy. Michael. Michael Cohen. My son. Born and raised in Befnal Green.'

'Where is he now?'

'God only knows,' she murmured, turning on to her side away from me. ''e'd be gettin' on now. A grown man, with kids for all I know. My grandchildren, just imagine.'

On my next visit, Sadie told me the story of what had happened to her son.

'Come closer. I want to tell you something and I don't want no nosy parker's over'earing,' she said.

I drew the chair to the edge of her bed and leant forward so that our heads were only inches apart. I could hear her breathing more clearly now. It sounded like the sea washing up against a pebble shore. In the background, ECGs bleeped, and pumps worked with hypnotic regularity.

'Many years ago there was this couple 'oo lived in Befnal Green and they 'ad one son,' she began. ''e was the light of 'is mother's eye, that boy. 'andsome, strong, intelligent and kind. Nine pounds 'e weighed when 'e was born.'

She smiled to herself and her eyes, which were by now yellow and sickly, blinked in slow motion.

''e was just like 'is father. Loved to climb trees and run around. When 'e was older 'e liked to box and all. 'e 'ad lots of friends in the neighbour'ood. Never got into much trouble, really. Once in a blue moon there'd be a tussle at school, or a football would get kicked through old Mrs Sampson's front window. But that was the sum total of it. Clean as a whistle 'e was.

''is father was a good man and all. A lovin' 'usband and 'ard workin'. 'e'd 'ad an 'ard child'ood . . .' Her voice trailed away and she sighed. Then she sat up in bed a little. 'Actually, to tell you the 'onest, 'e could be very strict. And 'e 'ad a temper. Ooooh, what a temper it was! 'e 'ad very rigid ideas about certain things. Like 'oo should marry 'oo for instance. 'e'd always say, "Like should be with like," and "You don't see the robin mating with the pigeon." Basically, 'e believed that Jews should be with Jews and Gentiles should stick to their own, and there was nofing more to say on the matter. Sometimes, when Michael was older, 'e'd tell 'im, "Michael, you can marry anyone just as long as she's Jewish." Thas 'ow 'e was,' she added. 'And when 'e got something into

'is 'ead, there was no changing it. 'e was a stubborn one, my Mendel.
Stubborn like a mule.'

Sadie's narrative was interrupted by a nurse who was distributing
medicine to the patients in the ward. She gave Sadie a few pills and
the old woman swallowed them with characteristic indignation.

'Anyway. Where was I?' she asked me after the nurse had gone, and
Sadie had not failed to tell me exactly what she thought of the nurses
in the hospital and what she would have them do with their pills given
a say in the matter. 'Well. When Michael was nineteen, me and
Mendel were out one Saturday night when we sees Michael walking
with a girl. They're arm in arm they are. She was a Welsh girl, a nanny
working for a posh family up town.

'At the time, my Mendel didn't say nothing. 'e waited till Michael
got home later that evenin'. And then Mendel told 'im that 'e'd 'ave
none of it, that Jews didn't mix with *goys*, you know – Gentiles.
Michael agreed. 'e promised 'e'd never see 'er again and we took 'is
word for it. As far as we was concerned, that was the end of it.

'But about a year later, me and my Mendel was up in Victoria Park
taking in the air when what do we see but Michael with the same girl
walkin' arm in arm. Well, my Mendel went irate 'e did. Slapped
Michael 'ard in the face and called 'im a liar. When we got 'ome, 'e
took all of Michael's belongings and 'e threw the lot out the winda.
Then Michael goes and says that 'e loves 'er and that they was plannin'
on gettin' married. And then 'e goes and says some things that no son
should ever say. Terrible things 'e said. Thas when Mendel goes and
tells 'im that 'e never wants to lay eyes on 'im again.'

There were tears in Sadie's eyes now; they gathered in her sockets
and soon spilled down her cheeks.

'Michael tried to mend fences a couple of times after 'e'd got
married,' she sobbed. 'But Mendel always refused to see 'im. Said 'e'd
betrayed 'is family and 'is people. Said 'e wasn't welcome in our 'ouse.'

Sadie wiped her face with her handkerchief.

'So what did you do?' I asked her after she'd regained her compo-
sure.

'Well,' she replied, blowing her nose. 'There wasn't a lot I could do.
In them days, people 'ad strict ideas about certain things. Mendel's
family and my Mum and sisters blamed me for what 'appened. Said I

was a bad Jewish mother; 'adn't brought Michael up right. Said I was no bleedin' good they did.'

'But did your son ever contact you directly?'

Sadie played with the end of her handkerchief, looking guilty.

'One or two times maybe. I can't remember,' she replied in a quiet voice. 'I wanted to see 'im, but . . .' She paused. 'Well, to be 'onest, I never 'ad the courage to go against the wishes of my 'usband. Mendel would never 'ave allowed it. 'e would 'ave seen it as a betrayal.'

There was another pause; this one was longer.

'I loved my Mendel,' she said eventually. ''e was a wonderful 'usband. 'e always looked after me. Always said I was 'is beloved. But . . .' And here she faltered and sounded cautious. '. . .'e 'ad a side to 'im, a side that wasn't so nice to look at. It was 'arsh, if you know what I mean, 'arsh and uncompromising.'

Sadie rested her head back on the pile of pillows behind her. Up on the TV on the wall, snooker balls clinked together. The woman in the next bed was asleep and snoring; the man to the left of her was doing a crossword puzzle.

'Where's your son living now?' I asked Sadie.

'I 'eard that 'e and 'is wife went to America. That was in 1977.'

Sadie pulled up her blanket and tucked the end under her chin.

'I'll never see 'im again. But there's not a day goes by when I don't think about Michael and wonder where 'e is and feel regret for what 'appened. Such a waste when you think about it, specially 'cause nowadays no one cares 'oo marries 'oo. There's English people marrying Africans, African people marrying Indians. Gawd only knows what else! The 'ole world's gone international. Globalisation's what they call it. Jews and Gentiles – what's the difference?'

I asked her whether she had tried finding Michael.

'I wouldn't know where to start, would I? Any'ow, Michael probably 'ates me. I wouldn't blame 'im if 'e did. I was a terrible mother. A bleedin' terrible mother, and thas the truth.'

I wish I could write that I managed to track down Sadie's son before the end, but I was unable to do so. There were too many Michael Cohens listed in the US, and not enough time to telephone or write to all of them.

Despite this, however, Sadie seemed to find some peace of mind. At my suggestion, she wrote a letter to Michael, which I agreed to keep safe until such time as I might be able to locate him. And despite her distaste for rabbis, she talked with one who listened to her life story (he was with her for some time) and said some prayers by her bedside.

Not long after, she asked me to do her a final favour.

'I trust you,' she said, a couple of days before she died peacefully in her sleep. 'You're a good man you are, and I know you'll see it done.'

It was then that Sadie told me about the fortune she had squirrelled away.

'It's my life savings,' she said. 'Every penny I saved over forty years. A few quid 'ere, a few quid there. I've been saving for a rainy day. I always fancied going on an 'oliday. Like on one of them lovely cruise ships. But it's too late for that now, so I'd like to see something good done with it. See it go to somebody 'oo'll make a difference. Maybe a charity – a deserving charity, mind you.'

I suggested that cancer research might be an appropriate cause and she agreed.

'They're good people they are. Deserving I'd say. Yeah. Give 'em the lot.'

Sadie motioned for me to come closer and I leant over her bed so that she could speak in my ear.

'The cash is up the chimney,' she whispered. 'It's in a shoebox. Inside you'll find a fortune! More money than you'll ever know!'

I nodded and sat back down in the chair beside her. And then for a brief moment, she was her old self again. Her fading yellow eyes narrowed and the edge returned to her voice.

'Just don't let that Mr Ali get 'is grubby 'ands on it. A bloodsucker 'e is. A bleedin' good-for-nafing bloodsucker!'

As soon as I returned to Brick Lane later that day, I used the keys Sadie had given me to her bed-sit and searched up the chimney. There, exactly where she said it would be, I found her shoebox. It contained just over fifteen hundred pounds, most of it in old one and five pound notes. These I took down to the Bank of England to exchange and then donated the sum to Cancer Research.

Mr Ali did not wait long before clearing out Sadie's room. A couple of days before she was buried next to her husband in Chadwell Heath Cemetery, a local junk shop owner arrived with a van and carted off most of her belongings.

I managed to save some of Sadie's personal possessions including her photographs, wristwatch and bracelet, and these I put away for safe-keeping, along with her letter, just in case her son should ever appear.

I also rescued Mr Begleiter and, although it took some explaining, managed to persuade some friends who lived near Victoria Park to allow me to bury him at the end of their garden.

Sadie's bed-sit did not remain empty for long. Within days, one of Mr Ali's second cousins, Shaik, moved in with his business partner, Muksood, and made it their 'corporate headquarters'. That is to say they furnished it with a couple of desks, a few chairs, a filing cabinet, two telephones, and a nylon rug stitched with the image of a Royal Bengal Tiger.

Shaik and Muksood, who I called 'S and M', had grown up together on a council estate just off Brick Lane. The latter's father was in the 'garment business' and ran a sweatshop in Whitechapel that employed anyone willing to work a twelve-hour shift without a proper break for three pounds and ten pence an hour. His workforce comprised mostly East Europeans and the occasional Somali, although he was generally disinclined to hire Africans and was unashamedly racist about his reasons why.

It was Muksood's father's wish that his son should work for him and eventually take over the business when he retired. This was something he hoped would happen before too long as it was his intention to return to Bangladesh, build himself a house, take a second – young – wife and indulge his passion for fishing. But in order to achieve retirement bliss, Muksood senior was unwilling to pay his son much more than his labourers. It didn't help, either, that his twenty-five-year-old son hated the 'garment business'.

'I'm, like, determined to make it on my own two feet, guy,' Muksood told me when he and Shaik moved in. 'I'm, like, gonna be someone 'oo can 'old is 'ead up 'igh round 'ere, man. None of this small time bullshit, yeah. Give me a few years, yeah, and I'm gonna be, like, rollin' in it, man. Just like Alan Sugar, the Amstrad geezer. Sugar, yeah, 'e started off as a stall'older on Petticoat Lane, man. 'e didn't 'ave two pennies when 'e was my age. Grew up poor, guy. Now look at 'im, yeah. Rags to riches, man. Owns football teams and shit. If 'e can do it, I can do it, guy.'

Muksood always called everyone 'guy' or 'man' – even women, regardless of their age. Teenagers, grandmothers, elderly aunties, it didn't matter to him. 'All right, guy?' he would ask them, ''ow's it 'angin', yeah?'

Shaik, twenty-six, was not as flamboyant by contrast, but just as passionate and cocksure. He had come from extreme poverty, having grown up in a family of eight crammed into a two-bedroom flat. His dream was to own a chain of restaurants. He had worked for eight years on 'Curry Mile' as he referred to Brick Lane, starting off as a dishwasher.

'I'm gonna be, like, the Bangladeshi Terence Conran, bro,' he told me the first time we met. 'I know, like, the restaurant business inside out and it's all about innovation, innit. The average British punter doesn't want no more of your Balti and Vindaloo. Thas the past, innit. We've got to look to the future. We're talking 'aute cuisine Indian-style, bro.'

For all S and M's enthusiasm and bluster, however, it soon became clear that they were starting off in business in a small way. A couple of days after they moved in, they had an electrician fix a flashing yellow emergency beacon to the outside wall of the building, and they hung a sign to one side of our shared front door, inviting anyone wanting a taxicab to ring their own doorbell at any time of the day or night.

Within hours, the sign and the light attracted EastEnders Taxi and Limousine Service's first customers. The only problem was that, initially, S and M didn't have any cars or drivers, let alone limousines. Instead, they relied on relations and friends in the local Bangladeshi community who were interested in making themselves a few extra pounds to take on jobs as they came along.

This was not the most reliable of systems. Often, the people they depended on were either unavailable or their cars were in the garage undergoing repairs, or they could not be cajoled or persuaded into getting out of bed at two a.m. to drive to the far side of London and back. Even when someone did agree to a job, it usually took them anything up to half an hour to reach Brick Lane, by which time the customers waiting down on the street had grown irritable and, despite S and M's assurances – and downright lies – shouted abuse at them and left.

Neither Shaik nor Muksood owned a car themselves, although the latter had a driver's licence and occasionally was able to borrow his mother's 1992 Ford Escort and drive fares himself. This was not something he minded doing when the job was local and it meant taking a Bangladeshi auntie to the supermarket or collecting some kids from school. But initially, most of the trade came at night and involved driving nightclub revellers who were invariably drunk or high. His experiences in the first couple of weeks did nothing to endear him to the occupation.

'The other night, yeah, this geezer like puked 'is guts out on the back seat, guy,' Muksood told me after the business had been up and running a short while. 'I've 'ad people, like, shoutin' racialist abuse at me and refusing to pay, man. One bloke, yeah, tried to steal my stereo, and I 'ad these two gay blokes, like, 'avin' it off wiv one another, givin' each other 'and jobs in the back seat. Straight up, guy! You wouldn't believe what goes on out there, man! There's, like, a lot of sick fuckers around, yeah.'

S and M soon set about trying to recruit permanent drivers. They tried poaching some from their local rivals and found one man this way: an elderly Pakistani called Mr Pushtun, he owned a fourteen-year-old Volkswagen Passat that he talked about as if it was an old race-horse that had been great in its day. Every morning, the car required three men to push it up Bethnal Green Road to get it started.

Mr Pushtun soon proved to be as unreliable as his car. He would often disappear for hours on end and fail to answer his mobile phone. Upon his return to Brick Lane he would make excuses about his car breaking down. But it soon became clear that he was on the fiddle and regularly lied about the distances he covered, cutting S and M out of hundreds of pounds in fares.

The next driver on the scene was a stocky Ukrainian who, it transpired, was in the UK on a forged Italian passport. He drove a new BMW with leather seats, a satellite guidance system and a ten-changer CD player. S and M were suitably impressed by the car and took him at his word when he told them that he had bought it with money saved while working as a doorman in the West End. For a couple of weeks, the Ukrainian drove long hours and brought in good money. But this run of luck came to an abrupt end when the police spotted him speeding down the A4 on his way to Heathrow, realised the BMW was stolen, and, after a high-speed pursuit, arrested both the Ukrainian and his passenger, a Bangladeshi businessman booked on a flight to Dhaka.

After this incident, S and M adopted a strict policy of hiring only Bangladeshi drivers, and started to consider buying a professional radio system. To achieve this, however, would require a significant investment.

'We're talking thousands, guy,' Muksood told me about a month after they had founded their taxi company. 'No company never got nowhere without, like, a cash inject, yeah. Business is all about risk, man – know what I'm saying?'

S and M did not tell me how they came across the thousands it took to buy the equipment. But the receiver, transmitters and aerials all appeared only a few days after they were paid a visit by a suave Bangladeshi man in his forties who arrived in a chauffeur-driven four-by-four Mercedes with tinted windows.

Their visitor spent about twenty minutes with S and M in their office. After he left, the smell of expensive aftershave lingered on the stairs.

<hr />

Anu was not best pleased with the arrival of the new tenants, who were noisy and smoked a lot and made the building smell like an ashtray. Even so, she took a liking to S and M and, being reasonable, they agreed to the new ground rules that she drew up.

From then on, none of their drivers were allowed to hang about on the stairs and they had to stop leaving their cigarette butts on the floor or flicking them out of the window on to our roof garden. Teasing of Puss was banned and there were to be no more incidents of tail pulling. Conversations shouted up the stairs or from the window were no longer permitted. And finally it was absolutely forbidden ever to use our toilet again.

At Anu's insistence, I also installed a small gate across the stairs leading up to the second floor and attached a sign that read 'TRESPASSERS WILL BE SHOT'.

With the arrival of the radio equipment, EastEnders Taxi and Limousine Service was quickly transformed into an altogether more reliable entity. But the operation was still flawed. The 'fleet' of cars was a sad selection of rusty jalopies fit for a demolition derby. And, worst of all, few of the drivers, who were mostly unemployed Bangladeshis, knew their way around London.

More than once, when I made use of the firm's services, I found myself guiding the driver with an *A–Z*. One of them, who had recently come from Bangladesh and spoke only a few words of English, drove with a piece of paper taped to his dashboard that was marked in English with 'left' and 'right'. Another thought that the M25 was a West End nightclub.

And yet thanks in great part to its location, S and M's business began to prosper. Its bread and butter were school runs, the late-night trade from the bagel bakeries, and regular airport drop-offs and pick-ups. S and M also drummed up extra local business by having cards printed in English and Bengali, which were distributed through letterboxes in the neighbourhood, and by offering backhanders to the waiters in the Brick Lane restaurants for putting business their way.

The biggest boost to the business came when S and M hired a controller who was both able and trustworthy and brought with him half a dozen drivers when he defected from another firm. His name was

Gullum and he was a local Bangladeshi East Ender who had studied the Knowledge, but failed as a taxi driver because he suffered from road rage.

Gullum had the mind of a general in that he could keep the movements of all his troops in his head, while at the same time working out advance strategies for their deployment. He would have made an excellent chess player. Like any successful leader, he also knew when to be firm with his men and how to inspire them. He put in very long hours. As such, he saw little of his wife of two years, who was a nurse at a local clinic and worked the graveyard shift. On weekdays, the two of them would share at most an hour at a time together at five in the morning.

Gullum had married the nurse, a fellow British Bangladeshi, against the wishes of his family, who had objected to the fact that she had a job. For his part, he had wanted, in his own words, 'a modern girl'. But now he was not so sure. Long working hours had put a strain on their relationship and aggravated Gullum's propensity towards paranoia. As the weeks passed, he became more and more convinced that his wife was having an affair. He started calling her at all times of the day and night to check up on what she was doing. Whenever she failed to answer her mobile phone, he would grow acutely agitated, start stabbing the top of his desk with the largest blade of his penknife, and share his worst fears with whoever was sitting in the office.

Gullum became so convinced of his suspicions that he started sending drivers over to the clinic to spy on his wife's movements. Sometimes, he would instruct them to masquerade as patients or relatives visiting ailing cousins and go inside and snoop around. None of them ever reported back anything untoward. But somehow Gullum always managed to draw a measure of suspicion from their intelligence and the paranoia continued to seethe inside him.

It did not help that Gullum's mother put ideas in his head. Hardly a day passed when she would not call him at work and tell him malicious rumours about his wife. 'She should be at home looking after my son! She comes from a bad family! To think that she will be the mother of my grandchildren!'

Matters finally came to a climax when Gullum's wife spotted one of the drivers following her home and forced a confession out of him.

This led to a huge argument which culminated in Gullum insisting that his wife quit her job. Later, at the divorce proceedings, she said that she could no longer stand living with a man who placed so little trust in her. She also denied having had an affair. But the controller remained convinced otherwise.

'She was always 'anging around all those doctors and working over-time,' Gullum told me after their marriage was formally ended. 'My Mum's right. It's important we stick to our traditions. Without them, we're nothing.'

There was no need for a night-time controller. After nine p.m. most of the trade came from people ringing the buzzer in the street and the drivers were left to divide up the work amongst themselves.

There were usually half a dozen drivers on duty overnight, and sometimes, when Anu was doing the graveyard shift at the BBC and I was home alone, I would go down to the office and sit with them as they waited between jobs.

Mr Chowdhury was my favourite. A gentle father of four, he was passionate about cricket and spent a fair chunk of his earnings placing bets on matches with an illegal bookie in Dubai. Mr Chowdhury's eldest son, Julhas, also worked for the firm and had leased himself a brand new nine-seater Volkswagen people-carrier, which was his pride and joy. It was the only decent vehicle in the EastEnders' fleet and because it was so spacious, Julhas was awarded most of the airport drop-offs and pick-ups. This was a blessing and a curse. A blessing because Heathrow and Gatwick jobs were the most profitable of all; a curse because more often than not, he had to transport an extended family of Bangladeshis travelling with hundreds of kilos of luggage packed with electrical items, designer jeans and perfumes for relatives in Sylhet. Picking these customers up at the airport upon their return to Britain was no less of an ordeal, as they would invariably arrive back with bags bulging with gifts for all their relatives in the East End, wedding jewellery for their daughters, and large quantities of rice from their home villages.

Julhas's best friend was another driver called Abdul who leased his car from one of the daytime drivers and paid him a percentage of his takings. It was generally recognised that Abdul was extremely unlucky.

He was always getting involved in car accidents although none of them ever seemed to be his fault, his wife had left him for another man, and he had once won a substantial amount on the lottery only to have the ticket stolen from him.

Consequently, nobody was that surprised when one evening, as Abdul was cleaning the inside of his car, he found a pistol lying under the driver's seat. He could not be sure which of his passengers had left it there, but he guessed that it had been a couple of Jamaicans whom he had taken up to Hackney a few hours earlier. The journey had stuck in his mind because his passengers had spent the time discussing how they very much wanted to see one of their adversaries killed.

The discovery of the pistol presented Abdul with something of a dilemma. If he got rid of it by throwing it into the Thames as Julhas suggested, the Jamaicans – if it was indeed they to whom the gun belonged – might come looking for it and be upset to learn that it was lying in fifty-odd feet of water under Tower Bridge. On the other hand, as Mr Chowdhury pointed out, Abdul was unlucky and so it stood to reason that if he kept the firearm, it would be the cause of some misfortune.

After much debate and a great deal of nervous cigarette smoking, it was agreed that the best solution was to keep the gun in the office overnight and, assuming that no one came looking for it, ask Gullum's advice in the morning.

Abdul spent a sleepless night on one of the couches in the office and, when Gullum arrived the next day, he told him the whole story. The controller, who was by now divorced and generally in a better humour, inspected the firearm, pointed it at the ceiling and pulled the trigger. There was a loud click but the pistol failed to fire and, as the drivers gathered round, Gullum started to laugh.

'It's a replica, you idiots,' he said.

Whitechapel Road was one place where I always got a sense that the East End had not changed as much as some people liked to suggest.

True, the hay market that was held there for centuries had vanished and the wide pavement that ran between Vallance Road and Cambridge Heath Road was no longer the Saturday night promenade of young Jewish men and women. The trams, horses and carts were gone, and the architectural landscape had been greatly altered: the old Whitechapel Bell Foundry (which has been in the same building since 1670 and produced the Liberty Bell and Big Ben) was now surrounded by ugly office blocks and the architecturally dull East End mosque.

I feel sure that Dickens's character, Sam Weller, who travelled along the crowded, filthy street in the 1830s with Mr Pickwick and remarked that it was 'not a wery nice place', would have barely recognised the physical aspect of the East End of today. But he would have found something familiar about the busy open-air market that operates on the same wide pavement along the Whitechapel Road. For it is here that the underbelly of London is most exposed, and although there is nothing glamorous about it and the rows of shops, the railings, the lamp-posts and litter combine to make it a distinctly un-exotic scene, the sheer volume and variety of humanity is as extraordinary as ever. Charles Booth's 'great stream of London life' surges down the pavements of Whitechapel Road as vigorously as ever.

As one stallholder put it to me when I was walking through the market one day and we got chatting: 'It's a zoo this place. Stand here for just one minute and it's amazing what you'll see.'

I decided to put this to the test and, taking out my personal journal, wrote down everything that came into view within the space of sixty seconds. I was hard pressed to keep up. Hawkers sold DVDs, smuggled cigarettes, perfumes and batteries. Stallholders flogged everything from fruit and vegetables to carpet offcuts and fake mink coats. An Albanian woman in a headscarf clutching a child and a dog-eared note that explained her circumstances begged for money. An Afghan wearing a *karakol* hat and a *patu* shawl with some kilims draped over his shoulder strode past with the purpose of the hill men of the North-West Frontier. A spotty white teenager selling cigarette lighters called out to the crowd. A Rasta stumbled out of the Seven Stars pub. Next came three Indian women carrying bulging plastic bags printed with the name of a Whitechapel sari emporium, followed by some Nigerians dressed in traditional *geles* and *ipeles*. A couple of black kids in hoods and baseball hats slalomed through the crowd on bicycles. A fishmonger selling unappetising hunks of frozen cod in plastic bags shouted out his prices. A young bank clerk with a Barclays name tag pinned to his suit walked briskly towards the underground station. Two Albanians started shouting at one another and it looked as if it would turn nasty. A heavily veiled woman scurried along the pavement with head bent forward. A couple of Chinese haggled over the price of a stereo. An Iraqi Kurd handed out anti-Saddam literature to passers-by. Two policemen strolled through the bustling crowd – either unbothered by the black economy that thrived around them or powerless in the face of it all.

S and M set up their new venture, an international call centre, on Whitechapel Road, a stone's throw from where Dr Frederick Treves discovered the Elephant Man in a freak show in 1884. The two entrepreneurs opened the business in mid-July and, like the cab company, it quickly proved a cash cow. There were nine booths in all, each with its own phone, an LCD counter that clocked the length and cost of each call, a chair, and an extractor fan. At the back of the shop, S and M had a new office. It was quieter than their one on Brick Lane and more spacious, but Muksood still had his sights set higher.

'This is, like, only temporary, guy,' Muksood told me the first time I visited their new establishment. 'Before long, yeah, we'll 'ave proper office space, man, with secretaries with wicked legs! I'm gonna 'ave one of them leather chairs that, like, spin arand, man, and a big mahogany desk that you can see your own reflection in, guy.'

As well as opening the call centre, S and M were planning to start their own estate agency as well.

'There's all these Bangladeshi families round 'ere that are, like, selling up their property, guy. At the same time, you've got all these yuppies paying crazy money to live 'ere, yeah. Fuck knows why, man. I mean it ain't Beverly 'ills, guy. Come to fink on it, it ain't even Stamford 'ill – know what I'm saying, man?'

The customers who used S and M's international call centre were all economic refugees and asylum seekers drawn from every corner of the globe. They came in their hundreds to the shop every day. The first always arrived just before seven in the morning when the doors opened; the last had to be turned away when the place closed at eleven p.m.

From the back office, I would sometimes sit and watch them come and go. They were the most unlikely assortment of people I had ever seen. Afghans, Burmese, Chinese, Congolese, Iraqis, Kosovars, Liberians, Nigerians, Senegalese, Sri Lankans, the occasional Lithuanian and many more besides. Few of them talked to one another; more often than not, language proved too great a barrier. And yet, their past experiences were chillingly similar, their current circumstances invariably the same. The victims of civil wars, political repression and economic hardship, they had fled or been driven from their homelands, travelled thousands of miles through the harshest of terrains, braved the most inhuman of conditions, and now found themselves part of the human stewpot of Whitechapel, the place George Orwell described in *Down and Out in Paris and London* as 'the land of the tea urn and the Labour Exchange'.

Some of those who came to use the call centre were worse off materially than others, to the point of destitution. It was not uncommon to see someone who was sleeping rough, and whose hair and clothes were filthy, carrying a blanket and a bag that contained all their worldly possessions. On one occasion, I saw a Liberian who had pieces of cardboard for inner soles and a half-eaten corncob protruding from the pocket of his frayed tweed jacket; another time, I saw an East European who smelt like bad fish, and had cuts and bruises on his face.

There were also those who, on the face of it, did not look so badly off, but whose awkward demeanours suggested that they had fallen far. Such was my impression of the Iranian man who visited the call centre one day with his wife and two young children. He was a quiet, polite man with a neat moustache and an air of pride who looked as if he belonged on a university campus. His children were well behaved and, while their father made his call, huddled around their mother as though on board a ship that was in danger of sinking.

From S and M's office, I watched the Iranian make his call and then go to pay his bill. But when he took out his wallet, he realised that he did not have enough cash and, standing in front of the counter, searched frantically through his pockets for a forgotten note or some loose change. Finding none, he turned to his wife, but she had no money either and started to cry, drawing her children ever closer around her, as if she was worried that someone was going to take them away.

I decided to step forward and settle the bill. But before I could do so, one of the men who ran the call centre on behalf of S and M – a Somali whose nickname was Wiil Waal, which meant 'Crazy Boy' – waived the remaining balance.

The Iranian man looked visibly shocked by this act of generosity and assured the Somali that he could return with more money in fifteen minutes. But Wiil Waal insisted that this was unnecessary and that the Iranian could pay back the money when it was convenient for him to do so.

Thanking him profusely, the Iranian shook Wiil Waal energetically by the hand and then shepherded his wife and children out through the call centre's front door and into the bustle of Whitechapel Road.

There was always a queue inside the call centre. Sometimes, when it was really busy, it extended out into the street and customers could wait up to an hour until a booth became vacant. Occasionally, those unfamiliar with the concept of queuing would lose patience and try to barge their way to the front. Pushing and shoving led to arguments and sometimes arguments led to fights. It was for this reason that S and M employed a Nigerian called Tokunbo who was handy with his fists, although he rarely had cause to use them as his size and build were generally sufficient to deter troublemakers.

When customers eventually gained access to a booth and closed the door behind them, they would reach into their pockets or search through their wallets and handbags and take out small phone books or scruffy pieces of paper with long numbers written on them. Then the process of dialling would begin and the digits would appear on the LCD mounted on the wall. Codes for some of the remotest towns and cities in the world would flash up: Chittagong, Jaffna, Kismaayo, Mazar-i-Sharif.

If a connection was made – and it generally took more than a few attempts to get through – the lines were often poor and customers had to shout to be heard, their voices penetrating the glass walls of their booth and disturbing their neighbours. Often more than one person occupied the same booth at the same time and people would stand together with the earpiece held between them, taking turns to talk or shout into the receiver.

It was unusual if a call did not engender some form of emotional reaction and, thanks to the lack of privacy, everyone was on display for everyone else to see. Sometimes the news from home was good and there were laughter and smiles and occasionally whoops of joy and hallelujahs. It was not uncommon for a customer to learn of the birth of a child or hear news of a parent's recovery from a medical procedure or be told that peace had come to their homelands or that the rains had finally arrived after years of drought.

But more often than not, there were tears – tears shed at the sound of a familiar voice; tears accompanied by deep sobs that indicated that some tragedy had occurred back home. And from time to time, the tears turned to hysterical sobbing or screaming, and customers would clutch their heads in their hands. Occasionally, they would sink down on to the floor of the booth.

Tokunbo always gave distraught customers as much time as they needed on the phone. But usually the house rules applied and use of each booth was restricted to fifteen minutes. The Nigerian kept a careful eye on each individual LCD counter to make sure nobody exceeded their limit. Once a customer's time was up, he would tap on the glass door and indicate to them that they should hang up the phone. Generally this action provoked a nod of resignation and the caller would quickly say their goodbyes. But sometimes people kept on talking or turned their backs to Tokunbo; worse still, some used offensive hand signals that were universally understood. Such responses could lead to people being abruptly pulled from their booths and shoved out on to the street. Only once did this course of action end in a fight, which was brought to a quick conclusion by one of Tokunbo's right hooks.

As well as overseeing the running of the call centre, Wiil Waal was responsible for organising international money transfers via Western Union on behalf of customers wishing to send home cash to their families. More often than not, the amounts were small: usually no more than fifty pounds at a time. The largest transaction he had ever handled was for five hundred pounds. The sum had been sent by a fellow Somali who had spent months saving up so that his brother in Mogadishu could get married.

'In Somalia one family can survive on fifty pound for one month easy,' said Wiil Waal during our first conversation. 'People must send money. It is their responsibility.'

Wiil Waal himself sent whatever cash he had to spare to his mother and two sisters who were still in Mogadishu.

'Without this, what will they do? There is no work in Somalia. Only war. If there is peace, then I love to return to my country. But if I go today, other men will shoot me for sure. The hour I arrive, I will be kill-ed.'

Like most of the ten to fifteen thousand Somalis living in Whitechapel, Wiil Waal had fled his homeland during the early 1990s at the height of the civil war. He had done so after his father and three brothers were killed in a blood feud. Wiil Waal had found himself the only surviving male member of his family and it had fallen to him to take up a Kalashnikov and fight. But Wiil Waal was a rare exception amongst Somali males: he was a coward or a pacifist, depending on your point of view.

'You must not tell any person,' he insisted when he admitted his secret to me one day. 'In my heart I do not want to kill people. I try many times to shoot. I cannot. In my country this is big problem. All men are fighting. So I run away. I said goodbye to my homeland. Perhaps I will not see it again. Only God can tell.'

After making his way through the Middle East and Europe, he had got across the Channel and claimed political asylum. In London, he had hoped to escape his past. But upon arriving in Whitechapel, he had found the streets crowded with fellow Somali refugees.

'Coming here, I think that I am in Mogadishu and I become very scared. I think maybe someone will try to kill me or I must kill another man. But in Whitechapel, Somali people do not have gun and RPGs' – rocket-propelled grenades. 'This is good because when Somali people have gun and RPG then they like to kill each other very much. Yes! I see you laugh. But it is true.'

Still, his community was not without its problems. Although there had been a Somali presence in the East End for more than a century, its number had ballooned in recent years. Many young Somalis, who had known nothing but war and starvation at home, were struggling to acclimatise to East End life. They faced a certain amount of hostility from the Bangladeshis, which spilled into occasional bouts of violence.

Wiil Waal was a rarity in that he was working for Bangladeshis (they needed him to communicate with their many Somali customers) and had made a conscientious effort to learn English as well.

'Somali men like two thing: fighting and football. All day they watch. Yes, they are watching every time.'

Wiil Waal said that his friends had all taken to following the British league and supported local London teams. On most evenings, they could be found gathered in select Somali-owned Whitechapel cafés and eateries with wall-mounted TVs to watch. But Wiil Waal rarely joined them.

'Football is stupid game,' he said.

Being football crazy was another characteristic of his fellow countrymen that Wiil Waal did not share.

On a Friday not long after it opened, S and M's call centre was robbed. At seven in the evening, three masked men armed with knives burst into the shop and forced Wiil Waal to hand over the hundreds of pounds in the till and safe. He cooperated without hesitation and, a few hours later, when I passed by, he was still wringing his hands with guilt.

'I am a coward,' he said. 'If I could fight, I could stop them. But I did nothing and gave them all the money.'

The robbery had been captured on the in-shop CCTV cameras, but surprisingly S and M had not reported the crime.

'Waas the point, guy?' said Muksood. 'The police are useless, man. I mean, they don't care. If I was white, it would be different, yeah.

But they're racialist, innit. They ain't gonna do nothing for me, man. We're gonna 'af to take matters into our own 'ands, guy.'

He wouldn't tell me what he meant by this. But as I left an hour or so later, I saw the suave-looking businessman who had visited S and M on Brick Lane pull up in his chauffeur-driven Mercedes.

Perhaps it was just a coincidence, but the next time I paid S and M a visit, a few days later, they told me that the money had been returned anonymously. Although neither of them would elaborate as to how this had come about, Muksood did say that it had been through 'connections, guy'.

9

The People of the Abyss

'As there is a darkest Africa, is there not also a darkest England?'
William Booth, *In Darkest England and the Way Out* (1890)

I THOUGHT SUMMER would make Brick Lane more tolerable. But if anything, it was worse. Sunshine did nothing to brighten up the street; instead it probed into every crooked crevice, highlighting the dirt and grunge which had lain camouflaged in shadow until now. Every wart and blemish could be clearly seen – from the black blobs of chewing gum ground into the paving stones, to the layers of filth that coated the windowpanes like volcanic ash.

The crisp blue skies and high, fluffy clouds contrasted sharply with sagging roofs, crooked chimney pots and rusting TV aerials. Suddenly the view from our kitchen window was less appealing than ever. The row of 1950s office blocks along Bethnal Green Road stood like beetle-browed Scrooges, uttering a defiant 'humbug!' to the sunshine that splashed across their façades. The brick hulk of the Bishopsgate Goods Yard as well as the glass and steel office blocks of the City combined to form an urban fortress impervious to Mother Nature.

Brick Lane was the last place I would have freely chosen to spend a summer's day. Still, the warm weather brought more trendy Londoners to the street than ever. The longer days also meant the tramps spent longer hours on their patch of pavement, which, thanks to the dry spell, grew ever filthier. Noise levels increased as every Bangladeshi teenager in the neighbourhood with access to a set of wheels took to cruising the street playing Gangsta Rap at full volume. And the lack of wind meant that pollution levels rose and the smell of A1 Halal Fried Chicken hung permanently in the air.

The arrival of a regiment of workmen armed with pneumatic drills who spent the best part of July punching holes in the junction with Bethnal Green Road only added to our misery, as did the strike by the local dustmen which caused mountains of black refuse bags to pile up on the pavements, attracting an army of rats.

Worst of all was the oven-like heat in the attic. At night, it was as bad as anything I had experienced in Delhi, except that here on Brick Lane we had to live without the luxury of air-conditioning. Two electric fans that Anu persuaded Mr Ali to lend us helped. But when the electricity meters ran out of money and switched themselves off in the middle of the night, we would wake up in a slick of sweat.

Our one reprieve from the heat, pollution and noise was Anu's roof garden. By now, it was the envy of our neighbours, a haven bursting with colour and scent. The jasmine had shot up ten feet. The passion flower vines were dotted with oblong, orange fruits. Broccolis and cauliflowers had begun to emerge from their nests of leaves. Honeybees buzzed amongst the roses and lavender.

It was here that we spent many of our evenings, drinking, reading, chatting, playing cards, and sometimes barbecuing and entertaining friends. Puss also spent a good deal of her time on the roof. In the mornings, she enjoyed stretching out on the warm asphalt. And once the sun dipped below the tops of the terraced houses, she would spend hours perched on the wall that divided our property from our asylum-seeking neighbours.

The hot weather did nothing to improve local dispositions. Tempers in the Sunday market were often strained, there were numerous incidents of road rage at the traffic lights, and whenever we went shopping on Bethnal Green Road, we heard people arguing and occasionally getting into fights.

Only Mr Singh seemed impervious to the heat. He stood at the back of his newsagents, which was uncomfortably hot and stuffy, dressed in one of the cardigans that his wife had knitted for him, puzzling over why everyone was making such a fuss about the weather.

'Personally I am not understanding,' he told me one day when all the newspaper headlines blared 'HEATWAVE'. 'Punjabi people are knowing proper heat. Not like your silly British summer. In India many people are dying from high temperatures every day. Real heat-wave is there.'

Mr Singh seemed to take a certain pride in this fact and nodded sagely to me as I stood on the other side of his counter.

'Certainly,' he continued, 'there is no pleasing you British. Always you are making complaint. When it is cold, you are making complaint, when it is hot, you are making complaint. Why not put up and shut up?'

He had a point. Only that morning, I had been in the post office where a couple of old women had stood in line moaning as usual about the weather.

'Aw! Ain't it awful? I've never known it so 'ot. Last night I 'ad to sleep with the winda open. It's like being in the bleedin' black 'ole 'a Cal-cut-a!'

But the phenomenon was not new. As I told Mr Singh, there is a passage in *East End My Cradle* by Willy Goldman in which he recalls summer descending 'like a scourge' –

> another burden from nature to add to those already imposed on us by man . . . The main problem was not to get in the way of the sun's rays but to dodge them. People continually moved their chairs to which-ever side of the street got the shade. They hated the sun. They talked about it in the same opprobrious terms they used for the rain and snow.

Mr Singh was thoroughly fed up with the British obsession with the weather.

'All day long I must listen to these people's negative sentiments,' he said. 'Really they are not knowing the half of it. If they spent one day in Calcutta, then their goose would be most definitely cooked. Sheer ignorance is there only.'

Mr Singh was equally mystified as to why many of his white customers insisted on walking around half naked during the summer.

'It is common to see these fat fellows standing bare-chested with no shirts on,' he said. 'I have noticed that many of them are low caste and congregate outside pubs. They have large hairy stomachs protruding most disagreeably over the tops of their trousers.'

He shook his head disapprovingly.

'Actually, I must say that it is a most unattractive sight,' he added. 'It is showing disrespectability also.'

———— ♦ ————

It was just such a sticky, disagreeable day that brought a change in my fortunes.

One morning, I ambled downstairs to collect the post and found a letter from the publisher, John Murray, lying amongst the usual collection of junk mail and pizza flyers.

I regarded the envelope, which was stamped with the company's crest, with trepidation. Most probably, I thought to myself, it was a rejection letter like the others I had received, saying that my manuscript was 'not quite right' for them.

Picking it up hesitantly, I took it upstairs and gave it to Anu to open.

She was sitting up in bed, listening to the *Today* programme and drinking a mug of tea. Her faith in the book had been shaken as much as mine and, as she opened the envelope, I could tell that she was bracing herself for the worst.

Her eyes widened on reading it.

'They want it, they want it! They want your book!'

I grabbed the letter from her and read it myself just to check that Anu's eyesight was not playing tricks on her. Then I let out a whoop of delight and the two of us jumped up and down in the middle of the room, being careful – as ever – not to bump our heads on the low ceiling.

The fact that John Murray was only offering four thousand pounds for the book did not matter to me. It was reward enough that my manuscript, *To the Elephant Graveyard* as it was to be called, was going to be published. Besides, the money would more than cover a deposit on a flat in a better area of London and pay off my overdraft.

I felt a new-found enthusiasm for the future. But I made the mistake of thinking this good news would lay Anu's fears to rest, too.

As we talked, she made it clear that while she was overjoyed at the prospect of escaping from Brick Lane, she was still not convinced that London was the place for her.

'When you asked me to marry you, I didn't realise what your country was like, or how much I'd have to adjust,' she said.

The next few weeks brought a new round of friction, arguments and tears. More than once, Anu's engagement ring came off and she packed her bags. Never before had we come so close to going our separate ways. At times I found myself wondering if perhaps our parents had been right after all.

In my heart I knew that if it came to it I would give up living in London for Anu. But I felt strongly that England was the right place for us to be. I just hoped that I could convince her, too – or better still, that she would find her own reasons to stay.

That month also brought good and bad news for my friends next door.

First came the bad news.

After all his efforts handing out flyers around London, Gul Muhammad had finally discovered the truth about the fate of his brother, Hamidullah. The information had come to him from another Afghan asylum seeker now living in London who had travelled with Hamidullah from Istanbul to Albania.

The Afghan told Gul Muhammad that in March the previous year, Hamidullah had paid a gang of Albanian people smugglers to take him to Italy. Under cover of darkness, he and about twenty others – including the other Afghan – had boarded a fishing boat and set off across the Adriatic. A few miles off the Italian coast, their vessel was intercepted by the coast guard, and as the unscrupulous smugglers attempted to make their escape, they forced their human cargo overboard.

According to the Afghan informant, the Italians managed to rescue half a dozen of the refugees; Hamidullah was not amongst them. Gul Muhammad said that his brother did not know how to swim.

Big Sasa told me the story one Sunday morning when we went to watch a football match on Weaver's Fields – off Vallance Road, where the Kray Twins grew up. The match was being played between a team of Kosovars and Somalis, all of them asylum seekers. Little Sasa was in goal, standing between two motorway traffic cones that were half his size. Big Sasa stood on one of the sidelines along with about a dozen of his fellow countrymen, shouting encouragement to their team.

It was a beautiful, clear day. Beyond the pitch, groups of teenagers kicked footballs back and forth. Parents pushing prams and men walking dogs passed along the pathway that cut across the wide expanse of grass. A couple of drunks sat on a bench soaking up the sunshine and cans of lager. Kids on mountain bikes practised jumps on a mound of dirt near the main gate.

'How is Gul Muhammad taking the news?' I asked Big Sasa, whose eyes were firmly fixed on the match and the progress of the ball.

'Really he is very sad and angry also,' replied the Kosovar, who was beginning to develop the first hints of an Estuary accent. 'He says he prefer to go to Albania for killing mafia people and he – '

Big Sasa turned suddenly to shout encouragement to Little Sasa, who had just made a spectacular save. Then for a brief moment he looked away from the pitch and shot me a concerned look.

'Really he is serious, I think. Afghan people prefer to make . . .'

'. . . revenge?' I added.

'Revenge, yes. It is their custom. I have worry for him.'

I watched the game, quietly contemplating what Big Sasa had just told me. I knew something of the Pushtun tradition of revenge; an Afghan in Peshawar on Pakistan's North-West Frontier had once told me how he murdered his brother-in-law for raping his sister. It was not inconceivable that Gul Muhammad would try to get back at the Albanians who had been responsible for his brother's death.

'We should talk to him,' I said. 'This isn't Afghanistan. He can't go round murdering people. He's bound to get caught.'

My last sentence was drowned out by the roar of approval from the fifty or so Somali supporters standing on the opposite sideline whose team had gained possession of the ball and pushed through the Kosovar defence. Their attack culminated in a kick by their star centre forward, which curled round the inside of one of the traffic cones, leaving Little Sasa sprawled across the grass. The Somalis hugged and celebrated and cheered. The Kosovars muttered their disappointment.

'Really Little Sasa is very good goalkeeper,' Big Sasa told me, apparently concerned lest I be left with anything but the most favourable impression of his friend's football skills. 'I think he can be profession, yes! Like your David Beckham!'

The score was now Kosovo two, Somalia one, with ten minutes left of the second half. The Kosovars' lead seemed remarkable given the obvious bias of the Nigerian referee towards his fellow Africans. Throughout the match, he had chosen to ignore a number of spectacular Somali fouls. He had also turned a blind eye to the fact that, before the match and during half time, most of the Somali players had been chewing qat leaves, which act as a stimulant.

'So what's your good news?' I asked Big Sasa, once play had resumed.

'Yes, I tell you,' he said, lowering his voice and taking a sideways step towards me. 'But please you must not to say to any person. It is secret, yes.'

I agreed.

'OK,' he said, trying to suppress a grin. 'Last week, I meet a woman.' The grin spread across his face into a broad smile. 'She is very beautiful and nice.'

I clapped him on the back. 'That's great. So who is she?'

'OK, I tell,' he said, still watching the match as he talked. 'Her name is Ravesa. I meet her at one café. It is where she work. I go for sandwich and after, I think about her very much.'

This first encounter had taken place nearly three weeks earlier; since then Big Sasa had returned to the café three or four times.

'When we talk first, she is very nervous. She is young woman. Twenty-three maybe. She tells me she is Italian. But really I know she is Albanian. I can see. So I tell her please no worry, I not tell no person. Then she make conversation with me and it is very nice.'

Had he taken her out on a date?

'No. Every day, she is working long hour. Mostly she is very tired. But don't worry, I have plan. I take her to one shop in Knightersbridge. It is named 'arrods. It is very luxury place, yes?'

'Yes, Harrods,' I said. 'It's a famous department store.'

'Yes, famous. I think Ravesa will be liking it very much. Next week, I ask her.'

He smiled again, but his expression quickly turned to displeasure as the Somalis pushed up the pitch and their centre forward, who was clearly offside, scored another goal. The Kosovar team surged around the referee, shouting some choice Balkan insults, while my fellow supporters bellowed their disapproval from the sidelines. Big Sasa kicked at the ground in protest.

'Really, this referee is donkey,' he said.

———————◆———————

As the month drew on, the two Sasas were offered work as casual farmhands. Big Sasa had to put plans to take Ravesa on a date on hold as he left for Cambridge, expecting to be away for a month or more. In their absence, Gul Muhammad, who seemed to be dealing with the news of his brother's death remarkably well, took in a room-mate called Salah al-din, a man in desperate need of help.

Salah, as he was known, shared the same name as the great Middle Eastern hero, better known in the West as Saladin. Like his namesake, he was regarded by most Westerners – including a number of officials in the Home Office – as an Arab. It was a misconception that he found both irritating and distressing, not least because he was a member of a proud race that had been robbed of its sovereignty and, for the best part of a century, struggled to retain its identity in the face of prejudice and ruthless persecution.

'It is true of course that the great Salah al-din spoke Arabic just as I do,' he said proudly the first time we met standing out on the roof, explaining that he was from Kirkuk in Iraq. 'But like him, I am a Kurd.'

Mention of the great Kurdish conqueror stirred bravado in Salah. But he did not cut the popular image of a warrior Kurd. An engineer with a degree from Baghdad University, he was short, stocky and bespectacled, with salt and pepper hair, and soft green eyes that betrayed the pacifist within. His voice had a calming quality and he often ended a sentence with a shy smile that pinched his burnished cheeks. His favourite pastime was to sit amongst Anu's rose bushes drinking iced tea and reading *The Rubáiyát of Omar Khayyám*. Sometimes, he would pick a marigold flower and tuck it into the buttonhole of his crumpled tweed jacket.

Yet despite Salah's quiet nature, he had been to war and killed his fellow man. The exact number was a question to which he would never know the answer. He had never been involved in hand-to-hand combat. But during advances into Iranian territory, he had seen the aftermath of Iraqi artillery offensives in which he had played a part: trenches scattered with shattered bodies; body parts rotting in the mud; the faces of the slaughtered frozen in panic and agony – hellish images that still crowded his nightmares.

'Saddam made me fight,' Salah told me a couple of days after we first met as we walked together along Bethnal Green Road towards Victoria Park where he liked to admire the roses and feed the ducks. 'He held a gun to my head and gave me no choice.'

'Do you mean Saddam personally held a gun to your head?' I asked him, my journalistic curiosity titillated by this detail.

'With Saddam there is no difference,' he answered. 'If someone in Iraq is murdered, it is on Saddam's orders. If someone is raped, it is on Saddam's orders. If someone has their tongue cut out, it is on Saddam's orders. If someone is executed as a deserter, it is on Saddam's orders. Everything comes from Saddam Hussein. So I should say, yes, Saddam personally held a gun to my head. He was not there in the room, but there was no need. Saddam is Iraq and Iraq is Saddam. There is no separating the two.'

Salah walked with his hands behind his back, absent-mindedly playing with his prayer beads, moving them one by one along their nylon thread. His face was dark against the sun climbing through the sky behind him, but I could make out the deep furrows that ran across his forehead and the twitch beneath his eye.

'I am sorry,' he said as we reached the entrance to the park, pausing in front of the wrought-iron gates. 'It is not right to burden you with my difficulties. Did not Khayyám say, "Your fate is fixed, and grieving will not cheat it." Let us talk of other matters.'

He pulled a newspaper cutting from his pocket and unfolded it.

'I have been reading in yesterday's newspaper that your House of Lords is to be reformed. This is most interesting. Tell me, does this signal the end of your monarchy as one writer in this newspaper seems to suggest? Are the Socialists plotting the overthrow of the Royal Family as they did in Iraq?'

It was typical of Salah to be so formal. Although in the coming weeks we spent many hours in one another's company as I tried my best to help him improve his circumstances, he always spoke to me in a modest, self-effacing manner that was charmingly old-fashioned. He regarded any gesture of friendship – even something as simple as an invitation to tea – as an act of immeasurable generosity, which he always had to be cajoled into accepting. Around Anu, he was like a fawning courtier. He always gave up his chair for her and invariably asked after her health and the well-being of her entire family. When she assured him that they were all fine, he would nod and smile, and then do his best to ensure that the conversation excluded anything he deemed unsuitable for her ears.

'Ladies should not be troubled with the worries of the world,' he once told me. 'It can be most upsetting for them.'

But since Anu had not accompanied us to the park, I persisted in questioning him about his past – that is, after a short digression on the controversies surrounding the House of Lords reforms, which, I assured him, would not result in the Queen and her immediate family being machine-gunned in the throne room. I persuaded him to tell me how it was that he escaped from the Iranian front.

'I was wounded in the leg,' he said. 'It was not serious, but thanks to Allah, the doctor made an error on my medical records and I was discharged from the army.'

Salah went on to explain – albeit reluctantly – that in early 1982, he returned to Kirkuk. At the time, life for the Kurdish and Turkoman population was growing ever more precarious. Saddam's programme to Arabise the city had already driven many into the hills. However, Salah came from a wealthy family with influence (his father was a university professor) and he landed a job with the national oil company. Soon after, he married and, within the year, his wife gave birth to their first child, a girl whom they named Serferaz.

Over the course of the next sixteen years, Salah steered clear of politics and, despite the ongoing Kurdish insurrection and the 1991 uprising, he retained his job. While many others suffered under the United Nations sanctions imposed during the Gulf War, Salah was able to draw on savings to feed his family and ensure they remained in good health.

Then, in 1999, events turned against him.

'My daughter, Serferaz, is a very beautiful girl,' continued Salah who had brought some stale bread with him to the park, which he picked apart and threw to the collection of pigeons, ducks, geese and seagulls that had gathered around us. 'She is as lovely as the morning sun and she has her mother's intelligence. Many parents expressed an interest in marrying her to one of their sons. But she was only sixteen and it was my wish that she should finish her education.

'One day a senior police officer came to my house. I knew him by reputation as a bad fellow. He told me that he wanted my daughter to marry his son. When I refused, he threatened me. He said that unless I agreed, I would be arrested and thrown into prison, and that my wife, my two daughters and my home would be taken from me. He gave me one day to think it over and promised to return the following evening to hear my answer.'

Within hours of the visit, Salah made the decision to leave Kirkuk and head for the Kurdish safe haven to the north out of reach of the Ba'athist authorities. He took with him his wife, his two daughters, his parents, the family jewellery and savings, and all the possessions they could pack on to one roof rack. They left Kirkuk in the dead of night and headed for the border. At the Iraqi checkpoint, they had to bribe the police and soldiers to be allowed to cross the boundary. Finally, they arrived in the city of Arbil and, from there, travelled to Zakhu where Salah had family.

'In this world I have seen no justice,' continued Salah. 'But it is comforting for me to know that, ultimately, Allah will be the judge of all our actions. There is no escaping His scrutiny. The hour will come when Saddam will answer for his crimes. In the end, he will not escape justice. Allah will see to that.'

A few months after reaching Zakhu, Salah had left northern Iraq, hoping to get to the United States and find a job in the oil industry.

In the past he had worked with many Americans and always found them friendly and positive, although often ignorant of his culture. He had felt confident they would help him now in his hour of need.

Leaving his family in the care of some cousins, he had crossed by land into Turkey and then, travelling on a forged passport purchased on the black market in Istanbul, by plane to London. At Heathrow, he had tried to board a flight to New York. But at the gate, an eagle-eyed airline official had stopped him and, for the past year, he had been trapped in London.

At first, the British authorities had looked after him. While the Home Office considered his application for political asylum, they had provided him with a room in a council flat in Peckham (which he had shared with two Turks masquerading as Kurds) and food vouchers to the tune of thirty-odd pounds a week. Salah had not sat idle during this time. He had written numerous letters to oil companies in the United States applying for jobs, and petitioned the American embassy in Grosvenor Square for a visa. He had also made the most of London itself, criss-crossing the city on foot and visiting its many free museums and parks. Salah had watched the Trooping of the Colour and fed the pigeons in Trafalgar Square. The highlight of his time in the capital had been the opportunity to watch 'the mother of all Parliaments' in action.

'That is something I will never forget,' he told me once. 'You have your freedom. That is the greatest gift of all.'

A couple of weeks before Salah moved in with Gul Muhammad, however, the Home Office had rejected his application for political asylum on the grounds that he was not a victim of political persecution.

'They said that my problems were personal and not with the regime,' he told me. 'They said that as a Kurd I would be safe in northern Iraq, because it is under the protection of the United Nations. They do not understand that I have no property or job in that place. I am a refugee even in my own country.'

The Home Office ruling meant that he quickly lost his right to housing, food vouchers and access to the National Health system. He was expressly forbidden from working in the UK. Bizarrely, however, the decision had not resulted in his deportation. The absence of diplomatic relations between London and Baghdad (not to mention flights to the country) made it impossible to send him back to Iraq. Returning him to Turkey (from where he had flown into London) was not an option either, given that Salah was not in possession of a genuine passport.

In short, the Labour government had cast him adrift. Salah had joined the ranks of thousands of refugees in London whom Mr Ali referred to as 'the nowhere people'.

'I don't understand their thinking,' said Salah. 'They will tell you that Saddam is a bad man, that his regime is responsible for gross human rights abuses and that he is an aggressor. These are the reasons why they have imposed years of sanctions on Iraq. But when I come to them and present my case, they say, "No. You are not being persecuted. We reject you. You must go back." It is extraordinary.'

Salah was now utterly destitute. When he moved in with Gul Muhammad, he had five pounds in his pocket and owned a few shirts, his tweed jacket which was crudely stitched together at the shoulders where the material had split, one pair of black shoes with soles worn wafer thin, some socks and underwear, a toothbrush, a comb, a razor, a bar of soap, a condensed edition of the *Rubáiyát*, a magnifying glass, three pens that protruded from the top of his breast pocket, a wallet that contained a few photographs of his family, and his set of prayer beads. All this he was able to fit into one Adidas sports bag. A twisted ankle, injured during a fall on Whitechapel Road, meant that he would be unable to work for some weeks to come.

'So what will you do?' I asked him, trying to think how I might be able to help.

'I must reach America. I will continue to make my appeal to them. I cannot go back to Iraq. How can I? I have no money and the people smugglers do not provide return tickets.'

Salah put a brave face on his circumstances and would often quote from Khayyám –

'Man, like a ball, hither and thither goes
As fate's resistless bat directs the blows;
But He, who gives thee up to this rude sport,
He knows what drives thee, yea, He knows, He Knows!'

But he missed his family desperately and wrote to them several times a week.

One day when we were together, he mentioned that he had not been able to talk to them for a fortnight, and I offered him the use of my phone. Typically, Salah resisted the idea at first and said that he could not possibly accept my generosity. But I insisted and eventually he agreed on the understanding that he would time the call and pay me back when he had the means. To appease him, I agreed, led him up to the attic and showed him the phone. Leaving him there on his own, I returned downstairs to the kitchen.

Ten minutes later, Salah came down and joined me. I could see that he had been crying. His shirt was stained with tears. I asked him what was the matter and more tears ran down his face. He wiped them away self-consciously.

'Sadly my father expired four days ago,' he said. 'He has been buried in Zakhu. I am sad that I could not have been there to pay my respects. But it is Allah's will that I am here, and who am I to argue with my fate?'

For the Sasas, the opportunity to work in the English countryside had, at first, seemed appealing. Like the Cockneys who traditionally spent their summers picking hops in Kent, they had been looking forward to putting the East End behind them and enjoying the fresh air of East Anglia. What's more, the ask-no-questions, cash-under-the-table employment agent who hired them had promised that the working hours would be shorter than those they were used to in London, and that they would have one day off a week. Big Sasa had pictured himself spending his Sunday afternoons snoozing in the sunshine in a lush meadow next to a meandering stream.

But only a couple of weeks after departing for Cambridge, he and Little Sasa were back on Brick Lane, and for once, they were relieved to be there.

'Every day we start working five-thirty o'clock and finish nine o'clock,' complained Big Sasa when I bumped into him on the pavement outside Mr Ali's shop, the morning after he returned to London. 'Sometime we eat nothing for twelve hour. If we stop the work, they deduct the money. We have no break. Really the conditions are very bad. We don't like.'

Big Sasa went on to explain that the dodgy employment agent had arranged for them to work for a man named Jim. Jim, in turn, was in the business of supplying casual labourers to farms across eastern England. A large man with two Rottweilers, he 'employed' dozens of illegal workers and asylum seekers at well below the minimum wage, housing them in sub-standard housing. The two Sasas had been forced to live in a derelict farmhouse without electricity, hot water or a functioning toilet. The kitchen had been filthy. At night, they had slept five or six to a room on lumpy, horsehair mattresses.

'Really it is very bad place,' continued Big Sasa. 'I prefer refugee camp. Very dirty and always the toilet is full of shit. Always bad smelling.'

Every morning, the two Sasas and the other illegal workers with whom they lived were picked up at five a.m. by a white van that transported them to one of a number of farms in the area. There were no seats in the back of the van so they had to squat on the floor for up to forty-five minutes at a time. They would then spend their days picking vegetables and fruit, loading bales of hay, or shovelling manure. Anyone who complained about the working conditions was fired on the spot.

'If you don't like, this man Jim, he tell you "fuck off",' continued Big Sasa. 'He is not good man I think. We are animal to him. Sometime, he is hitting the people, telling them bad thing, like your mother is whore or your father suck cock. This is not nice thing. Why he tell like this?'

One of the other illegal workers hired by Jim was a Chinese man who was financially indebted to the people smugglers who had brought him into the UK. He had been 'leased' to Jim, who paid all his wages directly to his 'owners'. In other words, the Chinese man was a bonded labourer.

'Why didn't he just run away?' I asked Big Sasa, amazed that this practice, so prevalent in India, should be going on in England.

'He is the scared person,' replied the Kosovar. 'He think they find him and beat him. Maybe worse. It is bad situation.'

'But what about the police? Don't they know what's going on?' Big Sasa laughed.

'Police! I think you make joke, yes? The brother of Jim is one policeman, so he say nothing. Really I think the police are the most corrupt people.'

As Big Sasa was telling me all this, Little Sasa emerged from their front door. His right arm was in a sling; he had fallen off a ladder a few days earlier and broken it in two places.

'Jim, he not care,' said Big Sasa, raising his voice in anger. 'I tell him take him for hospital, but no, he refuse. So I walk two mile and call one taxi to come. Then I go myself to hospital with my friend.'

Later that day Big Sasa had returned to see Jim and demanded to be paid the money owed to them as well as the cost of the taxi fare. But Jim refused and threatened the Kosovar with a beating.

'After that I make big problem for him,' said Big Sasa with a satisfied grin.

'What did you do?'

'OK I tell,' he said, lowering his voice. 'I wait until he is sleep. Then I put petrol on jeep. Then I light match and run away.'

The two Sasas exchanged a glance and grinned.

'Very big fire!' said Little Sasa, giving his friend a mischievous nudge.

'Yes! *Very* big fire,' added Big Sasa with a flourish of his hands. 'Really I think Jim is very pissed off person now, yes!'

During his time in East Anglia, Big Sasa called Ravesa almost every day from the payphone two miles from the farmhouse. When I had bumped into him on the street that morning, he was on his way to the café in Cricklewood to see her. But when the Kosovar returned to Brick Lane that evening, it was with more bad news. Ravesa had disappeared. For two mornings in a row she had failed to turn up for work, and in her absence she had been fired. Furthermore, her Greek boss said that he did not know where she lived and he did not seem to care what had become of her. He had told Big Sasa – who had spent nine hours waiting outside on the pavement in case she appeared – that if he came to the café looking for her again, he would call the police.

Given that I was the only English person that Big Sasa felt he could trust, he came to me for advice. I had never known the Kosovar so agitated. He paced up and down in my kitchen, chain-smoking and making himself endless mugs of instant coffee, which he drained in quick, sharp gulps. He was certain that the only reason why Ravesa would not have come to work was if she had been prevented from doing so. Despite her boss being lecherous and mean, she treasured her job. In a single ten–hour shift, she earned more than a doctor or a teacher in Albania brought home in a month. The money was helping to support her entire family – not just her parents and brothers and sisters, but three generations: from nephews and nieces to a full complement of grandparents.

'Perhaps she's sick,' I suggested.

But the Kosovar shook his head. Even if she had a temperature of a hundred and ten, she would still come to work, he insisted.

'Then perhaps the boss treated her badly and he's not telling you the truth.'

Again, Big Sasa brushed aside my suggestion. It seemed unlikely. One of the other waitresses had confirmed the boss's story. Ravesa had been at work three days earlier and she had been especially happy because her tips had amounted to forty pounds in cash.

'I suppose there is one other possibility,' I said cautiously, turning the end of my lit cigarette in the dross of the small bowl that served as an ashtray.

'Immigration people,' said Big Sasa with loathing in his voice.

I nodded.

'She *is* an illegal immigrant. Perhaps they picked her up and she's being held . . .' I was about to add 'for deportation', but the sad look on Big Sasa's face made me think better of it.

The Kosovar dropped into the chair on the opposite side of the kitchen table and sighed deeply.

'Yes, it is possible,' he conceded.

For a while we sat in silence, staring blankly at the space in front of us.

'If that's what's happened, it's better than some of the alternatives,' I said eventually.

Big Sasa nodded.

'Yes. I know this,' he said. 'But I think perhaps I not see her again in my life.'

I tried my best to help. I began by calling the Home Office to find out if they were holding Ravesa or knew of her whereabouts. But dealing with British officialdom proved a nightmare. I spent countless hours phoning numbers that either rang engaged, never answered or proved to be incorrect. Most of the officials I spoke to could not have been less helpful. After two days and dozens of calls, I was still none the wiser as to Ravesa's fate. The only thing I was able to tell Big Sasa with any confidence was that the main non-governmental organisations that provided assistance to asylum seekers and refugees had no record of her either. One of them advised me to contact the police and report Ravesa as a missing person.

Despite Big Sasa's misgivings about this course of action, I called Scotland Yard. But this proved futile too. The officer who took my call said that the best he could do was to put Ravesa's name on file.

'London's a big city, sir,' he said. 'We can't be expected to keep track of every illegal immigrant that slips into the country undetected and then goes missing, now can we?'

Big Sasa was not to be deterred, however. He followed Gul Muhammad's example and printed flyers that he and his friends handed out across London wherever Albanians were to be found.

A fortnight passed without a single lead. And then one day at the end of August, Big Sasa met two young Albanian women in the street who knew Ravesa. As my Kosovar friend had feared, she was being held against her will.

The truth about Ravesa's circumstances did not come as a complete shock to Big Sasa. But the news proved upsetting to him nonetheless, and rather than rushing over to the address he was given by the Albanian women, he returned to Brick Lane where he spent three or four hours sitting in his room in silence.

Ravesa was a prostitute, he would tell me later that day. She was working for an Albanian pimp who had brought her to England. A few months earlier, she had escaped his clutches and started working in the Cricklewood café. Since then, he had tracked her down. She was now being held by force in a flat near Baker Street.

'These ladies they tell me the pimp man is very dangerous. Always he beat the girls and make them do bad thing.'

Big Sasa looked pale as he sat back in my kitchen bringing me up to date with what he had learned. His voice had lost its determination and was vague and soft, as if he were talking in a dream.

'We have to do something,' I said eventually. 'We can't just leave her there.'

Big Sasa heaved his shoulders, looking miserable and tormented.

'No, really it is impossible,' he said. 'It is very bad situation I think. What can we do?'

It was Anu who made Big Sasa see sense. She argued that it was his duty to help Ravesa. The only question was how best to go about it. Personally, I was for calling the police or one of the charities offering assistance to women trapped in such circumstances. I argued that there was more at stake than Ravesa's future; there were bound to be other girls in the pimp's clutches and with any luck we could see him put away. If that meant Ravesa being deported, then so be it; at least she would be free of him.

Anu agreed. But before we made any calls, Big Sasa said that he wanted to talk with Ravesa face to face. He proposed going to the brothel himself where he would ask for sex with a girl matching Ravesa's description. With any luck, he would be shown into her room where the two of them would be able to talk. Then we could decide the best course of action.

The following evening, Big Sasa set off for Baker Street. He wore a suit, shirt, tie and shoes bought at a charity shop on Brick Lane, and he carried a briefcase. Little Sasa and Gul Muhammad went with him, looking their usual scruffy selves; they were going along as back-up and would wait in the street outside the brothel in case their friend needed help.

That at least was the plan. But things did not work out quite as intended and when they returned to Brick Lane a few hours later, they did so with Ravesa in tow.

She was a frightened-looking woman in her early twenties who, despite the roasting summer heat, sat trembling and chain-smoking on a cushion beneath the makeshift bunk beds in the asylum seekers' bed-sit. She had arrived on Brick Lane wearing only a cotton nightgown and Big Sasa's suit jacket; she was wearing no shoes. The soles of her feet were filthy, the red varnish on her toenails scuffed. Her face, too, was dirty. Tears had caused her eyeliner to run and she had smeared it across her cheeks with the back of her hand. Watching her discreetly from where I stood on the landing, I noticed tell-tale signs of the abuse she had endured: her arms and legs were badly bruised and she had a scar above her right eye.

Big Sasa came on to the landing outside his bed-sit and told me how he had gone to the brothel in Baker Street; how he had paid for sex and been shown into Ravesa's room; how, at the sight of him, she had broken down in tears and told him about many of the terrible things that had happened to her; how he had been overcome with anger and, taking her by the arm, fought his way outside.

'The pimp man, he is not there. One other man – he is Albanian also – is fighting with me, but I kick him and we run to street. Still, he come into street. But Gul Muhammad, he fight him and make bloody his nose.'

Big Sasa was shaking. He was excited and scared at the same time. One moment he would laugh out loud, then he would tilt back his head, murmuring to himself and running his hands through his hair.

'The pimp man, she say he do rape many time to her. Really he is fucker person.' The Kosovar kicked at the skirting board on the landing and cursed in his language. 'He is like animal! I like to kill him!'

I sympathised with Sasa's anger; I felt it keenly as well. I wanted to see the pimp pay for what he had done. But Big Sasa would still have nothing to do with the police.

'It is bad for her,' he said. 'She say, the pimp is knowing her family in Albania. He can kill her mother and father, maybe her sister for sure.'

'You mean, if he's arrested and she testifies, he has friends who will kill her family in Albania.'

'Yes. It is right. He is mafia person,' he said, kicking the skirting board again.

It angered me still further to think that Ravesa could not be protected in the UK; that the Albanian mafia could operate outside the law; that there was nothing we could do to help this young woman escape their clutches.

'So does she want to go back?' I asked Big Sasa, my voice betraying the frustration I felt.

'No. She does not like. But really it is bad situation. It is the big problem for her.'

'There must be something we can do,' I said.

'There is one thing. We can give pimp man money, then it will be OK.'

'You mean, if you buy Ravesa from him he will leave her and her family alone?'

'Yes.'

'How much?' I asked him.

'Too much,' he said and gave the skirting board another hard kick.

I spent a restless night, tossing and turning in bed, trying to consider the best course of action. In the morning, I again called one of the charities I had contacted and told them Ravesa's story. It was by no means uncommon, they said. Girls from East European countries like Albania and Romania were being lured to the West with promises of good jobs and then sold into prostitution. Thousands had been smuggled into the UK in recent years.

'They change hands between pimps like cattle,' said a volunteer manning the helpline at one of the charities.

Typically a girl had sex with a dozen or so men a night, she explained. Most did not attempt to run away from their captors because they feared for their family's safety at home.

'Unfortunately, the Albanian government does little or nothing to protect these girls or their relatives,' she added. 'It makes it very hard for us to bring them in. They're scared, and rightly. But there have been cases where girls have stood up to them and the pimps have been successfully prosecuted without the families being harmed.'

The volunteer offered to meet and talk with Ravesa and explain her options. I thanked her, put down the phone and went next door to suggest that I take Ravesa to the charity's local branch. But she was gone. In the middle of the night, while the Kosovars and the Afghan had been asleep, she had taken some of Little Sasa's clothes, sixty pounds from Gul Muhammad's wallet, and several packets of cigarettes.

'I still think we should report the pimp to the police,' I said.

But Big Sasa refused to tell me the brothel's address and insisted that there was nothing more to be done. After that, I never heard him mention Ravesa's name again.

Where Have All the English Gone?

'There is hardly such a thing as a pure Englishman in this island.
In place of the rather vulgarised and very inaccurate phrase,
Anglo-Saxon, our national denomination, to be strictly correct,
would be a composite of a dozen national titles.'

The Times (1867)

UNTIL SEPTEMBER, ANU'S work at the BBC was fairly mundane.
As a newsroom producer, she spent most of her long eleven-
hour shifts setting up phone interviews for correspondents and pre-
senters. Giving up her job in India, where she'd been reporting and
producing in the field, felt like a huge mistake. It was just another
thing she tried not to blame me for.

But one day in early September, she went into work only to find
the editor suddenly asking her to fill in for a presenter who had called
in sick. Anu jumped at the chance and pulled it off with relative ease.

That was the moment everything changed. Anu was offered more
presenting work and there was talk of her being sent abroad for
short-term foreign assignments.

In the coming days, Anu's outlook was transformed. Suddenly,
London didn't seem like such a bad place after all. With more money
in her pocket, she began dragging me to plays and concerts; and more
than a few nice restaurants a long way off Brick Lane. And as our
shared sense of desperation lifted, we began to look for a new place
to live. By now, I was finding more interesting and challenging work
and had embarked on producing my own freelance TV news stories.
Recently, I had sold an idea to Channel 4 News. But Barnes was still
out of the question, so we started doing the rounds of estate agents in

other areas. Eventually we settled on Stoke Newington where we hoped to find a one-bedroom flat, preferably with a south-facing garden.

Feeling less of an appendage to me, Anu started to explore London for herself, travelling more widely in the city than I had ever bothered to do and discovering places that I might never have seen. She got to know Southall, Wembley and Tooting Bec. And as a new member of the Royal Horticultural Society, she visited many of the capital's gardens and flower shows.

But undoubtedly her greatest find was the New Tayyab restaurant in Whitechapel. The place was owned by a Pakistani family from Lahore who lived upstairs. The menu was simple, authentic and fresh, and given that it was cheap and you could take your own alcohol, we started going there regularly. Ali, the nephew of the one-eyed proprietor, was always welcoming and friendly and would chat with Anu in Urdu.

New Tayyab was open only in the evenings and was housed in a converted pub next door to the derelict hulk of the Tower Doss-House where Jack London spent a couple of uncomfortable nights and, more recently, drug addicts had taken to squatting. It was popular with extended East End Pakistani families who required long banquet-style tables to accommodate them. Many were related or well-acquainted, and, as their children chased one another between the legs of the tables and chairs, they would mingle and exchange banter across the room. All of them were on first-name terms with Ali and his uncle and never bothered looking at the menu, which they knew by heart. They ordered sizzling platter after platter of tandoori chicken and lamb chops, and *naan* straight out of the tandoor oven. All this they washed down with mango *lassi* served in chilled pewter mugs, which gave the children milky yellow moustaches.

The Tayyab family also owned a kebab house a couple of doors down the street, which provided a different scene altogether. It was the older of the two establishments and the interior was simple and scruffy. The place was at its busiest at lunchtime. The clientele was an unlikely mix of men drawn from across South Asia, as well as Afghans, Arabs, the occasional North African, and a sprinkling of white workmen who fancied spicy mutton *karai* over egg and chips. It was a favourite hangout for Asian medical students from the Whitechapel Hospital who ate *biriyani* while debating autopsy procedures. And it attracted Islamic radicals who would arrive hungry after prayers at the mosque and sit discussing the concept of *jihad* while exchanging terrorist training videos shot in Afghanistan.

By coincidence, the Tayyab kebab house was also the favoured lunch spot of Aktar, the Bengali anthropologist, whom I had not seen for two months.

I found him there one day eating alone, which – as I was to discover – was most unusual for him. Indeed, Aktar's standard practice was to invite someone to lunch and then stick them with the bill. The wealthier the 'guest' the larger the order – up to four main dishes, as well as *naan*, *raita*, pilau, chutney, at least three salty *lassis*, two or three helpings of *kheer* and a couple of cups of *chai*.

Aktar usually got away with it because his hosts hailed from South Asian cultures where such behaviour is excused in aspiring ascetics. Certainly, amongst the Tayyab waiters and clientele, he was much talked about and even revered.

'He is a genius!' a local Pakistani businessman who had bought Aktar lunch on a number of occasions once told me. 'He is a deeply intellectual and spiritual man,' whispered another.

As such, Aktar never found himself wanting for a free place to live. Since arriving in the East End, he had slept in a dozen different beds and on at least as many couches. His hosts usually provided him with breakfast and dinner, too. In lieu of payment, he kept them entertained in the evenings with recitals of Urdu or Bengali poetry and played his *khol*. Yet he was never one to offer to do the washing up.

Fortunately for me, Aktar knew that I was broke and when he invited me to join him at his table that lunchtime, he ordered accordingly, keeping his requests to a minimum: a portion of fish tikka, which was served with a complimentary plate of chopped onion and tomato salad, an order of rice, one *kheer*, one salt *lassi* and a cup of milky *chai*. When the bill arrived, he pushed it across the table towards me, showing not the slightest sign of remorse or embarrassment.

'My funds are running somewhat short,' he said.

As I paid the bill, I took some comfort from knowing that I had got my money's worth. Aktar's study of the East End's Bangladeshi population was progressing rapidly and, although he was exceptionally long-winded, his findings were fascinating. He told me about the extraordinary collection of characters he'd interviewed – amongst them a Bangladeshi publican; the first British Bangladeshi millionaire, who drove a Rolls and lived in a mansion complete with swimming pool and landscaped garden in Bexleyheath, Kent; a young Bangladeshi import–export businessman with two wives (one in Poplar, the other in Sylhet neither of whom knew of the other's existence); and some of the last lascars who had worked aboard British ships in the days prior to Indian independence – and about his plans to turn his attention to the 'indigenous white population'.

'I have decided to cast the net wider, so to speak,' he said. 'I must gain a clearer picture of Cockney culture as it exists today.'

Aktar asked me if I might be willing to help.

'It is fortunate that you came along when you did,' he said. 'I would like to interview a dozen or so families, preferably from Bethnal Green and Whitechapel. They must be – and allow me to emphasise this – they *must be* one hundred per cent English. Thus far, the Cockneys whom I have met have all been immigrants masquerading as English people: Jews and Irish and so forth.'

I considered his proposition for a moment. It sounded interesting and, given that I was still only working a few days a week, I could afford the time. But was I the right person for the job? I didn't know a single white East End family. In fact, after almost a year living on Brick Lane, I knew only a handful of 'Cockneys'. Chalky was one of them, but I thought better of introducing him to Aktar. Then there was my neighbour Harry, who kept the pigeons, but he was unwell. I knew a plumber called Miles who had lived in Shoreditch for thirty years but he was Irish. And that was it. Everyone else who ranked amongst my new-found friends and acquaintances was either first, second or third generation immigrant or, like me, a new arrival in the East End.

'I'm not sure I'm the person you need,' I said.

'But you are English?' asked Aktar.

'Yes, but I didn't grow up round here. I'm a stranger in these parts, too. I have no more contact with the Cockneys of Bethnal Green than the average Bangladeshi does.'

'But they are your people, are they not?'

'You don't understand,' I said. 'I don't fit in. I've got the wrong accent, the wrong name. Everything about me sticks out. I'm perceived as being middle class. Sometimes, on Bethnal Green Road, when I open my mouth, I get strange looks. Once, when I went into one of the pubs, the man behind the bar asked me if I was a copper.'

'Of course I would not dream of putting you in the way of danger,' said Aktar.

'It's not dangerous,' I continued. 'It's just that the British are class conscious, and sometimes people from different classes can be standoffish with one another. The fact that I went to public school makes me a toff in the eyes of many working-class people. That can make them hostile. You'd have to live it to understand it.'

Aktar laughed.

'What's so funny?' I asked him.

'You British and your class system!' he replied. 'One day I should very much like to get to the bottom of it. But for now, I will settle for some Cockney families. Why don't we meet for lunch tomorrow and we can discuss the matter further. Shall we say one o'clock?'

Not long after Aktar enlisted my help, we heard again from Mrs Suri. She'd been out of contact for weeks – ever since Anu had bribed her parents' swami in India to say positive things about our proposed marriage and the fraud of an ascetic had given us his blessing. Now she wanted to help us organise the wedding.

'Delay cannot be there,' she told Anu on the phone.

Just for good measure, she had consulted with her own Manchester-based astrologer – one Bhagwan Ram – who had come up with a number of auspicious dates for us to choose from.

Anu, being none too fond of Orlando and not having any friends in Florida where her parents had moved only a year earlier, refused to entertain any suggestion of the ceremony being held there. As she put it to me, 'The reception will be above my parents' three-car garage with a bunch of motel-owning aunties whom I've never met before. They'll do stupid dancing and make us eat *ladoos* until we're sick. No thanks.'

Mrs Suri's response was to lobby Anu's mother to have the wedding in London and she soon proposed that we come to Upton Park for tea to discuss the arrangements. 'Making weddings is my expertise,' she told Anu on the phone during a sudden flurry of calls. 'Everything will be there. Beautiful thrones, *mehndi*, top quality DJ. Not to worry about a thing.'

Anu made excuses and put off seeing her; needless to say, neither of us was keen to have an Indian wedding in London organised by Mrs Suri. What Anu really wanted was a wedding in India with all her extended family in attendance. It was what every Indian and non-resident Indian girl dreams of. But the prospect of this happening seemed remote. Anu's father had told us that he took no joy in the prospect of our union, and my parents continued to be opposed to our relationship. For now, at least, our wedding plans remained uncertain.

<hr />

Strictly speaking, as I explained to Aktar a week or so later when I had done my research, there were no more Cockneys left in the East End. Virtually everything that had helped identify Cockney culture had vanished. The docks, the slums, the close-knit communities, most of the pubs and markets, and all but one of the music halls. Even Cockney rhyming slang was now, effectively, dead.

'In fact, it seems to have been in decline since the 1930s,' I said as we sat over yet another lunch in the Tayyab kebab house.

'Yes, I am aware of this,' said Aktar haughtily. 'However, Whites remain the majority in Tower Hamlets and I have observed that they continue to identify with the area. They are proud to call themselves East Enders. This is relevant, as I am trying to establish whether the

Bangladeshi community will be absorbed into the host culture as other immigrant groups have been in the past.'

It was Aktar's conclusion that the Bangladeshi community was going through a metamorphosis. The younger generation were fast shedding the values and interests of their grandparents and parents and adopting a 'hybrid identity'. He had interviewed dozens of young people who had never been to their homeland, spoke better English than Sylheti, and were lapsed Muslims.

'Unlike their parents, they are able to relate to the wider society. Even those who have wrapped themselves in a neo-Islamic identity – people you might refer to as fundamentalists – cannot accurately be referred to as "Bangladeshi". Mostly they identify themselves as "British Muslims", but I have observed that in many ways these young Sylhetis, having grown up in a Western culture, have absorbed Christian values and attitudes. Most significantly, they are starting to have smaller families and fewer are "importing" partners from Sylhet.'

Aktar saw economics as the principal driving force behind the transformation of the community.

'It is through private commerce that immigrants are inadvertently drawn into British culture,' he continued. 'Throughout the East End's history, every immigrant group that has settled here has been seized by this entrepreneurial spirit: from the Huguenots to the Jews and so on.'

He had found that, although the Sylhetis lagged behind other South Asian minorities like the Indians in economic terms, they were gaining ground.

'They control a major proportion of the British "curry" industry, which is worth some one and a half billion pounds a year – more than the steel, coal and shipbuilding industries combined. As they prosper, they are changing. The question I am asking is, what are they becoming?'

Aktar did not like the term 'British Asian'.

'It is true that many second and third generation East End Bangladeshis refer to themselves as being "British" or "British Asian" or even "British Bangladeshi",' he went on. 'However, we must ask ourselves what being "British" really means.'

He had met many an elderly Bangladeshi who carried a British passport but spoke little or no English and remained one hundred per cent Sylheti in mind and temperament.

'Officially they are "British", but in their case it is a term that denotes only legal nationality,' he said as we finished our meal and our plates were cleared away. 'This is England; the majority population, the so-called "Cockneys", are English. So surely, the question is this: are the Bangladeshis becoming "English" or are they becoming something else, something new?'

After lunch, Aktar and I left Tayyab and made our way through the back streets of Whitechapel towards Bethnal Green where I had arranged a series of interviews with white East End families.

We passed over Bethnal Green Road and into the neighbourhood beyond the grim-visaged estates where the odd row of terraces and mansion flats looked desirable – individual even.

Trevor and Flora Francis, the first couple I had arranged for Aktar to meet, lived in a terraced house near the Hackney Road. It was Chalky who had put me in touch with them. 'Archetypal East Enders' was how he had described them. 'They were born in Bethnal Green, they've lived all their lives in Bethnal Green and they'll die in Bethnal Green.'

Until the Germans flattened the far section of the Francis's terrace, adding to the list of 3.5 million homes they either destroyed or damaged across London, the street had been longer. Now it terminated abruptly at the foot of an apartment block that loomed over the remaining rows of two- and three-storey houses below. Net curtains hung in most of the windows, a sure sign that many of these houses were still home to white East Enders who had never moved out.

The Francis's home stood at the end of the street. The red cross of St George hung in one of the upper windows. Geraniums grew in the window boxes. An iron gate protected the front door. A sign attached to the red brickwork read, 'BEWARE OF THE DOG'.

I rang the buzzer, which played a couple of bars of *Land of Hope and Glory,* and the door was soon answered by Mrs Francis. She was in her late sixties with a frizzy, bleached hairdo that looked like a fancy sugar decoration on a minimalist, *nouvelle cuisine* dessert. She wore purple eye-shadow that matched the purple tint that ran through the plastic frame of her glasses, and a silk blouse with a butterfly costume brooch pinned through the top buttonhole. As she stood in the doorway in her pink slippers, her pet Pekinese circled around her feet, yapping incessantly and baring his teeth in a vaguely comical manner. The smells that wafted out into the street were of hair spray and perfume, and of fried bacon.

'Mr 'all, is it?' she asked me, pushing open the metal gate.

'That's right.'

'Come in, dear. Don't pay no attention to Freddy. 'e doesn't bite. Just likes to show awf when we 'ave people in.'

She leant down and spoke to the dog.

''oo's a silly then?' she said, scooping him up in her arms where he wriggled and licked and wagged his tail excitedly. ''e's been poorly lately. Went aat in the rain and got a cold Sunday last. Ain't the weather been 'orrible? 'spect you'll both be wanting a nice cuppa tay. Come in where it's warm.'

I stepped in through the open door, past Mrs Francis and her dog and into the narrow corridor beyond. Aktar followed cautiously, keeping as much distance between himself and the animal as possible, his petrified expression betraying his fear of dogs of all shapes and sizes.

'First door on your right, Mr 'all. Make yourselves at 'ome while I put the kettle on and fetch Trev. Won't keep you a moment.'

Aktar and I did as we were told and found ourselves standing alone in the living room. It was really two rooms that had been converted into one, with an archway linking them together. Chocolate brown carpeting was laid throughout. An enormous fireplace that looked like the face of a rock-climbing practice structure dominated the front room. It was as high as the ceiling and made up of chunks of uneven brown stone held together by thick seams of concrete. A variety of souvenirs, including a National Trust thermometer and half a dozen pewter beer tankards, sat on a slab of rock that served as a mantelpiece.

A floral three-piece suite was arranged in front of the fireplace, and above it hung a fake crystal chandelier with candle-shaped light bulbs. Against the opposite wall stood an antique mahogany cabinet with glass doors, which held a collection of porcelain Beatrix Potter figures, and memorabilia from the Queen's 1977 Silver Jubilee. Next to this, a side table groaned with framed photographs of family – children, grandchildren, weddings, picnics on the beach – and an old black and white enlargement of an East End street party with lines of tables arranged between rows of terraced houses and bunting hanging overhead.

'So waas this all about then?' said a sceptical voice behind us.

We turned to face a tall, fit man with broad shoulders and a thick neck whom we assumed to be Trevor. He looked us both up and down with barely concealed contempt. Unlike his wife, he had not bothered putting on his best to received us; he was wearing a red turtleneck, tracksuit bottoms and running shoes.

'Flo says you come round to ask us about the old East End. Well, let me tell you now, there's nafing you're gonna get out of us that 'asn't been said a million bleedin' times before.'

He shook our hands firmly but disingenuously and led the way into the other half of the living room. Here, another floral couch and two armchairs were arranged in a semicircle in front of a TV. A low table stood between them, laid with an embroidered, Irish-linen tablecloth and a blue-patterned China tea set that depicted emperors, concubines and dragons surrounded by bamboo groves, waterfalls and pagodas.

'Take a pew, ' said Trevor.

He moved aside a copy of *Hello!* and the *Mirror* and a half-knitted jumper, and slumped into the far corner of the couch.

'Flo won't be a minute,' he said, and he reached for the TV remote control and switched on the Saturday afternoon football.

I sat down in the middle of the couch, keeping my distance from him. Aktar took the armchair nearest to me. For a few minutes, the three of us sat there watching the game in silence until Flo arrived from the kitchen carrying a tray. It was laden with a pot of tea, a platter of sandwiches and a cream and jam-filled sponge cake.

''ere we go,' she said, as she placed the tray on the table and began to pour the tea. ''elp yourself to sandwiches and cake, Mr Actor.'

Aktar ignored the mispronunciation of his name; after eight months in Britain, it was something he had grown used to. Besides, his attention had been drawn to the sight of the cake and he reached out and took a piece and began to devour it with relish.

'So Mr 'all, 'ow can we 'elp?' asked Flo with a smile.

Trevor turned his attention away from the TV and stared at me in anticipation of my answer. I cleared my throat nervously.

'Well, Aktar here is an anthropologist,' I said, 'and he's making a study of people in the East End. He was hoping to ask you some questions.'

'Like what?' demanded Trevor.

'Like where your families come from, what sort of lives you've led, your views on immigration.'

Trevor suddenly sat up erect.

'Immigration!' he bawled. 'Thas a laugh! Yeah, I'll tell you what I've got to say about immigration. Write this down in your notebook.'

He made a gesture towards Aktar.

'Go on, you. Open your notebook and write this down!' He waited for Aktar to find a blank page. 'There's too many bloody farawners! This is England and it belongs to the English. You didn't like us over there and we don't want no more of you over 'ere. Got that? Thas my view and no one's gonna tell me no different. Right?'

He got up from the couch.

'Thas all I've got to say. End of story.'

With that Trevor left the room and made his way through the back door and into the small yard behind the house. I caught a glimpse of him through the sitting-room window going into his garden shed. And before long, we heard the sound of one of his power tools revving into action.

I was keen to make our exit from the house as quickly as possible, fearful that Trevor might return. But Flo, who had by now taken her husband's place on the couch and turned off the television, laughed nervously and insisted that we stay.

'Don't mind Trev. 'e can get all 'ot 'eaded about certain fings, if you knaw what I mean. 'e'll cool awf in a while.'

I looked over at Aktar who didn't seem the least bit fazed by what had taken place and was on his second piece of cake.

'So you was saying, Mr 'all?'

'Yes, of course,' I said, struggling to collect my thoughts. 'We were hoping that you might tell us something about your family.'

'Well, I wouldn't know where to begin,' she replied.

'Perhaps you might like to start with your childhood,' suggested Aktar.

That was all the prompting Mrs Francis needed. For the next twenty minutes, she regaled us with the history of her family. She told us about her father, a fireman who had died during the Blitz, racing to the scene of one of the hundreds of fires that blazed across the East End; and about her mother who worked in the Bow matchstick factory and died at the age of eighty-two. She told us how as a girl she herself had been sent to Scotland for much of the war and returned to find her home in rubble; and how she and her two sisters and three elder brothers lived with their Mum in a Nissen prefab during the late 1940s and early 1950s until they were relocated on to one of the new estates. She described her wedding to Trevor, a mechanic, whose family had been friends with her family and who had always lived in the same house. She told us about their honeymoon on the Isle of Wight, where it rained every day, and about the time an unexploded bomb was found buried at the bottom of her best friend's garden, years after the war had ended. She told us about her aunt Jess, who caused a family scandal during the war by getting herself pregnant by an American GI. And she told us about how, one by one, her brothers and sisters had all moved out of the East End – one to Australia, another to Debden in Essex, a third to Bermondsey, a fourth to Hartlepool, and the youngest to America where he now lived in Vermont.

'To be 'onest, I would 'ave been awf as well, given 'alf a chance. Don't get me wrong, I'm an East Ender, always 'ave been, always will be. But I've always fancied the country. Fresh air and greenery – that'd suit me. 'course Trev won't 'ear of it. Says 'e'll never live nowhere else. They'd af to drag 'im away from this 'ouse, I reckon.'

Mrs Francis had raised four children in the house. They, too, had all flown the coop and now lived in different parts of London and the Home Counties. One of her boys, Frank, the second eldest, worked as a stockbroker in the City where he made hundreds of thousands of pounds a year.

''e's always offering to buy us anover 'ouse, some place in one of them new developments with a new kitchen and bathroom and wall-to-wall carpeting. It'd be nice I reckon. 'course Trev won't 'ear of it.

To tell you the 'onest truth, the two of them – 'im and Frank – don't get along well nowadays. They 'aven't since 'e married that Trisha – a bit upper class she is – and they started sending little 'arry and Roga to that posh school. Trev says they're losing their working-class values. But I da' know. I mean, the world's changing ain't it?'

Aktar jotted down her comments in his notebook. He appeared pleased. But when he asked about her parents and grandparents, disaster struck.

'We're a right old mix,' she said. 'You wouldn't know it to look at me, would ya, but I'm one quarta gypsy!'

'Gypsy,' repeated Aktar who stopped writing and shot me a perplexed look.

'Yeah, thas right. My Dad's old man was a full-blooded gypsy,' she continued.

Evidently Mrs Francis was proud of her mongrel lineage.

'' e spoke their language – the gypsy language – and lived in a caravan with 'orses. 'e made 'is living in the rag and bone business – you know, collectin' used fings out 'a people's 'ouses.'

'And what about the rest of the family?' asked Aktar, hesitantly.

'What? On me Mum's side?'

'Yes.'

'Well, I reckon they must 'ave been Irish, 'cause 'er maiden name was Rourke. Mum told me they come to the East End during the potato famine. 'er father was called Michael. 'e worked down the docks and on barges and that. 'course, 'e died young. Most people did in them days, didn't they? There wasn't the propa medicine you get today. There wasn't supermarkets and 'olidays to Palma, neiver.'

By the time we left the Francis's home, Aktar was not in the best of moods, and as we made our way through the Bethnal Green estates towards our next appointment, he made it clear that, thus far, he was unimpressed with my abilities as a fixer.

'You assured me that the people we were to meet were one hundred per cent English,' he grumbled.

'They *were* English,' I protested. 'Believe me, you don't get any more English than that!'

'They were from immigrant stock,' he said angrily. 'Mrs Francis told us so herself. She is part Irish and part gypsy. I would not call that "English".'

It was a similar story at the five other households we visited that Sunday. All of the white East Enders we talked to had immigrant skeletons in their closets. Simon, a taxi driver living near Columbia Road, told us his mother was Maltese. Joe, who worked for the local council, said one of his grandparents had been Sicilian. Joe's wife, Anne, said her mother was Scottish.

We met Andrew Hoch, whose last name turned out to be German, and his wife, Rachel, who came from northern England and bore a Norse surname. Lastly we interviewed Chris, a pale-skinned teacher who had just finished eating a plateful of roast beef and Yorkshire pudding in front of *Songs of Praise*. He admitted his mother's father had been a Caribbean of Anglo-Indian descent who had married a Welsh woman whose maiden name was Blevin.

With each interview, Aktar became increasingly frustrated, and his mood was not improved when, later that evening, he looked up the origins of the surname Francis.

'It is French!' he bawled down the phone at around eleven o'clock when he called to tell me the bad news.

'What's French?'

'The name, Francis. In its original form it meant a "Frenchman". Your friend Trevor, the hater of "bloody foreigners", is a "bloody for-eigner" himself!'

'He's not my friend and you could hardly call him French.'

But Aktar wasn't listening.

'What about you?' he said, the tone of his voice accusing and sus-picious. 'Where is your family from?'

I had to admit that my genetic make-up was as mongrel as they came. My American mother was part English (her maiden name was Briggs), part Irish, with a splash of Cherokee. My father was part English, Scots, Cornish, Norman and probably a lot more besides.

'And you call yourself English?'

'Well, what else would you call me?'

I heard nothing from Aktar for a few days and when I sought him out later in the week in the Tayyab kebab house, I found him still despondent. He had not yet had any success finding twenty-four-carat English people, and his mood had not been improved by the fact that, for once, he had been forced to pay for his own lunch.

'I have been conducting interviews all week and I have come to realise that you people, you *English* as you call yourselves, are, for the most part, utterly ignorant of your own history and ancestry,' he said. 'What's more, I have not found a single person who can trace their ancestry back more than a few hundred years. It seems that everyone in the East End is from somewhere else – either their forefathers were immigrants or they came from another part of the British Isles.'

Aktar had been busy that morning looking up the origins of English surnames. He had discovered that 'Chaucer' was French, from *chausseur*, shoemaker.

'Even the father of English literature has a French name,' he said. 'It simply beggars belief.'

But Chaucer was not the only one.

'Your first great novelist, Daniel Defoe, was of Flemish descent, and Joseph Conrad's real name was Teodor Józef Konrad Korzeniowski.'

The Bengali had also been looking into the ethnic origins of English politicians.

'Did you know that a quarter of Margaret Thatcher's first Cabinet were descended from East End Jewish immigrants? Winston Churchill, the great British imperialist and, surely, the greatest Englishman of the twentieth century, was' – and here Aktar paused as if having to swallow a bitter pill – 'half American. His mother was from Massachusetts and, like you, she had Cherokee blood.'

He slouched back in his chair, looking beaten. It seemed an opportune time to tell him my good news.

'The last of the real Cockneys, the Pearly Kings and Queens, are holding a Harvest Festival tomorrow.'

Aktar had never heard of the Pearlies and, for once, I found myself adding to his knowledge.

'They're a kind of Cockney royalty,' I continued. 'They were traditionally costermongers who sold fruit and veg on the streets and did charitable work. From what I understand, their titles have been handed down generation after generation for hundreds of years. If they're not English, then I don't know who is.'

Aktar showed a glimmer of interest, but remained sceptical.

'How did you come by this information?' he asked.

'Everyone in London has heard of the Pearlies. They wear outfits sewn with buttons. I thought they'd vanished years ago, otherwise I would have mentioned them before.'

The next morning, Aktar and I took the number eight bus to the church of St Mary-le-Bow in Cheapside, on the western border of the City, which is home to the famous Bow Bells. Typically, Aktar had spent the previous afternoon and evening reading up on the Pearlies and had found my description of them seriously lacking.

'Once again, your information has proven inaccurate,' he said as the double-decker Routemaster inched its way down the narrow length of Threadneedle Street, past the Bank of England.

'How do you mean?'

'The Pearly tradition has not been around for hundreds of years. In fact, it can only be traced back to 1870 when Henry Croft, a coster-monger, discovered a cargo of pearls on the banks of the Thames and created the first Pearly suit. He used to wear this said suit in public to raise money for the poor.'

I shuffled uneasily in my seat. 'I see,' was all I could think to say.

'You might also care to know that although the costermongers of today are considered respectable, in Victorian times they were' – and here he produced a photocopy and read from it – ' "rough, quarrel-some, illiterate . . . much given to fighting, drinking and gambling and tattooing their arms and throwing bricks at policemen".'

Aktar put the piece of paper away; there was no mistaking the smugness in his voice.

'Shall I go on?' he said haughtily. I nodded my assent.

'Cockney rhyming slang has not been around for centuries. Or at least it was not in common use until the mid-nineteenth century and by the 1930s it was already in serious decline. Furthermore, Cockneys did not only live in the East End. Traditionally a Cockney was born within the sound of Bow Bells in the City. In the days before mass transport and tall buildings, it is estimated that they would have been heard as far away as Westminster. Virtually anyone born in London could have laid claim to being a Cockney.'

But that was not all. True to form, the Bengali had looked up the origins of the word, too, and brought along a photocopied page from *The London Encyclopaedia*, which he thrust before me.

Cockney Derived from the Middle English, *cockney*, meaning cock's egg, a misshapen egg, such as those sometimes laid by young hens. As applied to human beings it meant an effeminate person or a simpleton, particularly a weak man from a town as opposed to a tougher countryman. In the seventeenth century it came to mean specifically, pejoratively, or banteringly, a Londoner.

'So, to summarise,' continued Aktar, once I had finished reading, 'the word has come to mean its opposite. A Cockney is no longer an effeminate person or a simpleton but a tough, wily Londoner, generally from the East End.'

Aktar frowned before adding, almost to himself:

'If this is the case, who is to say what a Cockney might be in the future? Perhaps even the descendants of the Bangladeshi community will one day be considered true Londoners. It seems that here in London anything is possible.'

The bus soon pulled up outside St Mary-le-Bow in time for the arrival of the Pearly Harvest Festival parade. It was led by a donkey-drawn cart, much like the ones costermongers used to lead or push through the streets of London, and was piled high with basketfuls of fruit and vegetables bedded in straw. Twenty Pearlies followed behind – elderly kings and queens, some with walking sticks, and a few princes and princesses. All of them wore individually designed black suits sewn with thousands of pearl-coloured buttons. The women had on large floppy hats adorned with ostrich feathers and carried handbags sewn with pearls in Paisley designs. The men's outfits were the most magnificent of all, with jackets, trousers, waistcoats and caps covered in intricate patterns.

A small number of tourists and curious Londoners had gathered outside the church. To their delight, as the donkey cart came to a halt, a number of the older Cockneys formed a line on the pavement, and with arms linked and legs kicking out cabaret-style, they started singing *Knocked 'em in the Old Kent Road* and *My Old Dutch*. Cameras flashed and camcorders whirred, and a few of the younger Pearlies went through the crowd with collection boxes asking for donations for charity.

'All for a good cawse,' one of them called as he approached us. 'We'll take coins but we prefer the kind of money that doesn't clatter!'

Aktar and I soon fell into conversation with George Major, the Pearly King of Peckham, the most senior of the Pearlies present. His father and grandfather had both been 'in buttons', as he put it, and they had been costermongers as well. But Major had broken with tradition and become a plumber, and, worse, he no longer lived in his 'kingdom'; he was now a resident of Epsom, Surrey.

'I'll always be a Londoner and I'll always be proud to call myself working class,' he said. 'But it got to the stage where everyone I knew growin' up 'ad left Peckham and we didn't know our neighbours. So off we went. 'course I still miss the place something terrible. There's nothing like a walk down the Old Kent Road.'

Aktar asked him where his family had come from originally.

'I can tell you that they've been Londoners for as long as anyone can remember,' he said.

Major was joined by his granddaughter, Jade. She was wearing a hat covered in multi-coloured feathers and a beautiful Pearly jacket and skirt studded with buttons. Unlike all the other Pearlies, however, she had a dark complexion.

''er father's West Indian,' said Major. ''e's not interested in putting on the buttons. She's the first multi-ethnic Pearly. Aren't you, darling?'

The girl looked up at her grandfather and smiled adoringly.

'Yeah, granddad,' she said, before ducking behind him and running off to find her mother, also a Pearly Princess.

Major beamed. 'She's so Cockney cheeky,' he said. 'Everyone loves 'er. She just melts people's 'earts – most of all mine.'

'So you would describe her as a Cockney?' I asked him.

''course I would,' he continued, 'race 'as nafing to do with it. It's where you grow up that matters. She's an East Ender 'cause that's where she's from. She's part of the place. It may be a different kind of East End to the one we used to know. But the immigrants are taking on our traditions.

'Years ago,' he went on, 'when the first blacks and Indians started arriving in the East End, people used to come out into the street and stare at them. Now look at the place. I shouldn't be surprised if, ten years from now, we'll 'ave a black Pearly King.'

Major wished us well and made his way inside the church where the harvest festival service was about to begin. Aktar and I remained on the pavement, listening to Bow Bells ringing out from the belfry overhead.

Standing there, it suddenly occurred to me that, according to the original definition of the word, I qualified as a Cockney, too. I was a Londoner, born in the old Charing Cross Hospital within the sound of Bow Bells, and, even if Tarquin wasn't exactly a traditional Cockney name, I was pretty soft by rural standards.

'Come on, me old China plate. It's a bit taters. Let's go down the rub-a-dub-dub for a pig's ear,' I said to Aktar.

He shot me a puzzled look.

'Cockney rhyming slang,' I explained.

But the Bengali did not seem amused.

11

A Not-So-Diamond Geezer

'Walk along the Whitechapel Road . . . there you will see the peaceful invaders who have occupied a large part of East London . . . As for their children, you may look for them in the Board-schools; they have become English – both boys and girls . . . they are English through and through . . . Never yet has it been known that the second generation of the alien has failed to become English . . . I believe that our power of absorbing alien immigrants is even greater than that of the United States.'

Walter Besant, *East London* (1901)

MR ALI WAS not himself. He seemed depressed and worried, and on occasion, bad-tempered. Throughout late August and early September, he closeted himself in his office and rarely returned home before midnight. Slouched behind his desk, he took to drinking more than his usual daily dose of rum and refused to eat the home-cooked food that his wife prepared, opting instead for family-size bucketfuls of A1 Halal Fried Chicken.

Physically he looked terrible. He stopped shaving and the lack of natural light in his office, coupled with the effects of a diet rich in saturated fats, conspired to make his skin blotchy. With each passing day, his body odour and bad breath grew ever more potent, causing anyone who came into contact with him visible discomfort.

During these dark days in the life of my landlord, he also stopped coming upstairs to watch my TV. Even when Anu was at work (the two of them kept a healthy distance from one another) and there was a South Asian international being played, he refused my invitations.

Similarly, on the couple of occasions when I stepped into the shop to discuss a matter regarding the upkeep of the property or to make my usual excuses for being late with the rent, he made it clear that he was in no mood for one of the long chats that had become something of a custom between us.

When I asked what was on his mind, all he would say was, 'My life's going down the shit 'ole, innit.'

It was not until mid-September that I discovered what was troubling Mr Ali.

One Monday morning, I went to see him in his office to tell him that we would be moving out in a month's time and I wanted to make sure he would return the small deposit I had given him.

His office was messier than I had ever seen it. The dustbin had toppled over under the weight of rum bottles and empty chicken buckets, and its contents now lay strewn across the floor. Used, sticky tomato ketchup sachets lay trodden into the carpeting. The wall behind the bin was splattered with grease and ketchup stains where chicken bones tossed from behind the desk had impacted on the paintwork. On top of his desk, mixed in with the usual heap of junk mail, bulging files, fabric samples, back copies of the *Sun* and unopened brown envelopes from HM Inland Revenue lay empty cigarette cartons, a couple of ashtrays brimming with butts, used lottery scratch cards and mugs containing cultures of mould.

Mr Ali had his feet up on a box of fake football strips that he'd had his boys manufacturing in the sweatshop. He was staring blankly at the ceiling, the whites of his eyes bloodshot. For a moment, as I approached his desk, he looked at me blankly, as if he were trying to put a name to my face. But then his expression changed and he seemed pleased to see me.

'Waas the time?' he asked, his voice sounding dozy, as if he had just woken up.

I told him that it was almost ten o'clock.

'Bollocks,' came his reply.

He took his feet off the desk and rubbed his face in his hands. Then he stood up and groaned as he tried to straighten his crooked back.

'I'm starved,' he said. 'Le's go 'ave a fry up, yeah. I fancy some egg and chips and a cup of tea, innit.'

We were soon out in the street where even London's exhaust fumes offered relief from the stench of the shop. It was not a bright day, but Mr Ali squinted in the light, holding one hand up to the sky to shield his eyes. He had not been outside for at least seventy-two hours, he admitted, and had spent the past two nights on a mattress on the floor of his shop.

'I feel like a truck ran over my 'ead,' he said.

We made our way down Bethnal Green Road and soon reached Mr Ali's favourite greasy spoon. A wall chart in the window printed with photographs of variations of the English breakfast reminded potential customers what combinations of fried eggs, beans, sausage and fried toast looked like. Inside, he led the way to a booth where he sat with his back to the door.

'I don't want no one seeing me, yeah,' he said. 'They won't leave me alone. All them uncles and aunties. They're always sticking their noses in where it don't belong. Always stirring it up, innit.'

He ordered us tea, his accent more Estuary than usual: 'Oi! Doris! Bring us a coupla teas, will-ya-darlin.'

Then he sat back in the plastic upholstered seat and lit a cigarette.

'I'll tell you this, geezer,' he said, blowing a pall of smoke across the table in my direction, 'I've got to get away from 'ere, yeah. I can't take livin' round 'ere no more. If I stay I'm gonna go mental, innit.'

I asked him what was going on.

'Trust me, you don't wanna know,' he said, but then proceeded to tell me anyway.

'Iss family bollocks, innit,' he began. 'The Missis, yeah. She's driving me up the walls. I'm telling you, yeah, Bangladeshi women are a nightmare and my Missis, she's the biggest nightmare, innit. All day, all night, she's 'aving a go. "Mr Ali do this, Mr Ali do that." The woman 'as no mercy.'

Our tea arrived and he heaped an unhealthy amount of sugar into his mug, stirring the contents impatiently so that some of the liquid spilled over on to the table.

'Iss like this, geezer,' he said, swallowing a large gulp of tea and then wiping his wet lips across the back of his hand. 'My second youngest daughter, yeah. Turns out she's a genius, innit.'

I knew the daughter he was referring to; I had met her at her sister's wedding. Her name was Razia and she was eighteen, pretty and bright.

'A few weeks back, yeah, she got 'er A-level results, innit. Well, believe it or not, yeah, she got five "A" grades.' He held up the palm of his hand with all five fingers splayed. '*Five* "As", yeah. Thas more than anyone in my 'ole family put together in the 'ole 'istory of my family going back, like, centuries, innit.'

I congratulated him. 'That's incredible,' I said.

But Mr Ali looked uneasy.

'Iss not all cosy – if you know what I mean. All these universities – some of them big famous ones, yeah – they're offering 'er places for, like, the furtherance of 'er education, innit.'

The universities to which he was referring were Cambridge, which had been Razia's first choice, and Queen Mary's in Mile End, which had been number two on her list of preferences.

'So what's the problem?'

'Well, iss obvious, innit. I'm facing, like, this big fuckin' question mark, yeah. If she goes to Cambridge, she 'as to live away from 'ome and if she goes down Mile End, she stays with 'er Mum, innit.'

Mr Ali drained the rest of his tea.

'So you're saying you want her to stay at home,' I said.

He made a face and shrugged his shoulders. 'Personally I'm con-fused. But the *Missis*' – and here he raised his eyebrows – 'she's got it all worked out, yeah. Basically, she don't want Razia doing nafing 'xcept getting married. She says to me, "Oi! Mr Ali, your daughter needs an 'usband."'

As my landlord went on to explain, his wife had rallied the support of most of their relatives and many of their friends and neighbours. Since the A-level results had arrived, they had been canvassing him to prevent Razia from going to Cambridge. The more moderate amongst them had counselled Queen Mary's.

'I've got all these old bustards comin' round. They says to me, "Mr Ali, if you let your daughter go, yeah, she'll turn into a prostitute." "Mr Ali, they'll fill 'er 'ead with shit."'

He drew his hands down over his face and shook his head as if he were trying to wake himself from a dream.

'What does Razia want?' I asked him.

'Thas obvious,' he answered abruptly. 'She tells me it's a big opportunity, yeah, that it only comes once in a lifetime. She says to me, "Dad, let me go and you'll be proud, yeah."'

Mr Ali slouched forward in his chair, resting his elbows on his thighs and looking down at the floor.

'I don't know what to fink,' he added, his voice half choked. 'All I know is, like, the 'ole thing's doin' my 'ead in, innit.'

Over breakfast, I tried my best to help Mr Ali think through his problem and made an impassioned plea for Razia to be allowed to go to Cambridge. She should be given the chance to make up her own mind, I argued. Stifling her future would be nothing short of criminal.

But Mr Ali was divided on the issue. Like his children, he was caught between two cultures. Part of him recognised that Razia had been offered an extraordinary opportunity; while his 'Bangladeshi side' subscribed to the view that a woman's place was at home and that his daughter should be married off before she got 'any more funny ideas'.

Overshadowing all this was the pressure being exerted by his relatives, his wife's family, the neighbours and at least one local religious figure.

'Already, yeah, they're saying I'm, like, a bad Muslim, and a bad father,' he said. 'When I walk down the street or come into the room, I know they're talking about me, yeah. "Mr Ali did this, Mr Ali did that, Mr Ali's daughter's runnin' around with white boys."'

He dragged hard on his cigarette and exhaled.

'Well, I can't 'ave it, can I? I've got, like, a reputation and a business to worry about, innit.'

This seemed to me the worst of all reasons for preventing Razia from going to Cambridge. Let people say what they want, I argued. Children should be encouraged to think for themselves.

'What's it got to do with them?' I added. 'Why don't they keep out of it?'

But in saying so, I crossed the line. Suddenly, Mr Ali did an about turn and rushed to the defence of those whom he had been criticising only moments earlier.

'You don't understand. Iss our culture,' he said, dismissively. 'We've got, like, different values to you people, yeah. Us Bangladeshis look out for one another, yeah. Our families are, like, together. Iss all about community, innit.'

With that, the discussion came to an abrupt end. My landlord made his excuses and headed back to his shop and I was left sitting in the café, worrying that I had inadvertently done Razia a disservice.

On 1 October, the former East End gangster, Reg Kray, died of cancer at the age of sixty-six. The date of his funeral was set for ten days later. The newspapers speculated that tens of thousands would come out on to the streets of the East End to watch his coffin pass through Bethnal Green, the old con's 'manor', on its way to Chingford Cemetery. A crowd of at least fifty thousand had turned out to see off his twin brother Ron in 1995.

Bill, one of Chalky's drinking partners who frequented the Bethnal Green Arms, had been amongst them. A few evenings after Reg's death, I met him by chance in the pub. He was standing with Chalky at the bar, sipping a pint of Truman's and reminiscing about 'the Twins'.

'Ron's funeral was a special event,' he told me in a parental kind of way. 'There was dozens of limousines and 'orses, a beautiful Victorian carriage for the coffin. Young and old came out on to the streets to pay their respects. They lined the route all the way from 'ere to Chingford. London 'adn't seen the likes of it since Winston Churchill's funeral.'

Bill was not unique amongst East Enders of a certain generation in claiming a connection with Ron and Reg. In 1967, at the age of fourteen, he had once been in the same room with them. This, apparently, made him something of an expert on all matters Kray.

'They 'ad this unmistakable presence. What you might call magnetism,' continued Bill. 'No matter 'ow many people was in a room, they was always the centre of attention. People was drawn to 'em. Like moths arand a bright light.'

His comments were met with murmurs of 'thas right' and nostalgic smiles from the four or five other men standing around the bar.

'The thing that made Ron's funeral so special was that, for one morning, everyone got this glimpse of what the East End was like in the old days and what it stood for,' said Bill. 'See, what you af to appreciate is, the Krays was kings. They ruled over the streets. They 'ad responsibilities. When something needed sorting aht, they was the people you went to. They stood for certain fings, fings that 'ave been forgotten today. Fings like loyalty and 'onour and common decency. They was men of the people, like modern-day Robin 'oods.'

Another man at the bar piped up: 'Yeah! They didn't sell drugs or nafing.'

Then another chimed in: 'Thas right. They kept the streets safe! Never 'ad no rapes when the Krays was in charge.'

Chalky remained quiet throughout this impromptu Kray love-in. But he had the calm look of a hunter waiting to strike and, during a lull in the conversation a couple of minutes later, he went for the jugular.

''course,' he said with a grin, 'Ron and Reg were a right couple of poofs, weren't they? I mean, le's be 'onest, you didn't wanna go bendin' over to pick up anything awf the floor when them two were arand.'

His comment met with incredulous looks and shocked denials from everyone at the bar. But Chalky persisted:

'Come on! Everyone knows that Ron did teenage boys and Reg wasn't averse to taking it up the arse and all.'

This was too much for Bill who shouted over Chalky's words, threatening him with violence if he didn't 'shut it'. But the fish smuggler just laughed, apparently pleased with the stir he had caused. He drained his pint, ordered another, and lit one of his Castellas. Then with obvious relish and a wink at me, he added:

'The Krays were a right pair of vicious cunts and thas the truth.'

Chalky enjoyed debunking virtually everything except the Queen, for whom he had immeasurable respect. But he took particular pleasure in slinging mud at the Kray legend. The cult status the Twins had attained made them a tantalising target for his ego.

'Reg and Ron were amateurs and not exactly geniuses, neiver,' he said as we walked from the pub back towards Brick Lane. 'Compared to organised crime today, which is a multi-billion pound industry, they were nothing. All they cared about was getting their pictures in glossy magazines and that was their downfall. If they'd 'ave been smart, they would 'ave kept a low profile. There's plenty of successful East End villains 'oo no one's ever 'eard of. Why? 'cause they don't go round shooting off their mouths.'

I had heard some of this from Chalky before. For someone who was so dismissive of the Twins, he talked about them a great deal.

'So is it true they were gay?' I asked him.

'Bent as Boy fuckin' George.'

But Reg was married, I pointed out.

''course 'e was. Same as Ron – a number of times. It was all part of the act, make people think they was straight. They never wanted no one to know they was 'omosexuals 'cause being poofs didn't tally with their 'ard geezer image.'

Chalky told me about the long-standing relationship between Reg and a convicted bank robber called Bradley Allardyce, with whom he served time. The two of them shared a cell for a number of years in Maidstone Gaol. Apparently, both Allardyce and Reg's wife, Roberta, had been at the side of the old con's deathbed.

'Thas the Krays for you,' he said. 'Sick as fuck. Robin 'oods my arse.'

Despite all the uncomplimentary things Chalky had to say about the Twins, there was admittedly something strangely mesmerising about them. Even in death, they held a certain allure, titillating a primitive human fascination with criminality. I was by no means immune to its effects. Indeed, a day or two before the funeral, when I came across a couple of Kray biographies on the shelves of the Whitechapel Library, I found myself engrossed in them.

I soon discovered that Chalky was right about the Twins. Their criminal empire was founded on violence and extortion and, although they donated some of their ill-gotten gains to charity and loved their dear old mum, they were not the protectors of the community they claimed to be. What's more, both men appear to have taken particular pleasure in murdering their victims. Their trademark was to get up close and personal. When Ron killed fellow gangster George Cornell in 1966, he did so at close range with a pistol, blowing his victim's brains across the bar of the Blind Beggar pub on Whitechapel Road; and when Reg murdered Jack 'The Hat' McVitie on 28 October 1967, he drove a knife through his neck, impaling his victim to the floor.

Beyond the image of 'gangster chic' that the Twins worked so hard to promote – they were even photographed for *Vogue* by David Bailey – their personal lives were anything but glamorous. Reg terrorised his first wife, Frances (he once slept with a prostitute in the same bed with her) and drove her to suicide; and Ron was a paranoid schizophrenic who took medication to suppress his violent nature. Had the Krays not been put away by Scotland Yard's Detective Inspector 'Nipper' Read, there seems little doubt that both men would have claimed more victims.

As career criminals, the Twins could hardly be described as successful. They both spent more than half their lives behind bars and although the celebrity and money they earned through the promotion of their story brought them respect amongst their fellow cons, their 'Firm' did not survive their downfall.

Still, in their lifetimes, the Krays achieved the celebrity they so craved. Like Dick Turpin, who is remembered as a swashbuckling highwayman rather than the murderer, thief and rapist that he was, they became legends. Their 'cult of violence', as John Pearson has dubbed it, inspired dozens of books, a number of films, and it helped found an entire industry that allows criminals with charisma to promote their stories and attain celebrity (it helps if they love their dear old mum and she still lives in a humble council flat).

Reg and Ron Kray have been firmly established as Cockney folk heroes in the British – and to a degree, the international – psyche. They rank up there with Bill Sykes and Jack the Ripper, and public fascination with the Twins shows no sign of diminishing. Since Reg's death, yet more films and books have been produced and, as I had seen for myself, their deeds live on in the oral tradition of the East End.

'The important thing to bear in mind about a myth is that it has no direct connection with the truth . . .' writes Pearson; 'it can be endlessly reinterpreted and retold to exalt or terrify later generations – and therein lies its power.'

On the morning of 12 October, I walked the short distance from Brick Lane to St Matthew's Row, puzzling over the Krays' story and wondering whether it mattered if the Twins were remembered as heroes.

It seemed to me that it did, that the public should recognise such men for what they were: murderers whose evil deeds had been well documented. And yet, I had read enough history and been in journalism long enough to know that the Kray myth was nothing unique given that past and present continually manipulate us, muddying the waters of truth and playing on our ignorance and prejudice. The crowds who stood along St Matthew's Row and Bethnal Green Road that morning were guilty of nothing more than being human. For them, Reg Kray's funeral provided a dose of good old-fashioned London street theatre, and it was a show that they would not have missed for the world.

Amongst the crowd opposite the church stood Bill from the Bethnal Green Arms, dressed in his best suit and tie. He was standing next to his mum, Gladys – also dressed in her best. White-haired, short, tough as nails, she had a voice like a bullfrog.

'Diamond geezer Reg was,' she told me. ''andsome boy. Asked me aht once.'

With her were some of her lifelong friends, Bethnal Green girls one and all: Violet, Louise and one Mrs Jones. The latter had brought along a wreath of flowers and a thermos of tea. This she shared out amongst her friends as they waited for the show to commence.

And a show it was.

It began an hour or so before the service with the arrival of a couple of dozen burly thugs. To a man, they were all either bald or had shaved their heads. A good many did not appear to be in possession of necks. All of them wore long dark coats, black ties, Doc Marten shoes or boots, and, despite the overcast weather, black designer sunglasses.

One by one, they formed a long line with their backs to the church, facing the crowd on the other side of the street. There they stood, staring out at us with stern expressions and rigid jaws. Each time a couple of them exchanged words, they moved in close, shoulder against shoulder, and spoke directly into one another's ears, like spies swapping introductory codewords. Then they would nod gravely and shake hands firmly and give one another chummy pats on the back.

When I approached one of them and asked who he was and what he was doing there, I got a curt, one-word reply: 'Secure-it-iy.' The word was delivered with a look that was not conducive to further questioning. But as I backed away I wondered what on earth he could be providing security for. He and his associates would hardly have to worry about the old dears in the crowd, nor the fathers who stood with their children hoisted up on their shoulders. Besides, there was a considerable police presence on the street.

Could it be, I wondered, that these men, who looked like night-club bouncers, were there as window dressing? Were they there to do their bit for the promotion of the Kray myth? Certainly, most of them would have been in diapers when Reg and Ron ruled the East End.

Whatever the case, the press pack loved them. The couple of dozen still photographers and video cameramen covering the funeral crowded in around the thugs, capturing the image of the 'East End underworld' that they knew their editors wanted. It was an image that would appear on TV screens and front pages around the world. And it would help reaffirm Reg Kray in the collective subconscious as the great Cockney don. Still, the sight of these men brought a smile to my face. It was perhaps an odd reaction given that I was at a funeral. But to my eyes, they looked like a caricature of themselves, less *Reservoir Dogs* and more *Blues Brothers*.

The rest of the funeral also had a distinct air of pantomime about it. Next came the funeral cortège. Reg's coffin arrived by way of Vallance Road in a gothic Victorian hearse drawn by six horses, like something Count Dracula might have ridden in. Inside, through the thick panes of glass, the coffin lay surrounded by gaudy arrangements of flowers that spelt out the words 'FREE AT LAST' and 'RESPECT'. Behind the hearse came a long line of eighteen stretch limousines with tinted windows. These bore Reg Kray's widow, Roberta, various other mourners (including a number of men wearing chunky gold jewellery and bleach blondes with perma-tans in miniskirts and high heels), plus several D-grade celebrities to the front gates of the church. Amongst them I recognised Mad Frankie Fraser, an acclaimed psychopath who had recently featured in a TV series entitled *Hard Bastards*. The actor and playwright Steven Berkoff, who played Jack 'The Hat' McVitie in the film *The Krays*, also attended.

Some amongst the crowd cheered as the coffin was carried by Bradley Allardyce and three others into the church. The thugs remained out on the street, keeping an eye on the old dears in the crowd, presumably worried that they might turn rowdy and start lobbing their thermoses. And then, as the service began, loudspeakers broadcast the proceedings for the benefit of the crowd.

First came music, the theme tune to the gangster movie *Once Upon a Time in America*. Hymns were sung, eulogies read. An evangelical Christian who claimed to have converted Reg to Christianity (this despite the fact that the old con never showed any remorse for his crimes and said he was proud of what he had done) spoke of him as a child of God and a 'rare bird' who had 'flown his cage'. Reg's solicitor called him a man of honour and 'an icon of the twentieth century'. And someone else stood up and said something along the lines of, 'You was a legend and legends never die.'

The service ended with Frank Sinatra's *My Way*. Then the coffin was carried from the church, placed back inside the hearse, and the cortège headed along Bethnal Green Road where a huge crowd of people had gathered on the street. I followed the long line of limousines for a few hundred yards until I spotted Steven Berkoff standing near Pellicci's café, giving a TV crew a soundbite or two. Eavesdropping behind the cameraman, I heard him talk about the Krays' relationship with the East End, where Berkoff himself has long been a resident.

'The Krays played a vital role in establishing the mythology of the old East End,' he said – or words to that effect.

The actor thanked the camera crew for their time, then hurried off down the street, presumably on his way to Chingford Cemetery where Reg Kray was due to be laid to rest side by side with Ron.

I had decided not to go to Chingford. Instead, I stood outside Pellicci's watching the funeral cortège disappear underneath the railway bridge at the end of the road. Then I headed towards the

Bethnal Green Arms where I found Bill and his mother and friends having a lunchtime drink. The talk around the bar was about raising funds to pay for a public statue of the Twins and lobbying the council to have it erected in Bethnal Green.

———————◆———————

Over the course of the ten days between Reg's death and the funeral, Aktar left three or four urgent phone messages on our answering machine, but I chose to ignore them. Partly this was because he had not once thanked me for my help and instead did nothing but complain about how 'un-English' all my contacts were. But mostly it was because I was tired of buying him lunch.

Then on the Sunday morning after the funeral, he called yet again and said that he had decided to make his way back to India and that, before leaving London, he wanted to share a 'startling discovery' with me.

'I'm sure you will be interested to hear what I have to say,' he said.

Reluctantly I agreed to meet him, and an hour or so later found myself inside one of the curry houses on Brick Lane. The restaurant was packed with bargain hunters who had spent the morning in the Sunday market. Sylheti waiters in white shirts served them bowls of rich, incandescent balti dishes and chilled glasses of Kingfisher lager. Bollywood dancers pranced in unison across a giant video screen mounted on one wall, while the high-pitched voice of the legendary Indian playback singer Asha Bhonsle sounded over the speakers.

Aktar was sitting at a table at the back. He looked exhausted and said he had not slept more than a few hours in the past week.

'I have been working from dawn to dusk,' he said as I sat down at the table opposite him.

A waiter approached and Aktar ordered a beer for me and water for himself – as well as several dishes, none of which appeared on the menu.

'I hope you have no objections but balti is not Indian food as I know it,' he said with some disdain. 'I have taken the liberty of ordering some traditional Sylheti food.'

The drinks were brought to the table and we clinked glasses. Aktar took a gulp of water and then, for once, got more or less straight down to business.

'I should warn you that what I am about to tell you will not be easy for you to hear,' he said, looking me in the eye. 'Are you sure you are ready to hear it?'

'Well, without knowing what you have to say that's not a question I can readily answer, is it?' I said.

'Point taken. Then here it is: I have discovered that almost everything you consider "English" is foreign in origin.'

I groaned out loud. 'Not this English thing again. We've been through this already. You're obsessed!'

Aktar ignored me. 'You must listen,' he said, picking his satchel off the floor and producing the crumpled photocopy of a newspaper article. 'It says here that fish and chips, the English national dish, is not English or even British.'

'Fish and chips,' I repeated dismissively, snatching the paper from his hand. 'There can hardly be anything *more* English.'

'Precisely,' replied Aktar. 'This is my point. Fish and chips is considered quintessentially English. And yet its origins . . .'

He paused to allow me to read for myself. A section of the article was underlined in red ink. The headline ran: 'TOP UK DISH HOOKED FRENCH FIRST'. It went on to say that a professor at Leicester's De Montfort University who was studying the multicultural nature of the UK's cuisine had suggested that fish and chips were in fact 'French frites with Jewish fish dishes'.

I handed the piece of paper back to him. 'OK, so fish and chips isn't English. Big deal.'

It seemed obvious to me that Aktar was suffering from a severe case of disillusionment. He had been brought up with a certain image of England left over from the Raj and it had been shattered. But he denied it.

'I admit that I once saw the English very differently. That is exactly my point. I have been fooled along with everyone else.'

He implored me to hear him out.

'Fish and chips is just the tip of the iceberg, so to speak,' he continued. 'Your royalty have almost all been foreigners – Normans, Welsh,

Scots, Dutch, Germans and so forth. Queen Victoria's husband, Albert, was a Saxe-Coburg-Gotha and Prince Philip is Greek –'

'Everyone knows that,' I interrupted. 'The royal families of Europe have always intermarried.'

'But did you know that the sport of polo is not English but Persian, morris dancing came from Moorish Spain, and your patron saint was from Cappadocia in modern-day Turkey and never so much as set foot in England?'

I did know about St George; there had been an article about his foreign origins in a newspaper only recently. But the other examples had me stumped.

'Your name is not English either,' continued Aktar. 'The Tarquins were Etruscan kings with no perceivable connection to England. And yet, somehow, the anglicised version has become an accepted English Christian name. It has even acquired certain class connotations. As you have told me yourself, it has come to be associated with middle-class males from southern England.'

'Yes, I know all this,' I said, impatiently. 'But what are you getting at? I'm sure when you scratch the surface of most cultures you'd find foreign influences –'

Aktar stood firm. 'No. With you English it is different,' he continued. 'You are unique in that you loot elements of other cultures and then you make them your own. For want of a better word, you "English" them. And in so doing, you somehow convince yourselves that whatever it is that you have absorbed was English in the first place. Then you go one step further and present it to the world as such. Thus a Middle Eastern knight can become the patron saint of England, Jewish fish and deep fried French potato wedges can become the national dish. And the name Tarquin can come to be regarded as being English by the English themselves.'

Aktar paused for a moment to gauge my reaction. But I kept quiet and sipped my beer.

'The English language illustrates this phenomenon clearly,' he went on, now well into his stride. 'The language is packed with so-called "loan" words which nobody has any intention of returning – for example "cheroot", "cushy", "jungle", "pyjamas" and "pundit", all of them from Indian languages. "Blighty" is another one. It comes from the Hindi – "*bilāyati*", foreigner. But you English have made it stand for home, for England. Thus you hear British ex-pats saying how much they miss dear old "Blighty".'

Aktar had also compiled a list of foods and dishes that the English had 'plundered'. Baked beans came from North America where they were once eaten by Indians who prepared them with maple syrup; ketchup – *ke-tsiap* – was from Malaysia whence it was brought by British sailors; and the parsley "liquor" so beloved by East Enders and eaten with pie and mash originated in Holland.

'You've even hijacked my national cuisine,' added Aktar, accusingly. 'How else can you explain the so-called "curry clubs" that have been established in English pubs across the country. Or "curry nights" on Fridays that have replaced the Christian tradition of eating fish. Or the newspaper articles that talk of Chicken Tikka Masaala as the new "national" dish?'

The Bengali shook his head disapprovingly.

'You people are quite capable of making absolutely anything English if you choose to do so,' he said. 'I should not be the least bit surprised if, eventually, curry, like fish and chips, is considered "English". No doubt a day may come when the traditional Sunday roast will be replaced by the "traditional" Sunday curry.'

Aktar spent much of the rest of the meal confronting me with further evidence of my culture's thievery. The way he saw it, we Anglo-Saxons had been at it ever since we arrived on Albion's shores in the fifth century, miraculously metamorphosing ourselves from 'Garmans', as we were known to the Britons, into the English.

'From earliest times, your history reveals an ability to reinvent yourselves, to change your colours completely, and you have proven yourselves unconquerable,' he said

Aktar cited the example of the Norman invasion.

'Ultimately it was you English who won. But it was not a victory achieved by feat of arms; it was far more subtle. Quite simply, you "Englished" the Normans and a substantial part of their language. Within a few generations, the Norman conquerors became English themselves.'

Aktar was convinced that it was something in the English and not the British character that had achieved this. 'Otherwise, the Britons would have absorbed the Romans,' he reasoned.

'But how do you think this absorption is achieved?' I asked him.

Aktar drained his glass of water and placed it back on its coaster.

'On this point I am not absolutely clear,' he admitted. 'However, a clue may be found in the history of the Huguenots in the East End. At first when they arrived in London and set up in commerce, they found their foreignness an attribute. Society women flocked to tailors with French names – the more Gallic the better. But later, the second and third generation did not want to be seen as being French and so they Anglicised their names.'

'But why?' I asked him.

Aktar shrugged. 'Possibly because there was nothing to stop them doing so, the English mindset being predisposed to foreigners joining the fold,' he replied.

I asked him whether he believed the same fate awaited the East End Bangladeshis.

'Yes, it stands to reason that they will be "Englished" too,' he said gloomily. 'But it will take time – in the case of the Jews, the total assimilation of the community took a hundred years.'

Aktar found the prospect depressing. He believed that English culture would be greatly enriched by becoming 'truly multicultural'. He was against assimilation and believed ethnic groups should be encouraged to retain their own identities, practices and religious beliefs.

'It saddens me to think that the Sylheti community will disappear,' he said. 'Everything that makes it unique and colourful will be gone. Banglatown will vanish and its people will forget their roots.'

After paying for lunch and wishing Aktar a safe journey back to India, I left the restaurant. It was mid-afternoon and the street was crowded with Bangladeshis. They stood about on the pavements in groups chatting and gossiping. The sari shops, Islamic goods stores and restaurants were bustling with trade. The mosque was busy, too, the congregation making its way inside for afternoon prayers.

I stopped for a moment on the corner of Fournier Street and glanced up at the old Huguenot sundial hung with its inscription, *Umbra Sumus* – 'We are Shadows' – and wondered if Aktar was right. Would Banglatown eventually vanish, leaving only a few ghostly street names to mark its existence just as Weaver Town had done?

It was a question that would occupy my mind for days, weeks and even months to come, and as I went about my daily life, I remained on the lookout for clues that might provide an answer.

I found no shortage of examples of my fellow countrymen and women with foreign blood, amongst them some of the most famously English of all – such as Alistair Cooke (Irish mother), Boris Johnson (Turkish grandfather) and Geri Halliwell of Spice Girls fame (half Spanish). And I found no shortage of further examples of ostensibly English things with origins abroad.

Much to Aktar's delight, I also came across a plot to claim 'curry' as being originally English. The website menumagazine.com states that: 'There is much evidence to suggest the word "curry" was English all along.' It goes on to say that the word was in use as far back as Richard II's time.

But it was while reading up on the history of the Anglo-Saxons that I came across what is surely the most pertinent fact about the nature of Englishness. The word 'English' (as defined in the *Oxford English Dictionary*) is not derived directly from 'Angle' but, in its earliest examples, from 'Angelcynn', a group of peoples who comprised not just the Angles, who were in the minority, but the Saxons, Jutes, Roman Britons and Celts as well. In other words, the English have always been a composite of different peoples. Thus the definition of 'Englishness' is: 'The quality or state of being English, or of *displaying English characteristics* [my italics].'

Assuming that the absorbing power of the English was still hard at work – and Aktar was certainly of the opinion that it was – it was in keeping with the spirit of the Angelcynn that the Bangladeshis and other immigrants should become a part of the mix. Given this, it seemed only right that Banglatown's days be numbered and, in time, the chameleon that is Brick Lane change once again.

12

Come Hungry, Leave Edgy

'Whatever the East End is for you, whatever you can find within
its environs will depend upon what sort of chance you are prepared to give it. Much of it looks dead yet is alive and vibrant.
Much of it is depressing but wondrously gay. Although old it is
being reborn again.'

Roy Curtis, East End Passport (1969)

NAZIZ'S GREAT-UNCLE'S skin was the colour and texture of a
walnut shell, light brown with a waxy lustre. The wrinkles on
his forehead were smooth and soft as if, over his eighty or so years, he
had cared for his complexion with Oil of Ulay. His beard, too,
appeared to have received a considerable amount of attention. The
snow-white hairs, which ran in two symmetrical lines down either
side of his face and broadened into a Pharaoh-like tuft, had been
meticulously pruned.

His clothes were equally well-tended. A hole in his trousers, neatly
folded over his polished leather boots, had been expertly mended. His
blue mackintosh, worn buttoned up to his neck, was faded but spot-
lessly clean. His skullcap, thin and frayed, had been bleached so the
blemishes were barely visible.

Hajji Syed Ullah, as he was known, seemed remarkably at peace
with himself. He said little as he walked with Anu, Naziz and me to
Liverpool Street Station from Brick Lane where we had bumped into
him and I had suggested that he come with us on the train down to
the coast. And yet, Naziz was not exactly overjoyed at the prospect of
taking his great-uncle along with us for the day.

'He's always wandering off,' he moaned to Anu and me, being

careful not to let Syed Ullah hear his remark. 'He tells the same stories over and over again! I've heard them a million times. And he's always talking to strangers – especially good-looking birds. He'll walk up to them and start telling them about how he was lost at sea.'

Naziz made us promise that we wouldn't encourage Syed Ullah to tell his stories – to good-looking birds or anyone else for that matter – and we agreed to do so. After all, this was Naziz's big day: he was going to lay eyes on the sea for the first time and I wanted him to enjoy the experience.

As the train pulled out of Liverpool Street and passed through Bethnal Green, past London Fields, Anu and I sat opposite Naziz and Syed Ullah, staring out of the window. It was almost a year to the day since I had arrived on Brick Lane and I thought back to my first meeting with Mr Ali and the shock of being on the street for the first time. Even then, I had never dreamt that a whole twelve months would pass before I would be able to move on. But it was finally happening. Anu and I had spent the past few days packing up our belongings (by now, we had more plants than anything else) and that night would be our last in the attic.

We were not going to be living in Stoke Newington as we had hoped. The one-bedroom flats we'd seen there were too small and those with gardens too expensive. So we'd opted instead for a place in Dalston, Hackney, a fifteen-minute walk from Brick Lane and traditionally a step up for Cockneys escaping the East End proper.

Anu was now more her normal, cheerful self. Every morning for the past week, she'd bounced out of bed, yelling, 'Only a few more days until I never wake up in this horrible attic!' or 'No more fire alarm bell!'

It helped that her job at the BBC was proving increasingly challenging. Her producing days were now behind her and she was working as a full-time presenter and reporter. And she had taken a real shine to the capital. More than anything, it was the city's connections with its colonial past and its unrivalled cosmopolitan mix that appealed to her. She loved the fact that she could spend the morning sitting amidst hookah-smoking Lebanese and Iraqis on the Edgware Road; go to Drummond Street to eat *dosas* for lunch; spend the afternoon wandering through Southall window-shopping for saris; and spend the evening watching the latest offering by Iranian director Samira Makmalbaf in Soho.

Wherever she went, she saw mixed-race couples like us and found that the cross-cultural fusion was something she could identify with. She was also attracted to the fair-mindedness and common sense of the English she worked with and the tolerance of British culture. She no longer saw herself as a 'Little Princess' orphaned from her past, but as someone who felt that, in London, she had found her place.

The other passengers in our carriage were mostly East End Bangladeshis heading, like us, down to Southend for a reprieve from the Big Smoke. Amongst them, Naziz recognised a couple sitting four or five rows away and he got up to say hello.

'Now, don't start boring everyone with your stories,' he lectured his great-uncle before leaving him in our care.

But the moment Naziz was out of earshot, Syed Ullah seized his opportunity.

'Sir,' he addressed me, an old habit dating back to the days when he had served under British officers. 'Perhaps you are not knowing that nine-year minimum service I am giving as one lascar sailor in Her Majesty's Merchant Navy. All seas and oceans I am crossing. Atlantic Ocean, Pacific Ocean, North Sea Ocean. Many city I am seeing, also. Hong Kong, Mombasa, Sydney. London I am liking very much the most. Many lights, many people, many beauty lady.'

I peeked over the top of the seats to check that Naziz could not overhear our illicit conversation. I could see him chatting and laughing with his friends.

'Please tell us more,' I said to Syed Ullah, and the old lascar nodded, clearly pleased to have found a receptive audience.

'I am born in one home village in proximity to Sylhet town, my brother also,' he continued. 'No job there is for us. No money also. Sylheti people is poor people. That is why many men, they go for working on British vessel. All the world they are crossing. Some, they return very rich. One man – he is cousin to me – he tell many adventure story.'

Syed Ullah and his brother had been raised on the Sylheti legend of the mythical land of milk and honey that lay beyond seven seas and thirteen rivers. From an early age, it was their dream to sign up as lascars, find this promised land, and make their fortunes. When Syed Ullah was sixteen, they set out from Sylhet, travelling across Bengal to reach Calcutta, then the second city of the Empire.

With its imperial monuments and wide avenues bustling with horse-drawn carriages, uniformed sepoys and white sahibs in pith helmets, the capital of British India was unlike anything the two farmers had ever seen. Together, they spent their first hours wandering through the metropolis, marvelling at its sights and sounds, and later, in the evening, they sat on the banks of the Hooghly river, watching gigantic steamers ply the muddy waters, their great funnels belching out clouds of steam and smoke.

Soon they made contact with some of the hundreds of other Sylhetis working in the docks and were taken on as ship's hands aboard a vessel bound for Shanghai. Once at sea, they quickly discovered that the life of a lascar was anything but romantic. They had to labour in soaring temperatures, shovelling coal in the bowels of the engine room, and sleep in confined, cramped quarters. The air was stale, malnourishment and disease were rife, and the treatment meted out by the British masters could often be cruel.

But there were compensations. In their first few years at sea, the two brothers travelled across the Far East, visiting Hong Kong, Taipei and Tokyo, and being sailors, they made many lady friends. They also formed close bonds with their fellow Sylheti lascars. Amongst them was an older man who had seen the capital city of the British sahibs. It lay, he said, across many seas to the west and it was the greatest city in the world, greater even than Calcutta.

'He tell London is most rich city,' said Syed Ullah, as the train continued on through the Essex countryside towards the coast. 'After, I make dream for come Great Britain, my brother also.'

To this end, the two men spent the next few years stoking the fires and greasing the pistons of British vessels in the hope that one day they would secure work aboard a ship bound for London. Then finally, in 1937, after a gruelling journey round India and through the Suez Canal, they found themselves sailing up the Thames and docking within sight of Tower Bridge.

'I am very happy, my brother also,' he said. 'But British sahibs, they tell lascar sailor – no shore leave. We must to staying on board.'

Syed Ullah and his brother decided to jump ship. Under cover of darkness, they shinned down the anchor chain, dodged the security patrols and escaped into the East End. Upon reaching Shadwell, they found no trees bristling with golden leaves as described in the Sylheti legend. Instead, they had to sleep rough and, ever vigilant for the patrols sent to track down wayward lascars, they relied on their wits to survive.

For months, the two brothers peddled wares in the streets for fellow Sylhetis already established in the East End. They shared a room with a dozen others near Cable Street, then the lascar district where nightclubs were packed with prostitutes and criminals. Slowly but surely they learned their way around London, devising means to identify the city's buses: two eggs standing for the number 8.

London, they soon realised, was not the paradise that had been described to them; life was as much a struggle as it had been back home in Sylhet. But Syed Ullah had no complaints; he saw a future for himself and his family and soon he found a job as a stoker in the boiler room of a grand Park Lane hotel. It was there that he met Doreen Fishman who worked as a chambermaid.

'She was one beauty lady,' he said with a smile.

Syed Ullah started telling us about his courtship. But with the train approaching Southend and Naziz due back at any moment, I wanted to hear how it was that the old lascar had ended up in a concentration camp.

'So how were you captured by the Nazis?' I asked.

'I'll give you the short answer to that if you don't mind,' interrupted Naziz, as he returned to his seat, shooting me an exasperated look. 'He spent most of the war working on board ships that ran the U-boat gauntlet between Britain and America. In 1944, his troop carrier ship was sunk by a German submarine. He was one of the few survivors and spent five days at sea in a life-raft before he was rescued and taken prisoner.'

Syed Ullah nodded sheepishly, obviously disappointed to have had his storytelling cut short.

'Now that's enough of your stories, uncle,' Naziz said sternly as the train pulled into the station. 'And if I catch you trying to chat up any birds, you won't get any ice cream.'

———◆———

Southend-on-Sea used to be the preferred destination for East Enders wanting a day out by the seaside. Summer weekends brought thousands of Cockney families armed with their buckets and spades. Even during the war, they came and sat amidst the barbed wire, barricades and barrage balloons and ate their fish and chips.

But the age of the package holiday and the dispersal of the old East End communities had brought about a reversal in the town's fortunes. Southend remained as I remember the Brighton of my childhood, largely untouched by the middle-class revolution of the 1980s with its profusion of cappuccino bars and Body Shops. The lack of investment was evident in the cracks of the concrete boardwalk and the gutted pier. Along the waterfront, it was all pubs, chippies, video arcades and stalls selling sticks of rock. Hawkers flogged 'S Club 7' T-shirts. Posters plastered on boarded-up shopfronts advertised mostly forgotten entertainers like Freddie Starr. *Que Será Será* played over a public entertainment system.

The sea was something of a disappointment as well. It was calm and there were no rolling breakers, no sounds of waves crashing on the beach. There was not much of a breeze, either, and the pong of vinegar hung in the air, masking the smells of salt and seaweed. The beach itself was covered in pebbles and green-tinted mud. It was mostly deserted, but for a couple of Cockney diehards – the man in a cloth cap with trousers rolled up, the woman with a headscarf protecting her perm – who sat in deckchairs eating ham sandwiches and drinking cans of stout.

None of this seemed to bother Naziz. It was, after all, the first time he had ever laid eyes on the sea. And it was with some excitement that he took off his shoes and socks and rushed down to the water. He waded in up to his knees and insisted we do the same. He posed for photographs. He cupped seawater in his hands and tasted it. He collected a few pebbles, a couple of shells and a piece of glass worn smooth by the tide. He examined pieces of beached seaweed and put some in a bag to take home with him. And he told us that he wanted to bring his mother down to Southend for a visit.

'She'd love it here,' he said. 'Compared to Shadwell, this is paradise.'

We remained on the seafront until mid-afternoon. We ate fish and chips, visited the funfair where we went on the bumper cars and Naziz won a toy dinosaur, and we rode on the toy train along the pier. The weather was unseasonably warm and sunny, and after lunch the crowds grew larger. The majority were white and working class: shell suits, trainers and peroxided hair ruled the day. But there was also a significant British Asian presence. We spotted courting Sylheti teenagers walking hand in hand or sitting on the sea wall stealing illicit kisses; a gaggle of Punjabi aunties squatted on plastic sheeting on the beach, sharing *rotis* and *gobi aloo* out of tupperware containers; and a young Pakistani couple introducing their daughter to the sticky delights of candyfloss.

As Naziz had warned us, Syed Ullah proved a handful. He was forever attaching himself to strangers and, whenever our backs were turned, he'd wander off. For an old man who walked with a cane, he could get surprisingly far very quickly. At one point, it took me ten minutes to track him down to a pub where I found him sitting at the bar nursing a lemonade and chatting up a barmaid called Samantha.

'Captain Pugwash 'ere was just telling me about 'ow 'e took on the entire Nazi navy,' she said to me wearily.

After that, we visited the town shopping centre and at about four o'clock headed back to the railway station.

Syed Ullah said nothing along the way – clearly he was not best pleased at having been dragged away from the pub and from the well-endowed Samantha – and it was not until we were standing on the platform with our train approaching that one of us noticed the old man was missing his false teeth.

Naziz and I then had no choice but to leave Anu and Syed Ullah at the station while we retraced our steps to the seafront where we found the dentures in the pub. They'd been discovered in the men's room and were being kept behind the bar. We washed them out before hurrying back to the station.

Along the way, Naziz toyed with the idea of not giving them back to the old man.

'It would be one way to keep him quiet on the way home,' he joked.

It was nearly six o'clock by the time we boarded the train back to London. Syed Ullah was worn out by the day's events and, with his teeth back where they belonged, the rocking motion of the carriage soon put him to sleep. This left us free to have a good laugh at his expense.

'You can't take him anywhere. He's a right old Casanova,' declared Naziz.

'But he's so sweet,' said Anu, who'd heard more of his stories as Naziz and I had gone looking for the false teeth.

'That's what all the ladies say,' said Naziz.

'But are all his stories true?' I asked.

'Oh yes, all of them,' he nodded. 'He really is a war hero.'

Naziz leant forward to check that Syed Ullah was definitely asleep before telling us more about his great-uncle's life, his voice lowered to a whisper.

'He was already living in the East End in 1939 when war was declared and so he decided to sign up and go to sea again,' he said in his precise English. 'No one forced him to do it. But he was a British subject and he saw it as his duty to do what he could for the war effort.'

Syed Ullah, Naziz went on, was one of tens of thousands of lascars who served on board the British fleet during the war. As unsung heroes, they laboured in the engine rooms and galleys from where it was often impossible to escape a sinking ship. Thousands went down with their vessels, amongst them Syed Ullah's brother, whose frigate was torpedoed in the Atlantic.

'People forget the sacrifice the lascars made,' continued Naziz. 'But everyone in my extended family has a story: how such-and-such an uncle drowned at sea. I've seen the telegrams sent to their wives and mothers informing them of their deaths.'

There were Sylheti casualties in the Blitz as well. Syed Ullah lost his best friend who was on shore leave in 1940 when a Luftwaffe bomb landed on the house where he was staying. His first cousin died during a raid on the docks. And Syed Ullah's fiancée, Doreen Fishman, was also killed when a V-1 doodlebug dropped out of the sky and flattened her home.

'He showed me a picture of her once. It was old and cracked, but she looked very nice. I think they must have fallen for each other. You hear quite a lot of stories like that. You'd be surprised how many mixed couples there were, even in those days.'

The three of us sat in silence for a minute or so, listening to the sound of the train. The Essex countryside gave way to new housing estates and rows of industrial units. We passed through a couple of empty stations and alongside another train. And then as we reached the outskirts of London Naziz told us how, at the end of the war, Syed Ullah was sent back to Sylhet only to return to the UK in the late 1940s.

'It can't have been easy. There weren't benefits in those days and you didn't get council housing. He used to work thirteen – fourteen – hours a day in a Jewish sweatshop, seven days a week. Sometimes, in the evenings, he'd wash dishes in a restaurant as well.'

It was not until the late 1960s that Syed Ullah could afford to marry. His bride, who hailed from his native village, was twenty years his junior. When she left Bangladesh she had never been outside her district before. But the two of them settled down near Brick Lane and together they raised three children. Now in their mid-twenties and early thirties, one was a chartered accountant, another ran his own plumbing business, and the eldest worked as a GP in the National Health Service.

'Unlike the Old Man, my great-uncle always understood the importance of education,' said Naziz. 'He didn't want his children to have to do the menial work he did. He would always say they were born British subjects and that was something to be proud of.'

'Doesn't he ever think about going back?' I asked Naziz. During my time in South Asia I had seen Sylhet for myself; if anywhere matched the description in the legend of a paradise that lay across seven seas and thirteen rivers it was there amongst the lush paddy fields and tea plantations of Syed Ullah's homeland.

'He misses it of course,' said Naziz. 'But as hard as his life has been here, he's always told us that the opportunities have been far greater.'

The conversation petered out after that. Anu put her head against my shoulder and fell asleep. Naziz opened his copy of *Moby Dick* and began to read.

I sat looking out of the window, watching dusk fall over the east London suburbs and trying to imagine how Syed Ullah had accepted the upheaval in his life with such grace. He didn't appear at all troubled by the hardships he'd endured. To him loss and struggle were all part of the natural order of things.

It occurred to me that our expectations set us apart. I had never anticipated needing to struggle in London and I had made pretty heavy weather of a re-entry that had been by many immigrants' standards a cushy ride.

Did that make me spoilt, I wondered. Or privileged? No doubt a bit of both.

The train moved on through the architectural jumble of the East End, taking Anu and me home to Brick Lane for the last time. Terraced rooftops bristling with TV aerials and chimney pots gave way to industrial graveyards, where crushed cars and old fridges lay rusting. Towering council blocks dwarfed elegant church spires. Gasworks loomed over the canal, where the stagnant water reflected the subdued yellow hue of street lamps.

I caught a few glimpses of gleaming parquet flooring and exposed brick walls in renovated lofts. But for the most part, the view was still of crumbling Victorian terraces whose blackened windows offered murky glimpses of matchbox-sized kitchens beyond. In hundreds of cramped, dingy flats, immigrants like Big Sasa and Mrs Abdul-Haq were cooking their evening meals, dreaming of home and no doubt making the most of their hardscrabble lives. Even in the twenty-first century, the East End was showing few signs of change, forcing people of wildly divergent backgrounds to live side by side and adapt to one another.

'COME HUNGRY, LEAVE EDGY' read a sign I had spotted that morning in the window of a trendy new café on Brick Lane. Better than anything else, these words seemed to sum up the immigrant experience of the East End — and also my own.

Brick Lane had forced me to adapt to a London I would never have known and helped me to learn that Barnes was not for me. I now felt more in tune with my surroundings than I ever had done while living as a foreigner in other cultures. For this I felt a profound gratitude. But as the train passed the glistening edifice of Canary Wharf and rattled into Liverpool Street Station, I wondered if I could ever feel truly at home in London again, if I would ever be able to relax into a comfortable sense of my own Englishness.

Perhaps I would always remain something of an outsider. Perhaps that was not such a bad thing to be.

Epilogue

W HEN THE SECOND-HAND car dealer who owned the lot across the street sold up to a property developer for half a million pounds, it started Mr Ali thinking.

''e's laughin' all the way to the bank, innit,' said my ex-landlord when I stopped by his shop almost a year after Anu and I had left Brick Lane. ''e says to me, yeah, "Fuck this place for a laugh. I'm movin' to Malaga." Now 'e's livin' in a villa with a swimmin' pool. 'e's got a Range Rover and 'e plays golf every day. Lucky bustard, innit.'

A few days earlier, my former landlord had invited the new estate agents in Spitalfields to appraise his properties. They had concluded that he, too, was sitting on a gold mine.

'There's people offering crazy money round 'ere. I 'ad this Russian geezer come to me the ova day, yeah. 'e says to me, "Mr Ali, I'll give you three 'undred and fifty thousand in cash for the building!" I says to 'im, "You must be mental." But 'e says to me, "Take it or leave it, guvna."'

Mr Ali was not the only one who had grown rich off the recent East End property boom. With many cashing in, the face of Brick Lane was changing dramatically. Some of the leather jacket shops had disappeared already. One by one, derelict Victorian terraces were being renovated. There was talk of a multi-million-pound scheme to resurface the street with cobblestones.

At the same time, Spitalfields was changing. Plans had been drawn up to knock down half the market and replace it with city offices; and the Bishopsgate Goods Yard was facing imminent demolition. The profusion of 'FOR SALE' signs on the old Huguenot properties in the streets around Christ Church reflected the end of an era.

Bangladeshi families, who had occupied the properties since the 1960s, were now moving out and being replaced by a wave of yuppies and self-styled bohemians. Some warned that this new invasion threatened the very spirit of the East End, that the gradual march of gentrification was changing it for ever. But these critics saw no irony in lamenting the days when the East End was a byword for deprivation and poverty. Besides, Tower Hamlets had been through periods of affluence and deprivation before and away from the bright lights of Brick Lane's curry houses and trendy cafés, much of the borough remained severely impoverished by Western standards. It had recently been labelled the poorest place in Britain, with 64 per cent of the population suffering 'severe financial hardship' and the highest rate of tuberculosis in the country, six times the national average.

Certainly, Mr Ali felt no compulsion to stay if it meant a better quality of life for his family elsewhere. Some of his relatives had already moved out of London and he was considering following in their footsteps.

'In the old days, yeah, everyone built big houses back in Sylhet, innit,' he told me. 'But now everyone's keeping their money 'ere in Britain. Iss all about investment, innit.'

He had become particularly enamoured of Cambridge, which he had visited a couple of times in the past fortnight since his daughter, Razia, had – against all the odds – been allowed to take up her place at the university.

'I used to think Bow was all right, yeah. But Cambridge is, like, seriously beautiful, innit.'

Mr Ali had even ventured to suggest to the Missis that they move out of the East End. But she was not keen on the idea and, since defying her wishes and agreeing to allow Razia to go up to Cambridge, he was not exactly in her good books.

'The Missis says to me, yeah, "We're leaving over my dead body!"'

Still, he felt confident that if he could find a house grand enough, she could be persuaded.

'They 'ave this expression in Turkey, yeah,' said Mr Ali. 'My mate, Ozman, taught me. It goes, "*Yavash yavash.*"'

'What does that mean?' I asked him.
'It means, like, "Slowly, slowly", innit. All fings in their time.'

<hr />

At the time of writing, Mr Ali and his family are still living in Whitechapel although they are planning to move near Woodford. He is no longer in the leather jacket or sweatshop business, but remains a slum landlord.

Sadie's friend, Ethel, died a few months ago, but Gilda and Solly are still going strong. The last time I saw Mrs Abdul-Haq, she was studying English and being courted by Rafiq the Builder.

Mr Singh has recently been on a pilgrimage to the Golden Temple in Amritsar, the first time he has returned to India in some thirty years. He tells me that the country is much dirtier than it used to be during his childhood and that there are far too many people in it.

Chalky is still up to his old tricks. As well as doing the odd bit of poaching, he has designed a betting system based on the study of horses' biorhythms. He claims it is foolproof although he says investors in the scheme should be prepared for initial losses.

Since his journey to Southend-on-Sea, Naziz has been bitten by the travel bug and is planning to visit Bangladesh. It will be the first time he has left the UK. Meanwhile, his father has terminal cancer and is being tended by his wife. It seems it is only a matter of time before she will be free.

Much to Anu's amusement, Mrs Suri's son, Kunal, has become engaged to a Houston girl called Charlize. His decision has caused quite a stir amongst the aunties of Upton Park. But Charlize has written to her mother-in-law-to-be, saying she is looking forward to visiting east London and learning to make *rajma*, Kunal's favourite dish.

Gul Muhammad is working as a carpenter and is married to a second cousin, a nurse whom he helped escape from the Taliban. They live in Bethnal Green and have a one-year-old daughter.

The two Sasas are back in Kosovo trying to rebuild their lives.

Salah, the gentle Kurdish engineer, has finally returned home, too. After several gruelling years in London (at one stage he worked as a janitor in an underground toilet), he is employed again in the Iraqi oil industry. His prognosis for his country grows grimmer by the day.

Shaikh and Muksood are now successful property dealers and both own flash cars. They have finally bought a limousine which they rent out at weddings. Muksood recently married and spent his honeymoon in Mauritius.

Aktar is somewhere in India, but no one seems to know where. The last I heard from him, he was giving consideration to withdrawing from the world to meditate on the divine. Perhaps human anthropology had proven too disenchanting.

Anu continues to work as a presenter and reporter for the BBC and has become a British citizen. Her American accent is slipping and she no longer talks about her parents' sisters as 'ants'. Just recently, one of her listeners wrote to her wanting to know if she was Canadian.

We were married soon after leaving Brick Lane at the register office in Marylebone, just one of a number of mixed couples to tie the knot that day. The following year, we had a second wedding in India. It was held in a former palace in Jaipur, Rajasthan. Anu dressed up like a princess and looked ravishing; I rode in on a large elephant.

The two of us have yet to make it to Stoke Newington. We are still living in Dalston where Anu has created a beautiful garden and Puss makes the occasional, futile attempt to catch wood pigeons.

Glossary

balti	a hybrid 'Indian' cuisine introduced to Birmingham by Pakistani immigrants; not the 'national dish' of Baltistan in Pakistan as is often affirmed
beta	Hindi for child
Bhangra	a lively form of folk music and dance that originated in the Punjab, traditionally performed during harvest celebrations
bhel-poori	savoury puffed rice snack
bindi	a dot or mark on the forehead; for women traditionally a symbol of marriage but increasingly worn as a fashion accessory
biriyani	a rice casserole cooked with lamb, chicken or vegetables
burfi	a diamond-shaped milk-based sweetmeat with an ultra-thin layer of silver foil on top
burka	an all-covering garment with veiled holes for the eyes worn by a minority of Muslim women
chaat	a range of South Asian snack dishes consisting of chopped fruits, vegetables, spices, herbs, beans or lentils and sometimes meat or seafood
chai	the word for tea on the Indian subcontinent
chuni	a thin scarf worn over the shoulder with a *lehnga* or *salwar kameez*
desi	Hindi for native; in the Indian diaspora, a slang term used to mean Indian, or 'one of us'
Diwali	festival celebrated throughout India in late October or early November; known as the 'Festival of Lights' for the common practice of lighting small oil lamps around the house
dosa	a South Indian crepe or pancake made of fermented ground rice and lentils stuffed with fillings, usually potato
Dub	in popular music, a remix of a song emphasising the drums and bass

Eid Al-F'itr	the celebration of breaking the fast marking the end of Ramadan
Ganesh	the Hindu elephant god, revered as the remover of obstacles
gele	style of headgear worn by African women
ghee	clarified butter
gobi aloo	cauliflower and potato dish
goy	Jewish term for a Gentile
Hadith	the recorded teachings of the Prophet Muhammad, also known as the 'Traditions'
Hajj	the Muslim pilgrimage to Mecca
Hajji	honorific given to someone who has made the pilgrimage to Mecca
hijab	headscarf worn by Muslim women
iftar	the meal Muslims eat at sunset to break their fast during the holy month of Ramadan
imam	in the Sunni tradition, a teacher or leader of Muslim prayers
ipele	style of shawl worn by African women, usually draped over one shoulder
jellabie	also spelled *jalebi*; batter fried in a coiled form soaked in sugar syrup, orange-yellow in colour and three inches in diameter
jihad	literally, 'striving' or 'struggle', although often used in the theopolitical context of a 'holy war'; it must be either defensive or to right a wrong; its truer meaning is subjective and psychological, not objective and political; thus it is said that the 'lesser *jihad*' is the external war with an aggressor, while the 'greater *jihad*' is the internal war with oneself
jilbab	a long Middle Eastern garment for women that covers the body
Ka'bah	shrine located near the centre of the Great Mosque in Mecca and considered by Muslims to be the most sacred spot on Earth
karai	literally a wok, but also used to mean a South Asian dish made in a wok, usually including chicken or mutton
karakol	a type of Afghan hat
Kheder	Jewish Sunday School
kheer	sweet milk-based dessert
khol	a terracotta two-sided drum used in northern and eastern India

kitty party	a social gathering of South Asian women, usually at lunch, for the purposes of having fun, sharing gossip and pooling savings
Kshatriya	traditionally the Indian warrior caste, once the ruling class
kulfi	ice cream made with boiled milk, usually flavoured with pistachios
ladoos	round yellow walnut-sized confection, used as ceremonial dessert
lascar	in the past a sailor from Africa or India employed aboard a European vessel
lassi	a South Asian buttermilk drink either sweet or salty flavoured
lehnga	a skirt with generous flare often made out of bright, brocaded fabrics, worn with a matching *choli*, or blouse, at formal events and parties
Londhoni	Sylheti term for Bangladeshis who live in London; a play on words, *dhoni* meaning rich
madrasa	Arabic word meaning place of study; a *madrasa* is frequently but not always attached to a mosque
mehndi	henna leaf, ground into powder, mixed with water, coffee grounds and lemon juice and applied in intricate designs to the hands and feet; once dry, it is washed off and leaves behind a temporary red tattoo
mubarak	literally, 'blessed', thus 'Eid Mubarak' means 'blessed festival' or 'happy Eid'
mullah	a Muslim trained in the doctrine and law of Islam; the head of a mosque
naan	unleavened bread made from wheat and baked in a tandoor
namaste	greeting performed with folded hands; hello
niqab	a face veil covering the lower part of the face (up to the eyes)
paan	betel nut leaf laced with *katha*, a paste that produces *paan's* characteristic red colour, *supaari*, or areca nut, *mitha masaala*, a mixture of sweet spices, and *chuna*, or slaked white lime
patu	a type of Afghan shawl
Pir	a Muslim religious leader or saint
puja	worship or veneration of a Hindu deity
qat	the leaves of the shrub *Catha edulis* which are chewed like

	tobacco or used to make tea; has the effect of a euphoric stimulant
raita	yoghurt seasoned with salt, pepper and crushed roasted cumin seeds
rajma	red kidney bean dish cooked with fresh ginger, garlic and spices
Ramadan	the holy fasting month, during which Muslims must not eat, drink or make love from sunrise to sunset
roti	South Asian unleavened bread
Sabbath goys	Gentiles who work for Jews on the Sabbath
salaam aleikum	standard Muslim greeting meaning 'peace be upon you'
salwar kameez	baggy trousers and long shirt worn in various styles by men and women throughout the Islamic world
Shariat	term used to denote the system of ordinances given in the Koran and Hadith
sherwani	typical wedding attire of north Indian men, essentially a long coat buttoned up in front with wingless collars
swami	literally, 'master' or 'lord'; an Indian holy man or teacher
tiffin	a metal lunch box
Umma	Koranic word for people and community, today used to define the worldwide Muslim community

Acknowledgements

Special thanks to Tahir Shah for being such a supportive friend; to Judy Byrne for getting me through some tough times; to Jane Blackstock for her constant encouragement, and to The Society of Authors for providing me with financial assistance while I was writing this book.

I am also greatly indebted to Kath Hopkirk and Ramsay Wood for their invaluable advice; to Gail Pirkis, Caroline Knox, Gordon Wise, Howard Davies and Caroline Westmore; and to Rachana Shah for suggesting the title.

I would also like to extend my gratitude to the following for their time, help and input: Zafar Abbas, Naziz Afroz, Mohammed Ahmed, Muquim Ahmed, Soyful Alom, Ruhul Amin, Tanya Arsan, Tareq Aziz, Nazrul Islam Bashon, Hanima Begum, Rita Benzley, Shilpa Bhaban, Alf Cheesewright, Abdul Gaffar Chowdhury, Imamul Chowdhury, Ruhun Chowdhury, Bill Cousins, Notun Din, Sister Christine Frost, Simon Greenberg, David Harris, Simon Harrold, Dr Abdul Hasnat, Rob Hodge, Peter Hopkirk, Jim Howard, Bruce Hunter, Manjurin Islam, Khaled Mashud, Phil Maxwell, Shakoth Miah, John and Virginia Murray, Abdul Qayum, Abdul Rub, Safia Shah, Razia Newaz Shariff, Rahul Tandon, Ian Thomas, Nobab Uddin, John West, Andrew Whitehead, Layachi and Mehdi, and the many other people in the East End who gave me their time.

My thanks also to the Pearly Guild, and the staffs of the Bethnal Green Library and Archive, the Hanbury Centre and the Whitechapel Library.

The title of chapter twelve, 'Come Hungry, Leave Edgy', is used with the kind permission of Sukhdev Sandhu and the *London Review of Books*.

I have also quoted from:

Besant, Walter, *East London*, Chatto & Windus, 1901
Booth, William, *In Darkest England and the Way Out*, Salvation Army, 1890
Cox, Jane, *London's East End: Life and Traditions*, Phoenix, 1994
Curtis, Roy, *East End Passport*, Macdonald, 1969

ACKNOWLEDGEMENTS

Elek, Paul, *This Other London*, 1951
Goldman, Willy, *East End My Cradle*, Robson Books, 1998
Harding, Arthur, *East End Underworld*, Routlege & Kegan Paul, 1981
Law, John (pseud. Margaret Elise Harkness), *In Darkest London*, 1889
London, Jack, *The People of the Abyss*, Pluto Press, 1998 (first published 1902)
Mackay, John Henry, *The Anarchists*, Boston, Mass.: Tucker, 1891
Massingham, Hugh, *I Took Off My Tie*, William Heinemann, 1936
Morrison, Arthur, *Tales of Mean Streets*, Methuen & Co., 1894
—— *A Child of the Jago*, Methuen & Co., 1896
Morton, H. V., *The Heart of London*, Methuen & Co., 1925
Pearson, John, *The Cult of Violence*, Orion, 2001
White, Jerry, *London in the Twentieth Century*, Viking, 2001
Zangwill, Israel, *Children of the Ghetto*, Heinemann, 1892

Read more ...

Peter Hessler

RIVER TOWN: Two Years on the Yangtze

'If you read only one book about China, let it be this'
Jonathan Mirsky

When Peter Hessler went to China he expected to spend a couple of peaceful years teaching English in the town of Fuling on the Yangtze. But what he experienced surpassed anything he could have imagined – the natural beauty, cultural tension and complex process of understanding that takes place when one is thrust into a radically different society.

Poignant, thoughtful and utterly compelling, *River Town* is an unforgettable portrait of a place caught mid-river in time – a country seeking to understand what it was and what it will one day become.

'Written with great clarity and affection, *River Town* should be read by anyone with any interest in finding the Chinese less inscrutable'
The Times

'Studded with insight and humility, written with unshowy elegance *River Town* is about ways of seeing' *Daily Telegraph*

Order your copy now by calling Bookpoint on 01235 827716 or visit your local bookshop quoting ISBN 978-0-7195-6480-2
www.johnmurray.co.uk

Read more ...

James Chatto

THE GREEK FOR LOVE: Life, Love and Loss in Corfu

**Part memoir, part love story, part wildly scenic travel piece,
The Greek for Love is every bit as sumptuous as its setting**

The two-line ad in the *Sunday Times* advertising Villa Parginos in Corfu
conjured an image of long afternoons drinking wine on a marble patio
shaded by a grape arbour, looking out over an impossibly blue Greek
sea. Instead James Chatto and his wife Wendy found themselves in a
little pink bungalow with linoleum, a buzzing fluorescent light and
a patio separated from the village's main street by a wire fence.

Yet Corfu delivered so much more than their wildest fantasy had
suggested. There was the intoxicating warmth of the sun, walks along
sage-bordered byways and swimming naked off an idyllic beach. There
were olive trees that dropped their fruit into nets, as well as fresh
apricots, grilled sardines, marinated lamb and long evenings of
storytelling at the local taverna.

'This sensual love story about two young people and Corfu, which
became their home, is my book of the year . . . It is a book that will
touch the hearts of all who read it' *Daily Mail*

'A searing journal of grief and healing . . . a return journey to
numbingly terrible events that began in love and ended in love'
Toronto Globe and Mail

'This memoir will have you dreaming of idyllic beaches'
Closer Magazine

*Order your copy now by calling Bookpoint on 01235 827716 or
visit your local bookshop quoting* ISBN *978-0-7195-6862-6*
www.johnmurray.co.uk

Read more . . .

Dervla Murphy

SILVERLAND: A WINTER JOURNEY BEYOND THE URALS

Irish septuagenarian Dervla Murphy's intrepid midwinter journey from Moscow to the Russian Far East

Dervla Murphy travelled by slow train through the world's most desolate and beautiful mountain ranges to a remote land of lynx and elks, indigenous tribes and shamans, reindeer broth and taiga-berry pie. While her less fortunate encounters included a bear and armed robbers, she was met with great hospitality by local people who openly shared their often difficult life stories over samovars of sweet tea.

'A free-thinking traveller, at once a romantic and a realist, extraordinary for her determination to cross Eurasia at the age of 75 with only her walking sticks, a smattering of Russian, her indefatigable spirit and gift for good crack' *Sunday Telegraph*

'Indefatigable, indomitable, incredible' *Daily Mail*

'One of our most outstanding travel writers' *Traveller*

'Rather eccentric and supremely talented' *Sunday Times*

Order your copy now by calling Bookpoint on 01235 827716 or visit your local bookshop quoting ISBN 978-0-7195-6829-9
www.johnmurray.co.uk